Jewels
of Our City

BIRMINGHAM'S JEWELLERY QUARTER

Jean Debney

BREWIN BOOKS

First published by
Brewin Books Ltd, 56 Alcester Road,
Studley, Warwickshire B80 7LG in 2013
www.brewinbooks.com

ISBN: 978-1-85858-480-5

A Cataloguing in Publication Record
for this title is available from the British Library.

Typeset in New Baskerville
Printed in Great Britain by
4edge Ltd.

CONTENTS

The Chamberlain Clock which sits in the heart of Birmingham's Jewellery Quarter (by the kind courtesy of the Hockley Flyer Collection).

FOREWORD

For too long our people, the common people, were mostly hidden from history. Too busy working day after day so as to survive, they had no time to write down their stories or compile diaries. Accordingly their appearances on the historical stage are restricted mainly to mentions in official annals and concern events when they had committed an offence according to the laws imposed for their own benefit by the ruling class.

Sadly so much of our knowledge of the past is gleaned through these official reports that lack the verve of personal testimony and that relate to working people in an arrogant and insensitive manner. Or else our understanding of the past comes via historians who interpret what they have researched according to their own background, upbringing, beliefs and attitudes.

Of course, the voices of the past are the concern of every historian; yet some historians speak louder than those whom they study. They muffle the voices of the past, making them difficult to understand and to appreciate. Oral history is a valuable way through which we can overcome this problem and speak with the past more directly. It provides a vital and vivid first-hand source that allows us to engage with the past in a more democratic and emotional way.

Everyone has a story to tell – but too few actually tell it. There is a real need for the older generation to pass on their lives before their memories are lost forever. Therein lies the importance of 'Jewels of Our City'. Focusing on the internationally-renowned Jewellery Quarter, it allows key figures within this distinct and vital area to speak for themselves about their work, their craft, their roots and their futures. It has given a voice to individuals who together raise a collective voice about the importance of skills, manufacturing and adding value. As such it makes a valuable contribution to our understanding of Birmingham and its people.

Professor Carl Chinn MBE

"Birmingham, for want of the recording hand, may be said to live but one generation; the transactions of the last age, die in this; memory is the sole historian, which being defective, I embalm the present generation, for the inspection of the future."

(Hutton, 1783)

Part I

HISTORY THROUGH VOICE

The quotation from William Hutton (1783) that precedes this chapter, frames the whole of my personal project. To date, I have written three historical texts which concentrate on a specific area of the United Kingdom and are related to the manufacturing trades there, quite simply, because I wish to celebrate the amazing contributions that have been made by the people of Birmingham and the Black Country to the United Kingdom as a whole.

The subject of this book is the area of Birmingham designated for nearly two hundred years as the Jewellery Quarter. On any map of one hundred years or more, it is the north west quarter of the City, which illustrates the prominence that this place held within wealth creation and employment for Birmingham. For a long period in the history of the City, it was the second largest trade, employing thousands of people, and supporting thousands more as a consequence. The area holds an eclectic architectural mix, from houses of the Regency period and smaller Victorian terraces, interspersed with Victorian and modern factory premises; at its entrance stands the iconic Chamberlain Clock, to honour a man who served the area personally. The larger premises, can be viewed as 'manufactories' and can appear austere and unwelcoming (this is not the case), the smaller places which have a more residential feeling conceal many gems of the Quarter. For what is hidden behind those unremarkable frontages are what many describe as the 'rabbit warren'; a multitude of old work places, in most cases converted from old dwellings, housing ancient pieces of machinery that hail from a bygone age.

This hive of activity accommodates many different types of craftsmen and women, conducting a wide variety of different parts of the trade, that all combine to create items of beauty and luxury. There is not any one person who could do without the other, for many skills are needed to fabricate such items, as such, they all operate symbiotically, their individual skills complementary to many more. It has the sense of a hidden world, busy in its activities behind closed doors, all with a part to play.

This project to collect the history on industries like the jewellery trade comes from my own personal experience as a glass worker thirty years ago,

I have always been fascinated with why such a wealth of trades and skills should be so concentrated in one area of the country. What caused so many people to be drawn to establish business enterprise and manufacturing concerns around the central Midlands area? Additionally, there is a definite characteristic of the people of Birmingham that makes them industrious and hardworking, determined to 'get on' and achieve. In turn, this creates a pool of numerous small trades that work very individualistically, yet, service other skill-sets around: in the case of jewellery, jewellers sit side-by-side with platers, engravers, chasers, die-sinkers, stampers, enamellers and others.

These people all have an individual tale to tell and add colour and texture to any collection of narratives, which is my chosen method of data collection. Stories can weave a rich tapestry of history, something that cannot be found in a dry history book of facts and figures, people and places. All too often, histories are not researched and compiled until a generation or so after the events have happened, which is where the loss of detail arises. It only takes one generation for a life history to be lost. I found this with my own parents who had much to tell me about Birmingham before and during WW2, however, after they died I could only recall in scant detail what they had shared with me; as a consequence, I was driven to write 'The Dangerfields' which covers that time, and to give a 'truth' I interviewed some of the very few remaining munition workers. This was important in order to preserve their first-hand narrative, rather than depending on second-hand stories which have less detail. As each generation passes, even less detail remains, and then we are left only with what can be found in books, or from the internet.

In this book I have collected narratives once more. I have sought 'voices' from all aspects of the Quarter, whether that be from the MD of a company, or a stamper, or an enameller, or a designer/maker. I have tried to gather as many different interests, skills and opinions, in order to relay a story of what the Quarter is today, and through many of these voices, what they have known in their years of being there. I have endeavoured to paint a picture, of their working lives and experiences, of their concerns and thoughts for the future, and the objects that they make, that they are so proud of. I have spoken to those who have worked there all their lives, some who are very 'hands on' and others who manage others, also, those in the Quarter who seek to promote or conserve what exists.

Each person who contributed to this book, has something different to say, and although many opinions are collectively held, they are not the thoughts of all necessarily; each story should be read as an individual narrative. There are many conflicting tensions and interests that operate within the Quarter, and other external pressures which are brought to bear from outside. The area is very central, geographically to the modern city, and land values are high, this leads to those with interests in property development often casting envious eyes that way.

There has been some redevelopment of what were deserted factories, or areas of land into apartments, this has brought 'incomers' to live in the area, which is fundamentally a working place. As a consequence, this has been known to cause a friction between those that work there and those who have chosen to live there. Additionally, many beautiful old buildings full of heritage remain, and two cemeteries with some of the city's most celebrated incumbents, a few interested parties such as the Jewellery Quarter Association, the Victorian Society and English Heritage have focused their attentions on conserving what there is left for posterity. At the same time the City Council have founded two museums there; the Jewellery Quarter Museum and the Pen Room. These conflicting interests of a working environment, a place of residence and a conservation area do not always rest easy with one another. In this text, I will endeavour to explore these issues, and what the respective views are of those who have a vested interest in remaining there.

The narratives are framed and contextualised by a brief exploration of the history of how this Quarter came into being. In that history I have discussed the rise of the small-metal trades, which developed into the buckle, button and 'toy' industries. I have also explored the origins of the diversity of this City, with the arrival of many 'Dissenters' who were attracted by the unincorporated status which tolerated religious diversity, in the same way many entrepreneurs and businessmen sought freedom from guilds and traditional regulations to establish their business concerns. Birmingham brought many like-minded, driven individuals together into a concentrated geographical area, which bred even greater drive and aspiration. As a result, many working-class people surged towards the place where the work could be found, and where it was known, that with application and determination a man might make his fortune. This can be found in much of the character of the City over the last two hundred years; the hard-working Brummie, determined to 'get on'.

Undoubtedly, a significant player in this rise of the Birmingham industrial wave was Matthew Boulton, no book about the Quarter could ignore the profound influence that Boulton and his partners, Watt and Murdoch had on the City. With the Soho Manufactory sited a mile away from what would become the Quarter and his own determination to secure an Assay Office for Birmingham, to enhance his business as a silverware producer; the connections between Boulton and the Jewellery Quarter are obvious.

The Assay Office encouraged those who had been buckle and 'toy' manufacturers, or who possessed a high level of skill, to transfer their manufacturing talents towards objects of a more precious nature. As the upper middle-class inhabitants like Watt vacated their sub-urban villas for more rural locations; so the next social strata of crafted artisans moved in, and those who made jewellery, needed stampers to make blanks, and the die-sinkers to cut the dies to make the blanks, and platers and enamellers, and so on. First, they congregated around the area of St Paul's Church and soon they took the houses developed on the Colmore Estate (Chinn, 1999). Within a relatively short period of time the place was buzzing with many mixed trades, working and living, in a complex community; changing a room, or two, in a house into workrooms, for security and for convenience. Garret Masters and Small-Master, became small factory owners, small factories grew larger. They busied themselves in their creative enterprises, while the well established 'factor' system, found markets and customers in which to sell those wares.

All was conducted against a backdrop of national and international politics and drama. If a war happened, or a bank speculation failed, or a monarch died, the pains of recession could be felt, leaving business that depended on a wealthy economy to buy luxury items, on its knees. But, if metal prices were good, or a monarch acceded the throne, or fashions changed, the Quarter could boom. The diversity of production from silverware, to exquisite jewellery, to mayoral regalia, or commemorative medals, all of these markets were affected in different ways at different times. Some trades continue to this day, some have been transformed into other areas due to the vagaries of fashion (the end of the watch and chain became a boom for cufflinks), some trades have died out completely, such as the Pen Trade.

In 2013 we still sit in a global recession, when many have felt the severe effects of contracting economies and have very little disposable income to consider extraneous luxury. How has the Quarter responded to the current challenges? What effects have been felt by those who endeavour to continue their trade? Do the larger concerns fare better, than the 'outworker'? Do sixth-generation companies fall back on known experience, or do the modern enterprises find new ways to do things? These few questions form a key part of much that has been discussed with my contributors. They have been candid and generous in their responses, and I have ensured that what is published within this book is an accurate representation of what was confided in me. Every narrative has been written, negotiated and edited by the contributor, before the final draft has been published.

The book contains a multitude of images and photographs, many have come from the companies' archives themselves; their products and their histories. I am extremely grateful to them for providing so many images to add colour to this history. Also, I must thank the Jewellery Quarter Association and The Hockley Flyer for their contributions to illustrate parts of the text, and the JQA collectively with the Jewellery Quarter Regeneration Partnership for allowing me to use their wonderful three-dimensional map of the Quarter. To each and every contributor, I am extremely grateful for the giving of your time and opinion; this is your history, as honestly and as accurately as I can retell it. As Hutton (1783) writes, *"I embalm the present generation, for the inspection of the future,"* this is for all your heirs and successors, so that your thoughts and beliefs are never forgotten.

Chapter 1

A CITY OF TOYS

The City of Birmingham was the leading place for the manufacturing of metal 'toys' for the whole of the United Kingdom and as it leapt into the Victorian Age, the most productive manufacturing area of all things in metal in general. Three factors, can be firmly identified as to why this situation developed in a place that was insignificant on all maps of England for most of the second millennium. The first, was the huge availability of resources in abundance, the second, was the non-conformity of the town which attracted dissenters and entrepreneurs, and the third, were the people who came from many miles around, hungry, hardworking and determined to get on.

The subject of this book is the area that is called the Jewellery Quarter, I am going to endeavour to present a history of that area in this and subsequent chapters, by contextualising its growth and development within the history of the metal trades in general. This is not an easy task, as to make a comprehensive evaluation of the small industries would require considerably more discussion than a handful of chapters. I will be concentrating on the 18th and 19th centuries, as many of the narratives contained within this book commence in the mid 20th century. However, I will make a brief examination of what industry existed before the 18th century and how the Jewellery Quarter weathered the first tumultuous decades of the 20th century.

Matthew Boulton and his associates, will form a major part of this history, as it was through him and because of his entrepreneurial efforts that much of what we know in that area developed, including the canal infrastructure, which eventually led to the railways. The four main enterprises that he developed during his time; the Soho Manufactory, the Birmingham Assay Office, the Birmingham Mint, and the Soho Foundry, were all sited in a relatively close position geographically to the area, and there is no doubt that these astonishing enterprises attracted a considerable amount of attention to the luxury goods that could be produced in Birmingham.

The same could be said of what I consider to be the second wave of entrepreneurs to settle in, or near, the Quarter, the Pen Men, probably the most influential of these being Joseph Gillott. Not only did these individuals corner a very lucrative sector of the global market, but were some of the first major employers to settle in Birmingham, benefiting many people through direct employment.

It is also important to examine the peaks and troughs of the economy and how the actions of war and peace affected the markets in general. Also, how fashion drove the desire to have valuable items of adornment, or not, the rise and fall of the buckle industry, how the button industry boomed, and the death of Prince Albert and the detrimental effect that this caused to the Quarter.

Birmingham was known as a place of 'ironworkers' and 'ironmasters' as far back as the reign of Henry VIII. Hodder (2004) notes that on John Leland's visit in 1640, he recorded that 'a great parte of the towne is mayntayned by smithes', Hodder stresses that much of the archaeological evidence bears out the very high rate of activity that existed in and around the Bullring, Digbeth and Deritend, there is also considerable evidence for casting; the sand for this was taken from two pits, one at Key Hill and one at Warstone Lane, these pits would eventually become the cemeteries of the Jewellery Quarter.

Skipp (1987) gives a reason for this industry to arise, attributing it to the low 'capital outlay involved'. He goes on to say that the division between 'ironmongers' and 'ironmasters' was a natural development, as those who were making could not invest so much time in trying to sell their wares, as a consequence, the middlemen (or early factors) began to arise and fill the need for someone to market the finished products.

By the mid 17th century there were many ironworkers within the area, and the population had grown considerably, Skipp (1987):

"Birmingham's growth over the same period must have been in the order of 300%. Iron working was probably practised in something like one in every six households. The 1683 Hearth Tax lists 202 Birmingham properties with smith's hearths, of which 92, or almost half, were in Digbeth and Deritend."

The population was to expand at a much higher rate than all of the surrounding sites of urban settlement, by 1670 it had overtaken Coventry and become the largest town in Warwickshire, and for the next fifty or so years it continued to grow at an accelerated rate. Upton (1993) produced the following figures to exemplify this:

"In the 1670's the total must have been approaching 7,000, doubling again before the beginning of the next century. William Westley, who drew the first plan of the town, calculated that the population in 1700 was 15,032. In 1731, when he sat down to engrave his map, he estimated that it was 23,286."

Why Birmingham should grow to outstrip its long established neighbours is probably due to the geographical need of the location to be self-sufficient, thus driving the development of local manufacturing industry. As Skipp (1987) notes:

"The 102 square miles of land which is occupied by 'Britain's second city' is situated at the centre of a slightly elevated area known as the Birmingham Plateau and is drained by a 'hand' of small rivers flowing northwards into the Trent."

This accident of geography he argues, combined with the accessibility of 'iron ore and coal' (Hopkins 1998), meant that there was a necessity to manufacture products for use (initially for agricultural purposes) rather than trying to buy them in from elsewhere, with the state of the roads and tracks that fed the area, Skipp (1987):

"Down to the eighteenth century it was arguably to Birmingham's long-term advantage that, lacking a navigable river, it suffered from poor communications. The rise to pre-eminence of its metal industries could well have owed something to this deficiency. For costliness of road carriage must have been one of the factors which encouraged Birmingham craftsman to make as much as possible out of as little as possible: or in other words, to minimise their use of raw materials but maximise their skill."

The consequence of having to use small amounts of materials to their greatest potential, was to restrict the size of the wares manufactured, in order to recover the costs of labour and materials, this would mean an increase in complexity. According to Upton (1993) there was estimated to be '9,000 tons of iron' being used 'per annum', but obviously the local accessible mineral wealth could no longer be sustained to support that amount of usage, as a result eventually 'a third of which was imported'.

The first metal trade to display this combination of skill and material, was the gun making trade. There is evidence that Birmingham supplied arms for the civil war and from this the gun manufacturing industry was developed. During the 1690's, the gun makers of Birmingham were 'contracted to supply 200 muskets a month to the government' (Skipp, 1987). This trade developed exponentially, with the need to supply arms to the West Coast of Africa. By the end of the Napoleonic Wars Birmingham had supplied two-thirds of the arms to the army and navy (Skipp, 1987).

Hopkins (1998) notes that the supply of ordnance during the period between 1805-15 was 'very large' at 1,743,382.

According to Hopkins (1998) by the middle of eighteenth century the gun trade in Birmingham had become 'highly specialised', he notes that the first available Birmingham Directory of 1767, lists the various specialisms of manufacture, or different armaments, and parts of arms separately. It was because of the organisation of the industry, that it developed a very individual method of production, Hopkins (1998):

> "Usually a gun-maker did not manufacture guns at all; he was an entrepreneur who marketed guns made up of parts which had first been fashioned by specialist workmen (the 'material men', working on sub-contract), and then assembled by other workmen (the 'fabricators', or 'setters-up')."

This 'separate enterprise', very much defines the trades which Birmingham became both wealthy and famous for. The prescribed methods of separate artisans, manufacturing in relative isolation and then handing their work to another for the next operation became the main feature of all the metal trades, this method was practised particularly in the Jewellery Quarter. This also defined the workshops that they would work in, these were generally residential properties that had had one, or two rooms, equipped with the necessary benches and tools needed to make their parts of a gun. In the same way the original jewellers developed their small enterprises and it is no coincidence of proximity that the area that used to be defined as the Gun Quarter abuts the Jewellery Quarter, as many of these skills were transferable.

This difference of manufacture was punctuated by comparison of the rise of the large manufacturing businesses which developed in the cotton industry, requiring hundreds of people to work in factories in appalling conditions. Consequently, Birmingham developed an image as an area of high artisanal skill as the gun industry and its contemporary the 'toy' trade expanded rapidly. The reputation of the city increased and this encouraged many more to come, and this continued to perpetuate the high level of growth. Williams (2004) defines the characteristics of this emerging reputation thus:

> "Gun making was one or two of the earliest metal or 'hardware' trades of Birmingham; the other was the metal 'toy' trade. These craft-based trades established Birmingham's reputation as the 'other face' of the Industrial Revolution. One of the 'other face' characteristics of the industrialisation of Birmingham was the small bridgeable gap between artisan or master – leading to a culture of respectability, self-

improvement, independence and sometimes an unwillingness to confront the master."

The work was mainly manual and labour intensive, requiring a high-level of technical skill, they used hand tools in the first instance, but probably predetermined the need for much of the power machinery which was in use a century later. The growth of the industry and the numbers employed drove the need to gain Parliament's agreement to establish a 'Proof House' in 1813; up till that time all guns had to go to the London Proof House (Skipp, 1987).

The next metal industry which developed in parallel to the manufacture of guns was the brass industry. In 1740 the first brass works was established by Mr Turner in Coleshill. This was rapidly followed by a massive expansion of this trade to service the new fashions and demand for goods, combined with the wealth of pre-existing metal working skills (Hopkins, 1998). There was a large demand for all goods of an ornamental nature, such as; candle sticks, door handles, curtain rings, castors, furniture hinges, locks, keys, screws and bolts, eventually fittings for steam engines and plumbing. Hopkins (1998) emphasises the rapid development:

"In 1770 there were thirty-eight brass founders in Birmingham, by 1788 the number had risen to fifty-six, and in 1797 to seventy-one."

Not every man who came to Birmingham could work in these two trades, and as is the nature of the City, many who did arrive looked to find a living that may well grow into a sizeable income, as such, the further development of the one-man industries in metal evolved in another direction; again with consideration to using the minimum of materials, while at the same time maximising the opportunities to turn a profit.

The 'toy' trade as it was termed, was the manufacture of small articles fabricated in metal, such as; snuff boxes, trinket boxes, buckles and buttons (Hopkins, 1998). All of these things only required a worker to take a bench, and a handful of tools to start making the wares. This trade developed very rapidly, and as Skipp (1987) quotes Hutton on his visit in 1777 as noting that, Birmingham had become 'the great toyshop of Europe'. The main manufacture in this trade in eighteenth century was the fashion for buckles, of all manner, for all items of clothing (Skipp, 1987). However, fashions change and by 1812 this need was practically extinct and all energies turned to buttons, a sector of the 'toy' trade that had placed Birmingham very firmly on the map thanks to one self-made entrepreneur.

Known as 'the King of Buttons' by Hutton, John Taylor, developed a thriving industry (Upton, 1993). He was born in 1711 and was one of the 'ordinary artisans' which have been discussed in this chapter. Eventually he was to employ an army of workers numbering 500, in his factory in Crooked Lane, off Dale End (Skipp, 1987). He ran a very labour intensive operation, as button making requires many operations to assemble one button. This was at the time when only 'small hand machines' were available, he overcame this by employing vast numbers of people to carryout the many assembly operations. Hopkins (1998) quotes an observer who noted that he witnessed '70 different operations of 70 different work-folk'. He goes on to quote Lord Shelbourne's observations:

"According to him, a button would pass through fifty hands, and each hand would pass perhaps a thousand buttons a day."

This was the evidence that Taylor and his partner Samuel Garbett put to the Committee in the House of Commons, to encourage the development of powered machinery in the City to increase production.

There were some technological developments during this period, as they say, necessity is always the mother of invention, according to Skipp (1987):

"The stamping machine was replacing the die and hammer, by the mid eighteen century, together with the press, used for cutting out blanks, this greatly speeded up the production of a wide range of articles."

These machines are still the mainstay of the Quarter for producing blanks and embossed images. This is what must have attracted Gillott when he arrived in the early nineteenth century, it was most likely that these were the machines that he adapted to begin to generate pens in quantity and with speed.

Taylor used three main techniques for his decorating and finishing, according to Skipp (1987) they were; gilt plating, which he had been responsible for introducing to the city, japanning or enamelling, and painting. It is not hard to make the leap from the manufacture of buttons and other toys, to the manufacture of jewellery that would soon come. At his death in 1775, John Taylor left a sizeable fortune to the value of £200,000 (Skipp, 1987).

One of John Taylor's contemporaries in the japanning trade, was John Baskerville, who later became responsible for a revolutionary printing press, and the type font that still carries his name. He had a very ignominious end for a man of such influence and stature. When he died he was interred in his own mausoleum in 1775 on his property but because of his dissenting sympathies, once the house was sold in 1788, the new owner ordered his removal. He was then left unceremoniously for some years, moved around, buried and disinterred, his coffin upended and left against a warehouse wall, moved into a plumbers shop; until he was secreted away in one of the 136 vaults in Warstone Cemetery in the Jewellery Quarter (Uglow, 2002).

The 'toy' industry was large and employed many people in their own small environments trying to make a penny. This led to some of the work being particularly shoddy, in fact, the City got a reputation for producing 'cheap and nasty' goods (Hopkins, 1998). Hopkins continues with the old quotation that referred to bad workmanship that Birmingham was fast getting a reputation for:

"the old saying was that given a guinea and a copper kettle, a Birmingham workman could make a hundred pounds of jewellery."

The 'toy' trade of buckle manufacturers grew more, and more, concerned about the drop in their income, and not for the last time in the history of these products and the like they approached royalty; they tried to petition the Prince of Wales and the Duke of York to encourage them to wear buckles and not laces, but despite this and other entreaties, and some sympathy, the trade died off (Hopkins, 1998). All of these skills were transferable, and what the buckle industry lost the button industry gained, and this was a trade that would survive with some force for considerably longer. This transference of skills and ability to diversify, would characterise the 'hard working Brummie' at that time, as Skipp (1987) notes:

"It was during the eighteenth century, too, that Birmingham's own industry began to develop the flexibility of which it has been famous for ever since. The fact that its craftsmen possessed mastery over such a wide range of materials and basic techniques meant that when one line of business shows signs of failing, it was comparatively easy to switch to another."

Skipp adds to this that Birmingham outstripped its nearest rival Manchester, in the registering of patents, producing 'three times' more; there were many movements to improve manufacture, and make profit, so remained the ingenuity and invention of this rapidly moving city.

The expansion of Birmingham and its increasing productivity, now demanded a better system of transportation and communication, especially, to compensate for its elevated situation geographically. Upton (1993) emphasises the lack of accessibility for the City:

"Even Birmingham, whose energetic pursuit of trade and industry had allowed it to rise above its geographical restrictions, knew its limits: the nearest navigable river lay at Bewdley, some thirty miles away."

He continues, that the situation was so dire that 'eighty pack-horses were struggling in with fruit and vegetables from Evesham', this was because carts could not use the roadway. This was the picture on all the main arterial routes, including the Wolverhampton road.

The advent of the Turnpike Roads did much to improve this, enabling tolls to be paid to meet the maintenance. In 1726 a Turnpike Act was obtained to improve the Stratford and Warwick roads (Hopkins, 1998). This was followed in 1727 by the Wolverhampton road and 'in 1772 the Bristol road to Bromsgrove had £5,000 spent on its first four miles out of Birmingham' (Hopkins, 1993).

In 1768 a much better solution to the problem became available through the passage of the Birmingham Canal Act. It had followed considerable pressure from the leading businessmen and industrialists of the day, Matthew Boulton being one of the loudest spokesmen for the cause (Skipp, 1987). Much of this drive had come from the price of coal which was having to be transported in from the Black Country, Skipp (1987) notes that prior to the extensive canal building programme, coal had been retailing at 15s per ton, and by 1770 this had decreased to only 4s per ton. For the brass industry the coming of the canals was an absolute God send, the manufacturers were having to buy sheet material in from Bristol, and as copper prices began to rise dramatically, it was considered a necessity to manufacture their own brass from raw materials (Upton, 1993). According to Upton (1993) the first moves began:

"At The Swan Inn on 4th June 1767, James Brindley outlined the results of his survey for the cutting of a navigable canal between Birmingham and the Black Country coalfields. Canals would be unlikely to increase the speed of transportation, but the ability to carry heavy goods far outweighed this drawback."

It was decided to pay for the construction costs by selling shares at £140 each, by August of 1767 this offer of shares had managed to raise £50,000 and the plan for the Birmingham to Wolverhampton canal had been agreed (Skipp, 1987). This raising of capital proved highly successful, by the 1780's they were selling for £370 pounds each (Hopkins, 1998) and within 20 years of opening they were worth an astonishing £1000 per share (Upton, 1993).

In February 1768 the first part between Wednesbury to Paradise Street was opened (Upton, 1993). This was followed by a rapid building of canals that began to criss-cross the city, opening up access for all of the businesses that needed wharf-side facilities, to load and unload. According to Skipp (1987) the brass industry was able to gain great benefit from the canal that crosses Broad Street, Boulton too, had a stretch to serve his Soho Works. Canals enabled the raw materials, mainly coal in quantity to be delivered and more importantly the finished goods, to be carried out of the City, to connect with the burgeoning canal network across the country.

The Birmingham Canal Network grew rapidly and was fast becoming the centre, known as 'The Brindley Silver Cross' (Skipp, 1987). Many of these canals were built by competing companies and relationships were not always harmonious. Upton (1993) lists the many canals that were built by 1793, which included; the Birmingham and Fazeley (1783), the Worcester to Birmingham (1791), the Warwick to Birmingham (1793). He states that by that date over a hundred boats a day were using the main Birmingham canal.

It was very much the motorway network of its day, criss-crossing the country, serving all of the major cities and of course the ports, as Upton (1993) notes:

"The connections that this network provided were far-reaching. The Warwick and Birmingham canal for example, connected the Digbeth branch to Sri Lanka."

But as he continues later, just as the modern motorway network is under capacity for the amount of road traffic that it has to carry, so too the canal network eventually became choked by too many users. However, the BCN carried some startling statistics of its usage to the end of the nineteenth century, Upton (1993):

"The tonnage of goods transported on the BCN rose steadily until the end of last century, when it reached 8½ million tonnes per annum, almost 20 percent of the national total. A daily total of 31½ million gallons of water was recycled from the bottom of the system to the top."

Upton (1993) also supports the notion that there may be some truth in the claim that Birmingham had more miles of canals than Venice, but as he stresses it very difficult to prove, because of the infilling of so many of the linking waterways and basins that once existed, but without those the City could still boast 'roughly 33 miles of canal, comprising around 3.1 percent of all navigable waterways in the country'.

There is no doubt that the building of the network helped the economy to boom, even if it was only due to the transportation of coal at cheap cost, Hopkins (1998) is quite correct in his assessment that the slowness of the network, combined with the problems of freezing did not necessarily make it wholly reliable. The brass industry was one of the biggest beneficiaries and never looked back, as Upton (1993) points out:

"By Victorian times, Birmingham was the centre of the brass trade, with over 200 manufacturers and over 400 works in 1865."

It is safe to say that a City whose main trade was based on the fabrication in metal, all types of metal, the canal network gave opportunities for expansion and delivering to new markets, that had not been dreamt of before it was developed.

Certainly, for a man of Matthew Boulton's entrepreneurial strengths, to not have a canal would have been a very bad business strategy. Matthew Boulton can be assessed as one of the greatest leading industrialists of his time for Birmingham, but his national success far outstripped any local success that he achieved, and that was mainly due to a partnership that did not come to fruition until much later in his business life, that of the Boulton and Watt steam engine. I am devoting the next chapter to the Matthew Boulton story as he plays such a significant part in the map of the area near to where the Quarter sits. However, in this chapter I am going to deal briefly with the impact, if any, that their revolutionary invention had to the City of Birmingham.

It is important from the outset to try and understand why so many entrepreneurs and businessmen ended up in such a small area. The answers are as entwined, as the industries that they fathered. I have called Birmingham a City throughout this chapter, for that is what it is, however, that is a relatively recent title in its history. It grew so rapidly, that it was the size of a City long before it ever received the right to name itself so. Up until 1838, it was viewed as a town, and population was only recorded in terms of the most central area of what is now described as the city centre. It was incorporated as a borough in 1838 (Hopkins, 1998), when according to *www.visionofbritain.org* the population stood at in excess of 130,000. Prior to this Birmingham was unrestricted by laws of governance that affected the established cities, because of its lack of a charter, it could operate without the accepted practices of other places. According to Hopkins (1998), because of its lack of Charter it was not tied into restrictive regulations that governed the existence of guilds or apprenticeships, which allowed industrialists to operate without fetters. He continues in the same paragraph to quote Hutton when he acknowledged that 'A town without a charter is a town without a shackle'. This lack of restriction although positive in one way, caused problems elsewhere.

Without proper infrastructure and with the rapid growth of the area, it lacked 'control and governance' (Upton, 1993), he continues:

"The problems were the lighting and planning of the streets, pollution of the streets and the air, rising crime and bad housing."

In 1769, there was an Act passed to improve the road system, and this led the way for the creation of three main public buildings by the 1830's; the

Market Hall, Curzon Street Railway Station and the Town Hall (Upton, 1993), however, this was for the most part a slow process, until Birmingham had conferred upon it the status of a City in February 1889. That is not to say that little was done, it was just difficult to press for change without application to national Government prior to the 1830's but there was significant progress made during the nineteenth century.

It did offer more opportunity to those businessmen who wished to establish enterprise without shackles, and sanctuary to those who followed other religious doctrines, the Dissenters. The lack of restriction on religious freedom and the tolerance for other practices of faith, attracted many to arrive. Upton (1998) notes that by 1851 only half the population were practicing Anglicans and the other 50 percent consisted of; Quaker, Baptist, Methodist, Roman Catholic, Unitarian and Jewish practitioners. According to Upton, Quakers and the Unitarians were higher in social standing than the other non-conformists. This does account for the high concentration of wealthy well-educated people in a relatively densely populated area. Which of course would attract others of the same social standing with entrepreneurial drive to achieve.

In his book, Upton (1998) examines the place of the entrepreneur in the City, and has referred to the research that describes an entrepreneur in these terms:

"as any person who undertakes an enterprise for profit; but more specifically, he has been seen essentially as an *organizer.*"

He does stress that the City did have the propensity to produce 'vigorous businessmen' some who achieved political governance on the national stage. Through this he supports the notion that:

"It will not be disputed that the Industrial Revolution owed much to the initiative and drive of its leading industrialists, factors, retailers and bankers."

But he does stress that there are large differences between those considered entrepreneurs of their age as those of today, who nowadays are far more isolated from the activities that make them the profit. The industrialists then were very often involved in every sense and 'technically competent'. They were active in their premises and concerned (in the most part) for their individual workers. He concludes that:

"Finally, their active involvement in both their own enterprises and in the general business life of the community provides a fascinating glimpse of energetic entrepreneurship in an age of expanding opportunities before the coming of more easily obtainable limited liability, and the development of the larger industrial unit on a far greater scale after 1850."

That last point leads me to cast the waves of entrepreneurialship of Birmingham in two parts, those that aspired before 1850 and those that came after. Matthew Boulton was the last great entrepreneur before the transformation to large industry occurred, and for the most part was responsible for that.

It could be argued in terms of continued success that John Taylor achieved far more, and that his only limitations were caused by the lack of technological advancement to service his vision (Upton, 1998). Boulton was certainly not as successful in the earlier part of his business career, and was dogged by financial and labour problems, but as all great entrepreneurs he sought solutions continually, and was always on the look out for his next big venture that might result in fruitful return. The partnership with James Watt that began in 1775, had been driven by a business case to provide a better solution to power his manufactory at Soho; he knew through his many intellectual friends of Watt's invention and could foresee the business advantage that could be gained by encouraging their mutual association.

He had made advances to Watt prior to this in 1768, but at that point Watt had been in a partnership with his first financial backer John Roebuck, during which he had made some progress in testing and proving his separate condenser pumping elsewhere (Skipp, 1987). It was not until Watt's first partnership had dissolved due to financial difficulties (and Boulton, who had been consumed by his own financial problems turned his interests to power), that Watt decided to turn to his new backer. Boulton was a visionary and he could see a much greater potential for this invention than just the action of pumping; he realised that it must be possible to convert the linear motion generated by a beam engine into a rotary motion. There were many larger business operations, such as the cotton mills in Lancashire, that needed rotary power to drive their vast factories. Boulton continually pressed home the need to develop this new form of engine to Watt, and indeed some would argue, that he did much more than this, probably being actively involved in offering technical solutions (Andrew, 2009).

Once the machine was patented in 1782, Boulton set to applying the technology to his own works, as he could envisage a method of minting coinage that could be quick, efficient and above all accurate; and would challenge the monopoly of the Royal Mint. This he had achieved by 1788, powering six steam driven presses in his own mint (Skipp, 1987). Although, this radical invention was greeted with considerable enthusiasm nationally, as it did give the power that was needed for the larger factories, locally it was envisaged as a calamitous technology, arriving at a very bad time economically.

One of the first experimental rotary engines had been installed at Samuel Pickards, a button-maker on Snow Hill in 1779, to operate a mill. Once the technology was unleashed, it was an obvious transference for Pickard to utilise the mill to grind flour; this combined with the severe economic downturn that the country was experiencing due to the French Revolutionary Wars, the invention was perceived as a threat to personal income by the general public (Skipp, 1987). He continues that in 1795, a riot was sparked by the rising price of bread, turning the mob's attention on Pickard's Mill, who were accused of 'hoarding grain' thus inflating prices still further. This ended with the death of two rioters, who were shot by the dragoons. It was an uneasy truce that settled, for the following year there were more problems of a similar nature and worse to come.

This antagonism shown towards the steam engine in Birmingham explains in part the reason why Boulton and Watt found it difficult to establish a market locally, but this was not the only reason. As I have emphasised throughout this chapter, the nature of employment and the ways in which this was carried out, did not drive the need to use steam power. With so many small business concerns and one-man enterprises depending primarily on manual skill, there was neither the desire, or the capital investment necessary available at that time. Whereas nationally, Boulton and Watt had set themselves up as consultants to aid installation, and then before the patent expired, as manufacturers and had many buyers for their incredible invention; by 1800 they had 'erected around 450 steam engines' (Upton. 1993). The local picture was much slower and it was only with the advent of the larger enterprises, such as the Pen Men, that Birmingham began to exploit its own home grown technology.

It was the next generation that was set to the task of promoting the steam engine, James Watt (junior) and Matthew Boulton (junior), as James Watt (senior) retired to all intents and purposes, to his home initially at Harper's Hill, which existed in Regents Place in the Quarter; Watt died at Heathfield House (designed by Samuel Wyatt the architect of Soho House) in 1819. Matthew Boulton (senior) died in 1809, at his beloved Soho House, over-looking Hockley Brook; the site of the Manufactory, the Mint and the Foundry that he had created. Hopkins (1998) notes that Watt had always said of his friend, that 'he had always been more interested in fame than fortune'. Certainly, compared to the death of John Taylor some thirty years earlier, Matthew Boulton only left modest wealth at £15,000, but what he left in terms of wealth generation for the world is beyond calculation.

As the area around Soho began to subside in its prominence, especially on the death of James Watt (junior) in 1848, the Soho Manufactory only existing until 1862, the Foundry 1896. The area of the Quarter on the hill above began to rise. As with everything it was a slow evolution from trade to trade, from 'toy' making to more refined objects that required a higher level of skill. Obviously, many of the earlier jewellers who settled there were attracted by the proximity to such a vast enterprise; many affluent people were to visit Boulton in the valley below and take in his impressive works, those with the skill saw the opportunity to site themselves nearby in the hope of the passing trade. According to Hopkins (1998):

"In 1800 there were probably not more than a dozen workshops in the trade, employing 400 workers. In the 1830s the trade expanded greatly, and continued to grow in the 1840s, becoming concentrated in the St Paul's district of the town."

He confirms in his analysis that this coincidence of the rise of the Quarter coincided with the demise of the 'toy' trade, and that those skills had become 'absorbed' within jewellery production. It was a diverse trade initially, as it moved from the cheaper materials through to the precious metals and stones, so a vast variety of articles could be found in inexpensive gilt metals, through to the wide use of gold and silver. Any items could be purchased, from trinkets and 'cheap imitations' through to table ware and expensive ornaments. These enterprises operated as many had done before, first on a very small scale; one-man, or small employers, to the larger businesses with no more than fifty persons employed. The tools remained the same, apart from wide use of the press and the stamp, in much the same way as they are used today. It was an industry that encouraged the 'best of the best' to turn his hand to, if he worked hard and with great skill, there was a chance to make money (Hopkins, 1998).

To summarise this chapter, the rise of the metal trades which led to the development of the Jewellery Quarter, were driven in the first instance by the need to manufacture these items, due to Birmingham's difficult geographical location. The subsequent expansion and the exploitation of these trades, was inspired by the first wave of industrialists and entrepreneurs, who were not 'shackled' by a charter to restrict their practices. This lack of status also attracted many others of dissenting religion who were able to live in an atmosphere of tolerance, and this led to a concentration of well educated individuals of social status. The hard working environment that developed, which gave everyone a chance to aspire, attracted many to come to Birmingham, rapidly expanding the population; this in turn led to problems with the poor infrastructure and communications, many of which were solved through private collaboration and enterprise. As the place grew, so the problems of slow production drove the need to solve the issue of power generation, to be able to speed up mechanical processes, which until that time had been hand-powered.

In the next chapter, I will examine the story of Matthew Boulton and his many associates who led much of what could be considered the industrial revolution. I strongly believe that many of the jewellers chose to site themselves within the Quarter in an effort to profit from their profoundly influential neighbour. Certainly, James Watt lived there at Harper's Hill in Regents Place, and the connections to the place are very strong. Many of the products that Matthew Boulton produced in the Manufactory at Soho, where later emulated by producers on a smaller scale in the Quarter.

Chapter 2

POWER AND THE PHILOSOPHERS – MATTHEW BOULTON

There is no doubt that Matthew Boulton has left a legacy that was instrumental in driving much of what we know as the Industrial Revolution. His contribution towards the development of the technology to power the world through his association and partnership with James Watt, is a well known fact, but until recently understood as the facilitations of businessman and entrepreneur towards the invention, rather than as a direct contributor to the steam engine's development. However, much of that previous thinking is being reshaped by extensive research and analysis which has been carried out on the Boulton Archive which is held at Birmingham Library. Until a few years ago, he was dismissed to some extent, due to the lack of authorial accounts, whereas James Watt and others had been discussed in some detail. Now there has been a revisit by many authors to the papers and documents that have been left behind that has revealed much about Boulton, previously unconsidered. This evidence now leads to a strong belief that Boulton was more than just an innovator, or a business operator, he can be viewed in a new light, as a 'hands-on' engineer, or as described by Dick (2009) when reading Jones (2008), as a *savant-fabricant;* or in the direct French to English translation a 'scientist-manufacturer'.

In my own assessment and having some close experience of the character of entrepreneurial behaviour, it is driven from a need to primarily make money, by exploring opportunity through reading and knowledge and finding a niche, an idea that can be exploited to make that profit. It requires someone who can take risks, calculated risks, but often the vacillations of the market make it impossible to foresee all of the inhibitors to success; and when success is not forthcoming in the first instance, the character is not to give in, but to turn the blockage into a new opportunity and determinism. A person with entrepreneurial vision is a perennial optimist, who has no fear of failure, and always has an alternative direction to follow to find another advantage. There is a certain amount of luck required, of being in the right place at the right time, to have a product or service that is needed at that moment, and without the unforeseen economic downturns occurring. However, these people also understand that luck or advantage can be created and maximised, through knowledge gathering, facilitating strong business networks, and securing a good line of credit.

All of these characteristics were possessed by Matthew Boulton. He was a driven man of knowledge, he had some incredible luck being born to a father who established himself as a businessman, and making an advantageous marriage. He was able to establish very strong networks of supporters and intellectuals, such as the Lunar Society, by his general affability and social skills. Previously, some have commented that he was not a good businessman in his earlier years as an independent manufacturer, I will argue that as an entrepreneur he suffered the same vagaries of the market and various inhibitors which he successfully overcame, and far from lacking in acumen, he was working towards an eventual success. Everything that he did, from building the Manufactory at Soho, to pursuing the need to establish an Assay Office in Birmingham, and to his push to establish a partnership with Watt, were all driven by a business case to solve various problems for Matthew Boulton. However, many of the things that he did do, required a knowledge and an understanding that goes far beyond a basic comprehension; all of his advances were built on an absolute technical competence.

Unlike John Taylor, who had come from nothing and worked his way to the top, upon his death leaving a considerable fortune, Boulton had been born to a family that had been moderately well off, had fallen into some hard times and was working back to wealth. We know that his father, Matthew Boulton senior, had been moved from Lichfield to Birmingham and been apprenticed in the 'toy' trade as a button and buckle manufacturer (Mason, 2009). He married in 1723, and his first son Matthew died, so on the birth of his second son (third child) in 1728, he too was named Matthew Boulton. At that time, the father's small firm had become well-established in Snow Hill (Mason, 2009). By 1745, Matthew Boulton (junior) had left education, of which little is known and joined his father in the family concern (Dick, 2009).

Mason (2009) records that his notebooks as a young man reveal that he possessed a 'wide-ranging curiosity' and a thirst to gather knowledge. He could not take advantage of the more formal education that someone of his intellectual capabilities would have thrived upon, due to the present family circumstances, so for the most part, his education was self-acquired. He must have realised that to get on, and to be able to climb the ladder in social context would require the same broad understanding as achieved by that class he aspired to; he read everything from astronomy, to the classics, geology, accountancy and the sciences (Mason, 2009).

His internal drive to learn and personal charm, combined with the family associations and a certain amount of good fortune, enabled him to marry well in 1749. He first wife Mary Robinson was the daughter of a Lichfield man of money (he was to die the following year leaving his daughter a large inheritance). This placed Matthew Boulton junior into that social standing that he had so desired to achieve, he was able to build his first networks of influence, that were to assist in his business progress, with people such as, Samuel Garbett, John Baskerville and John Taylor (Uglow, 2002). Uglow continues later that 'Garbett taught Boulton how to finance ambitious projects', combined with his good fortune all things were now possible. Uglow (2002) describes the young businessman in these terms:

> "Matt Boulton was neat and dark and dapper, with curly brown hair, keen eyes and a broad grin. Frank and humorous, always with an eye to the main chance, he was a man on the make like his town."

For what he had gained in business, all was loss in his personal life, in their 10 years of marriage they lost three children and Mary died in 1759, and Matthew Boulton senior shortly afterwards. Matt was undoubtedly thrown into deep grief and other authors speak of the friendship that blossomed between him and his dead wife's sister, Anne. They shared a common bond of the loss of a loved one, this developed into a very fond affection, and it is clear that Matthew pursued her vigorously in love letters, much against family approval. According to Uglow (2002) this was quite a feverish exchange of letters and affection, and it was inevitable that it would lead to marriage, and on the 25th June 1860, they were married in London, well away from family interference. Much of the obstruction had come from Anne's own brother who viewed Matthew as a fortune seeker, for each of the girls had stood to inherit £14,000 from the family estate, Anne was now worth £28,000 the equivalent of one and half, to two million pounds today (Uglow, 2002).

It was about this time that the group that would be called the Lunar Society had begun to meet frequently. This group of men, were made up of academics, intellectuals, scientists, and industrialists, their common ground was all things of scientific extraction. It was much a group of friends that met, as a discussion group, though these societies were developing in many places, what set the Lunar Society apart was the sheer concentration of knowledge and understanding contained within. The man considered to be more of the leader, (though that was through his personality than by any definition) was Erasmus Darwin (the grandfather of Charles Darwin). Darwin was a doctor, with a love for all things flora and fauna, who had a predilection for writing all of his thoughts in verse. Uglow (2002) records the principal members in order of age who made up the substantive body of the group for the next thirty years; John Whitehouse, Matthew Boulton, Josiah Wedgwood, Erasmus Darwin, Joseph Priestley, William Small, James Keir, James Watt, William Withering, Richard Lovell Edgeworth, Thomas Day and Samuel Galton. Boulton, Wedgwood and Galton were manufacturers, Whitehouse a clock and scientific instrument maker, Small a medic like Darwin, Keir a chemist primarily, Priestley a Unitarian minister, Withering a medic and botanist, and Edgeworth and Day had a strong interest in social science among other things. This group claimed their title from their habit of meeting around the time of the full moon, allowing a well lit night for the men to travel on bad roads. This network of individuals was not just a group for discussion, but very often commercial interests were promoted and encouraged, and they shared a passion to change things for the better in every way.

Matthew Boulton was deeply influenced by the business success of John Taylor, and probably wished to emulate this, or surpass it if he could. Uglow (2002):

"Taylor was a role model for budding manufacturers. A real pioneer, he had broken with the old practice of 'putting-out' work, whereby a manufacturer received an order and then delegated the work to different craftsmen – to one man who made the button 'shells', another who made the thread rings, a third who made the decorated tops... For old-established merchants such as Taylor and for young bucks such as Boulton, these were promising times. Taxes were minimal; trade drove prosperity, and commerce became a badge of patriotism."

John Taylor had caused many to want to visit the City to take in the spectacle of his extensive business enterprise, this patronage that he received would have a positive affect on his profitability. Boulton knew that this ability to market not just the product offering, but the place where it was produced was an absolute necessity during that era; he set his heart on building the most impressive Manufactory that anyone could ever hope to see. His first move towards his new venture was to purchase the lease on a large amount of land at Soho in 1761 (which included a house which had been built c.1857, and a mill) for which he paid £1,000 (Birmingham Museum and Art Gallery, 2002). The house was unfinished in the interior, but he was not to turn his attentions to this until the construction of his new works were underway; initially his mother and sister lived there as he continued to live at Snow Hill. For a while his new business partner would take up occupation, before grumbling and complaining, he was removed by Boulton who chose as always to live near to his premises (Uglow, 2002).

The site had been carefully chosen, it was two miles from the City centre and in a very rural location, but adjacent to the Turnpike Road. In 1762, with the expanding business at Snow Hill having outgrown the premises he went into partnership with John Fothergill, who had extensive continental experience. Their association was to be dogged by financial difficulty, with cash flow and liquidity presenting a constant challenge; Fothergill was a very serious man and a worrier, unlike Boulton's more optimistic outlook.

It was not until 1764, when Anne Robinson came into her inheritance, that Boulton was able to raise enough money to be able to build his dream. Through his continued good fortune, John Baskerville was able to arrange a large loan 'of £3,500 (later increased to £10,000) from the London publisher Jacob Tonson' (Uglow, 2002).

Boulton opened the Manufactory to the greatest of fanfares in 1765, according to Uglow (2002):

"Fothergill estimated that it could hold four hundred workers – although Boulton, in flamboyant mood, upped this to seven or eight hundred."

The Soho Manufactory caused a sensation amongst society countrywide, it was his intention to create as much public interest as he could. Which is why it was built in such a spectacular style, and within a rural idyll which would be landscaped extensively. Boulton wanted to offer all of his visitors an amazing and enthralling experience, it was very much a theatrical stage that was probably more 'smoke and mirrors' than a serious money machine, although one day he would make that too. He had it built with the intention of challenging the Taylor monopoly on thrilling visitation to the City, as Jones (2002) comments:

"But Matthew Boulton was about to outstrip him inasmuch as his new Manufactory was a purpose-built edifice, rather than a series of workshops located in the crooked back alleys of the town."

This I assess as the biggest gamble that Boulton took in his career, he knew he had to speculate to accumulate, and he also realised that if he possessed the most spectacular operation that was so accessible to view, that he could develop the business potential still further. Hutton (1783), writes a glowing description:

"The proprietor, invited by a genius, a fortune of 30,000*l.* and a little stream, which promised to facilitate business, has erected the most elegant works in these parts, said to accommodate seven hundred persons. Upon the hungry ground, where, in 1758 stood one paltry cottage, we now behold, a city in miniature."

I do believe that he also knew that he would indeed over-extend himself financially; for the high cost of capital outlay in machines and premises could never be recouped through the potential turnover, but to him this was a first stage of a longer game. Of course, things were extremely difficult with mounting losses that had been accumulating since 1764, when they were assessed at £3,000 (Uglow, 2002), but Boulton was not to be perturbed and he set about finding ways of improving his situation and building the business.

There were two main problems that Boulton was confronted with. The first was the generation of power needed for the Manufactory, which was being powered by a watermill that was subject to inconsistencies due to freezing weather or drought. The second was caused by his product development. By now Boulton had broken away from the image as a 'toy' manufacturer and was manufacturing more exclusive larger items, initially in Sheffield Plate and then silver; the silverware would always present problems due to the fluctuations of bullion prices and the continued bad payment of well-off clients. These more exclusive items and the smaller things in precious metals required hallmarking, a very complicated and time consuming process, as this had to be done in Chester. The roads were intolerable, and very often work was being damaged, even lost and stolen, on its perilous trip to and from Chester. This complication to the process of manufacture added weeks to fulfilling any orders, and led to numerous letters of apology from Boulton to his clients (Uglow, 2002). The lack of accessibility to a local Assay Office was going to cause problems for a few more years, but the development of better provisions of power could be solved, and Boulton had read enough to know who might help in this endeavour.

In 1768 Boulton resolved to improve his power advantage in the first instance. Watt had some association with the Lunar Society prior to his eventual move to Birmingham, being the intellectual academics that they were, they were well versed in his work to improve on the Newcomen steam engine, through his network of like businessmen and backers in Scotland. John Roebuck (Watt's financial partner) had raised money through Garbett, to finance his experiments; Darwin was fascinated by the application of the steam engine to a 'fiery chariot'; and it was said that the Birmingham society was as much part of the Edinburgh circle as the Scottish incumbents were (Uglow, 2002.)

Watt spent years wrestling with the problem of how to improve the energy efficiency of the beam steam engine. It was obvious to him that a considerable amount of energy was lost by the cooling of the single cylinder, which became a condenser by the dousing of cold water to create the vacuum. The energy loss from the cooling of that one cylinder at boiling point to cold, and then to reheat was a considerable waste of more energy, which reduced both potential and speed. Watt's solution was to apply a separate condenser, which could be attached to the cylinder, thus reducing the severe energy loss as the steam would be cooled in there. Watt was dogged by manufacturing problems of producing a well-machined and strong enough chamber once welded, that did not fracture or leak. Finally, he secured a 14 year patent for his process in 1769 (Upton, 1993), and installed a successful engine in Kinneil in Scotland.

In the previous year, Watt had finally made his first of two visits to Birmingham, greatly encouraged by all in the Lunar Society, it was on his second visit to the City that he came to the Manufactory, according to Uglow (2002):

"He was astounded, to put it mildly, at the variety and modernity. He saw the watermill 'employed in laminating metal for the buttons, plated goods etc., and to turn laps for grinding and the polishing steel work'. He heard that Boulton was the first to use a mill this way, and saw several other ingenious improvements."

Boulton used the opportunity to share his concerns regarding the inconsistencies in the power supplied through the use of the wheel, and no doubt Watt was already aware. Sometime during that year, Watt and Roebuck (who had been facing increasing financial difficulties) offered limited rights to Boulton to manufacture the reciprocating engine, they specified the three counties of Warwickshire, Staffordshire and Derbyshire only. Boulton could see a business case, but realised it required a business mind and did not perceive that 'engineers' could drive the successful application of the technology, so he held out 'for all or nothing' (Uglow, 2002). He played the game of flattery and enticement with Watt, and waited, probably knowing that John Roebuck needed to raise money, and that without financial security, Watt would be seeking another funding opportunity eventually.

In March 1773, Roebuck was declared bankrupt, within a short time Boulton (who had been a creditor) made Watt an offer to take Roebuck's shares in the steam engine. Watt was probably somewhat reluctant at this stage, and suffering some personal distress, he knew that he would probably have to leave Scotland and relocate to Birmingham, but his financial situation was dire and this was the only offer available, he had even had to resort to work as a canal engineer. The very same year the full-size engine that had been based in Kinneil, was moved to Soho, but remained in pieces until Watt finally arrived the following year to settle (Demidowicz, 2009).

Then the engine was reassembled in an 'engine house' to add the desperately needed power for the Manufactory, while at the same time the Boulton and Watt partnership was first mooted, for the installation of steam engines and their continual design improvement. There is much evidence to suggest that Boulton was not the 'technically disinterested entrepreneur' that has been assumed, but was actively involved in making suggestions for progressing the design in various ways. From the documents and letters that Andrew (2002) has analysed within the Boulton Archive, 'Boulton wrote of the testing of parts of the engine, trying various components for excessive frictions', this he would continue to do even through the process of the rotary engine development later.

Considering that Boulton, had been a manufacturer since 1746 in metal, having much knowledge of fabrication and the basic machine tools available (many of which had been developed by his business ventures), why it should surprise anyone that Boulton did not have keen technical interest is the issue? Boulton could not devote as much time as he would have preferred, because he had to be involved in the business concerns, that Watt as an engineer would have had very little aptitude for. In fact, in 1775 Boulton actively pursued an extension of the patent through Parliament, as he realised that the only way to preserve his investment and to protect his business interest, was to prevent any other manufacturer from gaining the technology.

For Boulton his primary inhibitor to his eventual success with the Manufactory had been solved, he had managed in the intervening years to bring a successful conclusion to the secondary problem, the need for a local Assay Office. In 1771, Boulton had finally come to the end of his tether through the lack of adequate facilities locally, he had already experienced too many difficulties sending work to Chester and the final tipping point was the severe damage that a pair of candlesticks endured on their arduous journey. He had explored the alternative of sending them to London for assaying, but the risks of his designs being copied were too great (Uglow,

2002). He realised that the only way to ensure his desire 'of becoming a great silversmith' was to bring a petition before Parliament in 1772, to establish an Assay Office in Birmingham.

According to Baggott (2009) Boulton had always been aware that the need for an Assay Office would be paramount to his business success, and that for the campaign to succeed he knew that he must bring his full weight and that of his networks of influence behind it. He also knew that Sheffield was waging a similar campaign and he had no desire to weaken Birmingham's case by joining forces with the northern town; he considered that the real battle would be against the London interests in keeping all of the business to themselves. He left for a stay in London of some months in 1773 before the petition was to be read in Parliament, with an armoury of argument and written support behind him. His many advocates included a long list of aristocratic connections, and a supreme parliamentary lobbyist – Samuel Garbett (Uglow, 2002).

He fought for the petition tirelessly which put the case thus:

"The petition from Birmingham stressed the inconvenience, expense hazard and delay of sending silver to Chester, along with the limitations placed on the Birmingham trade, and the lack of success to domestic and foreign markets caused by the absence of Assay office in Birmingham."

(The Assay Office Birmingham – Independence, integrity, innovation.) The main force of objection came from London manufacturers, who believed that there was insufficient skill, in either of the two towns that had petitioned; in their view, this would lead to a dilution of quality and fraud. Boulton was thoroughly fed up with the London snobbery and the constant slurs on Birmingham quality, he was able to persuade the MP for Lichfield – Thomas Gillbert – to purchase twenty-two pieces of silver which had been produced in London and assayed, these were then presented to the Committee considering the petitions. All but one of the pieces were found to have silver quality well below the standard that was required (Uglow, 2002). Boulton had won his case, on the 31st August 1773, The Birmingham Assay Office opened on New Street.

There is no doubt that this establishment of the needed Assay Office, shifted the emphasis of manufacture in the City and encouraged the expansion into precious metals, consequently more and more, would come to Birmingham who possessed these skills and from that the infant Jewellery Quarter came into being; beginning in the St Paul's district very accessible to the New Street Assay Office and a mile from the Soho Manufactory with the many visitors of influence along the Turnpike Road. Boulton was the first to take advantage of the Office, to have his makers mark 'MB' stamped on his silverware, he was also the first to fail the quality standards 'the scratch test'.

According to The Assay Office Birmingham on the first day of opening, Boulton was the first to admit pieces:

"That day Boulton and Fothergill were the first to register their Sponsor's or Maker's mark as they submitted 104 articles for assay and hallmarking, in addition to tea vase furniture and 30 pairs of buckle rims. Boulton's campaign in London had been conducted in the Crown and Anchor tavern in the Strand and Birmingham and Sheffield chose to adopt the sign of the tavern for their respective marks. It was written into the Act that Sheffield's mark would be the Crown and Birmingham's the Anchor."

The Boulton and Fothergill trade in silverware improved, week on week, and rose steadily and reached the peak of production around 1776 and 1777 (Uglow, 2002), this coincided with the rise in his interests in the steam engine business with Watt. At that time his business emphasis shifted towards the engines, and there was a marked decline in his production of silver though it remained as a 'staple' business for Boulton (Uglow, 2002).

Boulton managed to extend the patent on the steam engine until the end of the century, by a private Act of Parliament in June 1775, which is when the official partnership with Watt began (Upton, 1993). The reciprocating engine (an engine that repeats and returns using linear motion) was in demand and things moved very quickly, by the following year two engines were installed one in the Black Country at Tipton for a Colliery and one at Broseley for a blast furnace. The next few years were dizzy with progress as the pair conquered the Cornwall mines with their reciprocating pumping engine. They were constantly under threat from those who would try to copy the technology, but the patent protection ensured a certain amount of security.

At this time, Boulton employed a talented engineer from Scotland, William Murdoch, he impressed Boulton to the extent that he was put to work immediately in the pattern shop, but then given greater and greater roles of responsibility, in installation of the engines. Finally, Watt felt that Murdoch was the only person that he could trust to oversee operations on behalf of Boulton and Watt in Cornwall. Murdoch was a very affable and fine fellow, who was evidently trustworthy; he befriended all that he met, being tall and extremely fit and he had a presence which gave him authority.

By the late 1790's Boulton's mind had turned to exploiting this technology to the optimum and he had long believed that the rotary, 'rotative' engine was the way forward and pressed on Watt the need to develop ideas in this direction. This was as much due to the death of his second wife and his need to throw himself into his business for distraction, as any indications that were coming from untapped markets. Late in 1779, Watt wrote to Boulton informing him that he would begin to work on the principles of 'circular motion' (Andrew, 2009). It is obvious that his progress was not as fast as Boulton would like, for by the summer of 1881, he was imploring Watt by letter that the people of the big cities were 'steam mill mad' (Uglow, 2002). Watt was somewhat irritated by this pressure and Uglow states that his response was to try and dismiss this as a passing fancy, in his opinion the reciprocating engines were enough for their enterprise. Boulton persevered with a barrage of good natured protestations to the contrary.

In 1882, Watt applied for a patent for a 'rotary motion' application to the steam engine. The same year the Boulton and Fothergill partnership was officially dissolved, when Fothergill passed away. Boulton had just one partner now, James Watt. Possibly encouraged by his elevation in status, when Watt made the application for the patent he suggested five methods of conversion of motion from linear to circular; although only one would eventually prove successful, this was called the 'sun and planet gear' (Upton, 1993). This technology had been first suggested and designed by Murdoch, although Watt developed it further, but he continued to encounter technical difficulties in finding a resolution due to his over-complexity of design. It was Boulton according to Andrew (2009) that suggested a 'much simpler arrangement' another example of why Boulton as an engineer should not be dismissed out-of-hand.

It may have been due to the injection of optimism at finding that he was now in profit through the partnership with Boulton in 1883, by the sum of £4,000 (Uglow, 2002), that galvanised Watt into some assertive action, for by 1884 he was writing excitedly to his partner revealing that he had found a way forward. In 1886 and 1887, they were able to erect two rotary steam engines at Albion Mills near Blackfriars Bridge in London. Their eventual success had coincided with a particularly bleak time in the economy of the country. It was during the period of the French Revolutionary Wars, which had caused a massive inflation in living costs, particularly the cost of grain. As bread was the staple food of most of the population, effectively more money bought less bread, and anything that was viewed as adding to this disaster was immediately under threat from the mob (Upton, 1993).

There were further problems for the likes of the Lunar Society as their own Dr Priestley was far too vocal regarding the revolution itself, and saw this solution as what was needed in England to shake off the shackles of oppression. Unfortunately, he was either not in tune with the mass of opinion in the City, or there were others of higher status who had a vested interest in keeping revolution at bay, and so actively did nothing to prevent the rising mob. As with Pickard's Mill four years earlier, Albion Mills was attacked by the rioters and destroyed by fire, at the same time Birmingham erupted into anarchy and Priestley's house at Fair Hill was sacked, he fled the City and was never to return. Boulton had his own insurrection to deal with amongst his workers within the same year, in the form of an industrial dispute.

The strike amongst his engine-fitters at Soho, caused Boulton to produce a pamphlet entitled 'The Rights of Man' that was linked to a newly established Insurance Society. Uglow (2002) notes that despite the mass availability of work in Birmingham, that his workers stayed loyal. She speculates that this was due to his optimism and exuberance, and the constant flow of new and visionary ideas. He had already begun to establish yet another opportunity, by identifying a need for a Mint to compete with the Royal Mint, by 1789 this had been established and was minting coins and medals for overseas markets.

This manufacturing diversion is another fine example of Boulton's profound understanding of his business and the applications that he could turn the plant, equipment and the skills of his workforce to. The state of the nations coinage had long been deplorable (Symonds, 2009), with coins that were easy to counterfeit and workers actually finding themselves being paid in this illegal money, a situation that Boulton found intolerable. He knew that his new steam driven presses and stampers could manufacturer a considerably better quality coin, that would be harder to counterfeit, if the opportunity was allowed for him to break the monopoly of the Royal Mint. This was a campaign of persuasion that would take time, while waiting he set about proving the case, by having dies cut and coins produced, and offering similar products to other countries (Jones, 2009. Tungate, 2009).

By 1784, the two senior partners admitted their sons into the business and it was renamed Boulton, Watt and Sons. For both Matthew Boulton (junior) and James Watt (junior) this was their opportunity to learn all aspects of the business from their fathers, allowing a time for an eventual, planned hand-over to the next generation. It enabled both Boulton and Watt (senior) to explore other interests which had either been neglected, or had not been best served, by the intensity of the years that they had been through.

Ballard, Loggie and Mason (2009) explain that one of the challenges that Boulton took on at that point, among his other continuing business interests was to landscape the grounds around the Manufactory to add to its already impressive façade:

"In 1795 he decided to 'Form a Terras at the front of the Manufactory so as to be always clean and neat'. A new retaining wall was built and the ground levelled and then gravelled."

This and the extensive landscaping of the grounds around the house, were always a passion of Matthew Boulton since the late 1780's, and when his daughter Anne was forced to convalesce at Soho following a falling accident, it was even more important to him, to make the place as pleasing as possible for his beloved daughter.

Boulton could never neglect his first drivers, that of the constant desire to expand and improve. He knew that the present situation of engines being fabricated elsewhere with other manufacturers and then being assembled by the fleet of 'Boulton, Watt and Son's' engineers was an unsatisfactory one; additionally the patent was going to expire at the end of that decade, opening the floodgates to every competitor and potentially removing all of their markets (Upton, 1993). He realised that the only way to keep the business profitable for their sons was to expand into the manufacturing of the machines.

In 1796, the Soho Foundry was opened with a generous 'celebratory lunch' for all of the workers. Boulton had sited this on the banks of the Birmingham Canal, for the access to the needed supply of coal, and besides the foundry, there was a smithy, a boring mill and turning shops, all was complete to proceed into the next century as a manufacturer of the steam engines (Uglow, 2002). The following year, he finally 'broke the home markets' in coinage receiving a contract to manufacture pennies and half pennies, which proved a very successful enterprise.

Murdoch is not to be forgotten. As far back as the early 1880's he had been suggesting new and exciting ideas, one of which was an application of the rotary engine towards transportation. That idea was not particularly well received by Watt, who was always very possessive regarding his inventions (Uglow, 2002), in order to keep the stability Murdoch did not pursue this further and turned his attentions to other ideas. He had been particularly interested by the possible applications of coal gas towards lighting and after some experimentation in Redruth in Cornwall, he was able to turn his application to lighting the Soho works, and in 1802 the place was illuminated in a great public display and spectacle (Upton, 1993).

There is no doubt that the most successful aspect of Boulton's career in the main perception of the public, was that of the steam partnership and the use of his business acumen to protect these interests (Andrew, 2009). What I have tried to stress here, is that these things should not be regarded in isolation as is the tendency to write, in single aspects, snapshots of business concerns. When all of his pursuits and achievements are viewed in a holistic way, as an on-going process, rather than separate entities, it becomes clear that not only was he prolific in all of his achievements, but he managed to accomplish more in one working business life than most entrepreneurs could achieve in three lives.

He was as much victim of the twists and turns of economic upswing and downswing due to the unforeseen, as any other, but he took each challenge head on. Sometimes this would lead to delayed progress, or suspension of that particular enterprise until the opportunities arose again. He never faltered from his drive to move on and find another diversification or development, and altogether he can be seen as one of the most driven men Birmingham has ever known.

As Boulton lay dying, the Jewellery Quarter one mile a way was beginning to develop and attract those new talents that would come. By the time James Watt (junior) died in 1848, signalling the end of Soho, the Quarter was well-established, manufacturing many of the articles in silver that had first been produced in the Manufactory. Would there have been such a Quarter without these innovations in machining and the application of power? Unless there had been the Manufactory would any of the 'new comers' have decided to settle there, in such a close proximity to it, with the opportunity to capitalise on its glorious success, from passing trade? But it is most important to remember that this new area sat firmly between Soho and (probably the greatest attraction to workers in precious metals) The Assay Office. The Birmingham Jewellery Quarter owes much to Matthew Boulton, I firmly believe that but for him, and all the contributions that he made, the next chapter in the history of the area would never have occurred, with such an explosive intensity.

Chapter 3

A QUARTER OF THE CITY

The development of the Jewellery Quarter in the nineteenth century was an evolution rather than a revolution of trade in the City. For all the skills and the methods of working were common practice for hundreds of years, as I have discussed in the previous two chapters. Birmingham had evolved around the small trades, these small artisans developed considerable skill-sets which enabled them to move to more exclusive and luxurious items, away from the image of small, poorer quality 'toys', buckles and buttons. The phenomenon that had been the Soho Manufactory was a very unusual happening in manufacturing processes for the area, and was not to be repeated on that scale again before the Pen Trade arrived. In many ways the Pen Trade still would not be exactly the same as Matthew Boulton had established his processes, for many of his workers were individual artisans working collectively, whereas, the large pen factories would require minimal skill, and sub-divided all the tasks into repetitive organisation.

The small artisanal community which would develop around the area of St Paul's would mirror much of the Manufactory but not be under the ownership of one individual. The whole concept of many skills working collaboratively within a small geographical area, would become the trademark for the place. In this chapter I will examine why that distinct part of the city developed in the way that it did. What attracted so many to come to a particular area and settle their individual trades there. Also, how the progress of the trade was furthered (or inhibited) by the vagaries of the national economic profile, whether that be economic depression, war, or fashion. The recent conservation strategies which have done much to preserve the historic architectural heritage have highlighted the unusual working environments that evolved there, here I will draw attention to particular features that have become established landmarks upon the map of the Quarter. Many of these buildings were residential dwellings which had been converted through necessity and enterprise, some of the more grand establishments came with the rise in larger industrial processes such as the Pen Trade, or through growth in niche areas that would establish the Quarter nationally, such as medals and regalia (Mason, 1998).

As Gledhill (1988) remarks, there is a correlation between the rise of the jewellery trades and the coming of the Assay Office. Matthew Boulton had desired to be a great silversmith and without the Assay Office, he viewed that his ambitions and those of many of his peers were being stifled. Assaying is a process that costs money, and the further away from an office the greater the cost, through transportation to and from, and loss of income in the time that it takes to fulfil an order. For the likes of Boulton, these costs could be absorbed, although as I have discussed, his success as a silverware manufacturer was constantly dogged by financial difficulty. For the small manufacturer, working in precious metals these delays were prohibitive, the costs of assaying elsewhere would exclude any prospect of development towards more luxurious wares. The foundation of the Assay Office in 1773, opened the doors to many to seek a more profitable trade, using the skills that had already been accumulated over several generations (Mason, 1998).

Those that had made buckles, already had much skill in silver, and but for the fashion trends changing to laces and killing a very lucrative trade, they would have continued. All the silver buckles would have to have been sent for assaying. In the same way those that had made 'toys' first in cheaper base metals, and then in gilt and gilding metals, had an opportunity to establish a trade that would offer them greater return for smaller well-crafted objects.

The geographical progression to congregate around one particular area of the City, I believe was driven by three factors. Firstly, the accessibility to the Assay Office, secondly, the availability of property as the City continued its urban expansion outwards, and those well-to-do inhabitants moved to more rural locations, and thirdly, because of the attraction of many visitors to the City because of the Soho phenomenon; the Wolverhampton turnpike road leading into the City passed Soho and then St Paul's. The land itself had been part of the estate of Ann Colmore, who in 1746 had 'obtained a private Act of Parliament' to enable her to develop this area (Haddleton, 1987). According to Chinn (1999) the street pattern for the Jewellery Quarter was originally laid out by the Colmore Estate and is clearly visible in the Street Commissioners map of 1810. This enabled many of the small manufacturers of 'toys' and buckles to settle, but it also allowed for some considerably grander town houses to be constructed for the upper middle class in society (Mason, 1998). Watt's house, Harper's Hill, which had stood in Regents Place, had been one of them (English Heritage, 2002). It is a feature of parts of the Quarter now, that there are some fine buildings that remain which are the remnants of these larger middle-class, detached and semi-detached villas.

Wright (1866) explains that:

"It is curious to note how this trade located itself in one part of the town – the St. Paul's district – which has in fact become the 'jewellers' quarter', the boundaries being almost as clearly defined as the Ghetto (or Jews quarter) in Rome and many continental cities. There is scarcely a workshop to be found in any other locality – and yet, twenty-five years since, this site was almost entirely occupied by small gardens."

Allen (1929) analyses that the settlement in the area was a slow but progressive one. As those upper-middle class aspired to move out of the urban sprawl which was beginning to envelop them, so the next rank in the social structure – the skilled artisan – took the vacant property; in much the same way as any city expands outwards. According to Allen, most of the jewellery trade up to the 1820's had been conducted in and around, 'Great Charles Street, Church Street and Newhall Street'.

Another advantage had been gained in 1824 'when further powers had been conferred upon the Birmingham Assay Office' to assay gold as well as silver (Ryland, 1866). Unfortunately, the following year a stock market crash (which had been precipitated by over speculation of the Bank of England in Latin America) caused a tremendous economic downturn, almost wiping out the jewellery trade; as is so common in experience, in times of severe financial constraints luxury goods suffer. The fortunes of fate changed the economic trend, for by the late 1840's demand for jewellery had increased substantially, mainly due to the accession of Queen Victoria in 1837 and her popularisation of the fashion to wear jewellery (Gledhill, 1988).

Many of the highly skilled artisans, that had been settling in St Paul's began to turn part of their domestic dwellings, towards their manufacturing, for several reasons. Primarily security, to live where you manufactured expensive items meant that you could discourage thieves who were very attracted to the ease of being able to acquire riches from insecure premises. Secondly, each artisan tended to be quite specialised and would require other artisans with complementary skills to assist in their manufacture. If you were a die-sinker, or a silver spinner, an engraver or a chaser, it would be natural to live where you could take most advantage of work, thus, many skill-sets began to co-habit in one small area. This kept the overheads of many lower than could be expected, and ease and speed of production high; in turn, this lowered all of the associated costs, yet kept the intrinsic value high. Finally, many of these businesses operated as family interests, as a consequence, working from home was in every sense more economically viable (Allen, 1929).

The combination of working in more expensive material, with higher levels of skills, in a close network of fellow artisans, combined with family help, gave many of these small artisans a very good income. In 1866 Wright reports that a jeweller was 'one of the best paid Birmingham artisans':

"The rate of course varies considerably, but he is a poor workman that can only earn 24s. weekly; 30s. to 50s. may be considered the average of wages. Some obtain much more. Enamellers frequently gain as much as from £3 to £5 weekly. Boys are usually apprenticed at fourteen, when they earn 4s. per week, which is increased annually until they are twenty-one, when in time they generally receive 10s. or 11s., working as a rule from eight to seven."

Wright (1866) notes curiously, that 'comparatively few females are employed in this trade; its cleanliness, and the delicate manipulation required, would appear to adapt it especially for women'. He continues by discussing the only two aspects of the trade that they are to be found in; one the production of 'guard chain' and the other using presses to create 'roughs' or blanks.

To analyse this further, needs some consideration of the lack of any accepted position of women in employment prior to the twentieth century; to some extent driven by the organisation of male workers and the prescribed moral standards of that society (Debney, 2010); combined with the emerging industrialisation of the mid-nineteenth century with the demand for cheap semi-skilled labour. The manufacture of 'guard chain' was one of the first trades in the Quarter to become an industrialised process. In order to produce the volume of chain required for lockets and other such items, steam operated machinery had to be utilised, however, this required a multitude of low-skill manual tasks such as; soldering, cutting, engraving and polishing to be employed. Such tasks could not command a high wage, thus, men would not consider this to be a reasonable employment, however, it was a good wage for a woman (Hutchins, 1915). As women could not be 'organised' and were not recognised as having individual rights due to the Parliamentary Reform Act of 1832, which had excluded them from the right to a franchise; the right to vote. This made them an underclass of workers, with no rights to be protected and no regulations regarding their wages (Debney, 2010).

As a consequence, women could be exploited to work on semi-skilled or unskilled work for very little pay. It must be added that the jewellery trade was one of the least exploitative trades, as were some of the Pen Manufacturers which were emerging at that time in the Quarter; there were much worse practices happening in the City, where armies of women were being used as 'sweated outworkers'; making boxes, carding buttons, hooks and eyes, and all other manner of menial (but very labour-intensive tasks) for very little remuneration (Black, 1907, Cadbury and Shann, 1907, Hutchins, 1907).

The establishment of apprenticeships is a further development which was not common to the City, due to its unincorporated status. This freedom from guilds and regulations had attracted many of the enterprising entrepreneurs and Dissenters to settle originally (Allen, 1929). It appears that the jewellery trade was one of the first industries to promote this practice in order to secure a supply of committed young men to train, who were not liable to drift elsewhere after having had considerable investment made in them. Hand-in-hand with this, was the recognition that an appreciation for art, form and function was essential in the trade of a jeweller; an education in any form of aesthetics was most desirable.

Many of the artisans that filled the void left by the departure of the middle-class villa owners, were themselves originally working for a 'small master' elsewhere. It was the desire to aspire to self-employment that was the same with many of those that chose to come to Birmingham, where it was viewed a man could make his own life and fortune through the opportunities available. In 1866, Wright was commenting that there were a 'great number of small but independent manufactories', he continued further that:

"Probably nine out of every ten of the master jewellers, who are now working on business on their own account, were originally workmen."

He noted at that time there were 'not less than twelve' businesses operating all employing a number of men and apprentices within each, and all of this had been established since 1840. He observed how comparatively easy, compared with other trades, it was for a jeweller to found his business:

"All that it is needed for a workman, to start as a master, is a peculiar-shaped bench and a leather apron, one or two pounds worth of tools (including a blow pipe), and for material, a few sovereigns, and some ounces of copper and zinc. His shop may be the top room of his house, or a small building over the wash-house, at a rent of 2s. or 2s. 6d. per week, and the indispensable gas jet, which the gas company will supply on credit. With these appliances, and a skilful hand, he may produce scarf-pins, studs, links, rings, lockets, &c., &c., for all of which he will find a ready market on Saturday, among the numerous 'factors', whose special business is to supply the shopkeepers throughout the country."

By carrying out a simple survey of the signboards in one street in the Jewellery Quarter in 1866, Wright was able to study the wide range of skills that sat cheek by jowl, in their mutually-beneficial provision of skills for one another. He determined that in one street alone:

"15 are   Jewellers
2   -   Stone dealers
4   -   Stampers and die sinkers
3   -   Lapidaries
2   -   Silversmiths
1   -   Glass cutter
1   -   Medallist and die engraver
4   -   Chain makers
4   -   Chasers and engravers
2   -   Electro-gilders and platers
2   -   Black ornament makers
1   -   Jewellers' case makers"

From this and other small scale surveys he was able to make estimations of the numbers that were employed at that time:

"Masters	500-600
Jewellers proper	3,000
Silversmiths	1,000
Gold and Silver Chain makers	1,500
Gilt Toy makers	1,000
Box makers, Die sinkers, and subsidiary trades	1,000
	7,500"

He was able to extrapolate, that by allowing for three others to be supported by each one, that upwards of 20,000 were 'supported by this trade alone'.

Allen (1929) noted that at the same time as Wright was conducting his surveys, that two trades within the Quarter had 'attained the small-factory stage'. Unsurprisingly, as already discussed one of these industries was the manufacture of gold and silver chains; the use of powered machinery combined with low-skilled cheap labour had made this a competitive business. The other was the manufacture of electro-plate, in 1840 George Richard Elkington and his partners, perfected the method of application of silver plate to base metal, which started a revolution in the trade (Gledhill, 1988). Having stimulated a market in affordable, good quality, plated-ware, with a fast process, it became a factory-driven method. According to Allen (1929) 'Messrs Elkington operated a factory in which no less than a 1000 persons were employed'.

The 'factor' was a critical part of the supply-chain for any small-manufacturer in the City. It had been a system that had operated for centuries, even when items were made in iron. It allowed the artisan to devote his time to the manufacture of the product while another man sought the markets to sell the wares. In Birmingham it was an honourable process on the whole, whereas, in the case of the Black Country Chain Makers, the 'foggers' (as they were known) gained a reputation for being highly exploitative and enslaving their outworkers (Debney, 2010). 'Factors' generally, distributed the wares for sale, and controlled the supply of raw materials to the maker, however, the jewellery trade was able to operate more independently, due to the availability of sovereigns as a good supply of gold. The factor's role here was merely to collect the finished products from the small-masters and sell on (Allen, 1929). Some makers, were also factors, able to source the products that they did not make themselves from others in the Quarter and sell on; some who started as factors, expanded into manufacture themselves.

The 1860's can be viewed as one of the boom periods for the jewellery trade, according to Allen (1929), by 1866 the population of workers had increased to 9,000 and as the decade turned 10,000. He analyses that there were several reasons for this sudden surge in employment. Firstly, the growth in electro-plating and chain making which required significant numbers of people to be employed. There had been a decline in button making and associated industries, which had encouraged a migration across trades, and across the City to join the community of jewellers. There were the large gold finds which caused the Gold Rushes of 1849 and 1851, and significant discoveries of silver in Nevada, increasing the availability of precious metals, he quotes that:

> "the world's average output of metal, rose from nearly 29,000,000 ounces between 1851 – 1860 to 35,000,000 ounces between 1861 – 1865, and to 43,000,000 ounces between 1866 – 1870."

Allen notes that this increase in silver led to the beginning of the 'silver jewellery period', this also had a significant impact on the production of 'mayoral regalia and civic insignia', due to the emergence of municipal authorities around the country; a trade which is a key part of the Quarter of today. Another fashion was driven by the use of precious stones, which would require faceting and setting, these finished stones previously acquired from Amsterdam, now could be produced in Birmingham.

During this early development of the Quarter, many of the more forward-minded, small-masters saw an advantage in encouraging their young apprentices to take the opportunity of the fine art education on offer through the School of Art which had been established in 1821 by the Royal Birmingham Society of Artists and drew much of its fame from its later associations with the great pre-Raphaelite artists of the Victorian period. Wright (1866) notes that this motivation to educate and train, had led to a transformation of the industry, to produce far more delicate and thoughtful products, to respond to more critical purchasers. This combination of aesthetical appreciation and extensive associations in the continental markets, had created a distinct style and range of products which could now be attributed to the City; far from being 'copyists' they were being viewed as fashion leaders (Mason, 1998). There is an interesting note that there was very little evidence of the Birmingham Jewellery Trade in either the Great Exhibition of 1851, or the Great London Exposition of 1862, because of the system of 'factoring'. As Birmingham was principally a manufacturer, it would supply to the London jewellery shops, as such to exhibit would have diverted the attention away from their principal customers. This is a situation that would continue through the use of middle-men buying wholesale and supplying the retailers, until the advent of ecommerce. It is also interesting to note, that Wright (1866) alludes to the London snobbery of the shopkeeper failing to 'admit that his articles are of Birmingham manufacture', yet at that time half of all the gold jewellery on sale in London had been made in the Birmingham Jewellery Quarter.

The second industry that sat in the area had risen to prominence by this stage, the Pen Trade. In a chapter later in this book, I shall discuss in some detail, the key facts regarding the emergence and development of this trade. Timmins (1866) writes of some 'Sheffield artisan' being responsible for the development of the pen, and specifically he applauds Joseph Gillott, for the manufacture of 'a first-class pen', and 'improvements in manufacture with which his name is associated throughout the world'. For Timmins, James Perry and Josiah Mason, have an equal position to Gillott, through their abilities to market and transform the desire for 'steel pens' away from the quill, and special praise for the introduction of the 'Perryian system of education'.

The rise of the trade from nothing within forty-five years to when the text by Timmins is written, causes some awe in the author, who notes that:

"When the British association first met in Birmingham (in 1839) steel pens were almost unknown; but when the second visit was made, in 1849, the steel pen trade had risen to a very important place among the manufacturers of our town. Between the two periods named there had been eighteen makers of steel pens, but these had been reduced to twelve in 1849; and although the number is now twelve, the quantity of pens produced has enormously increased."

He reports that based on his estimations at that time that 360 men were employed across the twelve firms, and 2,050 women, the approximate horsepower (collectively including steel rolling outwork) was 380. He believed that the production of pens weekly was 98,000 gross, using 9½ to 10 tons of steel, the approximate value of a gross of pens being 1½ d. to 1s.

Allen (1929) draws the reader's attention to point out that the large size of manufacturing premises were not in fact due to the use of powered machinery, but due to the fact that there were so many operations that were necessary in order to make one steel pen. These operations were very simple, and highly repetitive, and again demanded minimum skill and as such would command the lowest of wages, hence vast numbers of women in employment (Drake, 1917). By 1901 the figure of women employed by the pen trade would be an astonishing 7,000, or 85 percent of the entire trade (Ward, 2001), and that despite the fact that the trade then was in the descent due to the advent of the fountain pen, and later the ball-point pen.

Before this period, a mixture of good fortune and good economics caused the Pen Trade to boom and make an impact on the City and the world. The American Civil War had meant there was no significant competition from there, or the European continent. Allen (1929) writes that:

"Of the minor Birmingham manufacturers the pen trade not only maintained itself, but extended its output, which in 1886 was 60 percent greater than in 1865... The employment in the trade rose by 70 percent between 1871 and 1881, and the last years of the period 1885 – 1886, found the industry as prosperous as ever."

This is counter to the experience of the Quarter as a whole, as an area of Jewellery manufacture, which suffered a recession. This downturn in fortunes and been precipitated by another unfortunate event, that of the death of Prince Albert, consort to Queen Victoria. This caused her to go into an extended period of grief and mourning, when she would not (or allow anyone closely connected to her) wear anything but black, and she shunned all ostentatious personal adornment. The Queen set the trend for all, and certainly for the first ten years of that period, no one would deviate from this, the hardest hit sector was that of gold and precious stones, although silver jewellery remained reasonably consistent. Another field that remained significantly robust was that of the manufacture of regalia and insignia, Vaughton's were medallists at that time. It was not enough to keep the trade buoyant according to Allen (1929):

"Consequently, in the second period of the great slump – in 1885 – 1886 – jewellery was declared the most depressed of all local industries."

The rise of the Pen Trade in the Quarter with its great demand on low-paid female workers and the coincidental slump in the jewellery trade, heralded a transformation in the demographic profile of the area. Many of the back-to-back courts constructed from the 1820's to 1860's – that existed at one time to the west of the Quarter – in roads such as Camden Street, Tenby Street and Carver Street, attracted those poor workers desperately needed to keep Gillott's, Albert Works and Wiley's Victoria Works turning over (English Heritage, 2002). This influx of the poor would change the profile and image of the area, for the next century but at the same time (as the jewellery trade changed) the back-to-backs would provided a competitive supply of cheap labour.

The City itself was being transformed throughout this period, by 'The Great Municipaliser', the mayor Mr Joseph Chamberlain. He would revolutionise Birmingham by municipalising supplies of gas and water, street lighting, and education. All was done to great acclamation that it was 'the best governed city in the world'. He would in time, come to the aid of the Quarter, with his charisma and stature.

Chapter 4

WINDS OF CHANGE

This chapter will chart the development of the area from the Great Depression, when Queen Victoria's years of extended mourning had almost killed off the trade, to the end of WW2 and the decades of reconstruction which followed. It was by far the most complex, and disruptive time, which for some brought fortune and for others personal pain. The Quarter itself took on a new urgency and identity, there was a drive to work collectively in order to divert calamity and seek even greater opportunities.

This period saw the rise of larger enterprise, whether that was from the generations of established families, or those that chose to come to the area for their business advantage. Women began to become an integral part of the workforce, in those trades that they were encouraged to undertake; and because of regulations of marriage and children, became a significant part of the army of outworkers that would drive successive periods of prosperity.

The two World Wars had very different effects on the Jewellery trade, the first brought great wealth through the manufacture of 'keep sakes' and photograph frames. The second emptied the Quarter of key workers and subsumed those that remained into the Total War Economy of all production devoted to the war effort. It also brought waves of destruction, whether that was the constant bombardment of the Luftwaffe for eighteen months, or the personal loss of individuals (mainly men) who still formed the main body of skilled artisans that maintained the economy of the area.

The key to this whole period was a transformation of the attitude of collective working through close-collaborative networks of skills that individually served small enterprises; to a much larger vision of cooperation, as the 'Quarter' as an identity in its own right, driven by large privately owned workshops and factories. Through this bolder approach it became possible to seek a national and international profile, that until that time had to some extent been inhibited by the 'factor' system; manufacturing for outlets elsewhere who declined to acknowledge the provenance of their wares.

The turning point came with the desperation of the Great Depression of the late nineteenth century, that drove a few of the most enterprising to make pro-active moves to change the dire situation that they faced. Charles Green and Jacob Jacobs made a personal appeal to the Princess of Wales about the state of the trade. The appeal was met favourably and she agreed to support the industry by wearing selected items in gold at 'morning functions' (Mason, 1998). This had the effect of reviving the fashion for buying and wearing jewellery. Allen (1929) comments that this was mirrored in the increased figures of employment, which had only risen from 14,000 to 16,000 between 1840 and 1886, but rose steadily from then to 1914, when 30,000 were employed in the area. In 1901 according to Cadbury and Matheson (1907) nearly 6,000 of these workers were women.

1887 marked a significant year both nationally and locally, for all who worked in the jewellery trade. That was the year that Queen Victoria celebrated her Golden Jubilee, and Allen (1929) notes that this 'created a demand for medals and badges, insignia for corporations and presentation caskets for the Queen'. It was also the same year that a group of sixteen enterprising businessmen, composed a letter to all others in the Quarter to meet, regarding the serious issues that were affecting the trade at that time; lack of training, crime and business insolvencies (Haddleton, 1987). After various discussions that ensued in the following month, the group of 200 businesses and factors, resolved to form an umbrella organisation to undertake six main objectives:

"1) To promote art and technical education.
2) To secure uniformity of action in cases of failure.
3) To watch legislation affecting the Trade.
4) To secure prosecution of thieves and receivers.
5) To assist development of foreign and colonial trade.
6) To seek through Parliament or other competent authority the removal of all measures for the development of trade."

(The British Jewellers' Association – 1987)

The body formed under the title of the Birmingham Jewellers' and Silversmiths' Association; offices were provided in the first instance by Charles Green and Son, in Augusta Street, and Charles Green was the first elected chairman. There is no doubt that the formation of this body made a profound difference within a very short time. Another wave of depression was imminent (1893-94) the problem of insolvencies was a pressing one, the Association assumed a negotiating role in obtaining the 'best terms' for those facing these calamities. Further to this, they proceeded with their first aim to promote the need for education. They supported this initiative by providing 50 percent of the fees to pay for any members who wished to send their staff for training at the Birmingham Municipal School of Art, in Ellen Street. By September 1888, 60 young people had enrolled on the course, and the following year in February, the Association offered the first honours for the best students (The British Jewellers' Association, 1987).

The Association realised that the facilities and premises were woefully inadequate for their aspirations and numbers of students that they wished to train. The body made a strong appeal to the Corporation for help in funding a school dedicated to the trade in premises which had been identified in 82 – 84 Vittoria Street. The Association produced some most convincing arguments regarding the wealth generation that was created for the City within the Quarter and the potential that could be achieved by a significant investment:

"It is computed that between 14,000 and 15,000 persons are employed in the jewellery trade in Birmingham alone, and that from 14,000 to 15,000 are directly supported by it. It has thirty distinct departments or branches – related to the trade, which, as a whole, employs more hands in Birmingham than are to be found in any other trade in our city. The capital employed is larger than in any other trade carried on in Birmingham. About fifty factors, by themselves or by their travellers, carry jewellery as their principal stock. The names of 1,000 master-men appear in the last Post Office Directory issued as being engaged in some one or more of the departments referred to. It is estimated that close on one million pounds of sterling gold, weighing about six tons, are annually worked up by the trade in Birmingham alone. The value of silver used in Birmingham annually, including that used in the manufacture of watch-cases, is estimated at from £300,000 to £350,000, or about 45 tons. Thus, over 50 tons of precious metal are manufactured into jewellery and watch-cases in our Birmingham workshops in the course of a year. Further, the Birmingham Post Office statistics show that 300,000 registered letters or parcels are transmitted to, or go from, the jewellery district. This number is three times that of any other town or city in the United Kingdom, London alone excepted. In addition to the precious metals, there remain to be added the precious stones of all kinds used in the trade. No exact figures can be given of the value of these worked up annually; but it is estimated that it cannot be less than £500,000 or £600,000, and the quantity of precious stones used is increasing year by year. In a word, we have in our city an industry, comprised within a very limited area, which annually works up material of the total value of nearly £2,000,000."

(The British Jewellers' Association – 1987)

The new school opened 18th September 1890. The Jewellers' Technical School, offered courses in; engraving, enamelling, chasing and mounting. More significantly, the school would admit girls as long as they were educated separately (The British Jewellers' Association). According to Gledhill (1987) the Association invested heavily in the educational interests that they had, even selecting and paying for the first teachers, and calling on all of their members to make contributions towards the running costs.

From 1889 onwards, Joseph Chamberlain became closely attached to the Birmingham Jewellers' and Silversmiths' Association. He had lived in Frederick Street, and understood the importance of the trade to the City. At the very first Annual Banquet he was introduced to the Association, and made a speech that set him as a charismatic ambassador for the trade for the next few years, when he became the public face of the Association:

"The jewellers are so original and so independent, that no one jeweller could be represented by any other. In order to know the jewellery trade you must know every member. There is some inherent peculiarity in the business of dealing with the precious metals and making personal ornaments of this kind that causes every man engaged in it to be unique. But still our friends have succeeded in this great work and they have got together a representative association. Now that they have done it, everybody will feel as they did when Columbus stood the egg on end – that it was an extremely easy thing to do and that the whole wonder is that it was not done before. I have read with very great interest and attention the rules and regulations – the statutes of this new organisation and I must say they seem to me to be extremely well devised for the object which you have in view. In fact you are reviving in principle, at all events, an ancient trade guild, without, however, its exclusive pretensions and protectionist heresies."

(Mr Joseph Chamberlain – British Jeweller 1937)

It is ironic that he makes an indirect reference to the past of the City, the unincorporated status that gave so much flexibility to the early entrepreneurs (as he himself had been before his political career; subsequently, his meteoric rise politically caused by his rebuilding of the City infrastructure from which he sought the incorporated status). According to Gledhill (1987) he led a campaign against the foreign competition from other jewellers, on the grounds that the wares from

Birmingham were 'honest', and that by supporting the Quarter, the buyer was maintaining high standards of quality. His support to abolish the plate duties – an indirect taxation – won him great support across the City not just the Quarter, Marie Haddleton (1987) writes that he was viewed as the 'guardian angel' of the area. So much so, that the Association honoured him in 1903, and commemorated his visit to South Africa as Secretary of State for the Colonies, by erecting the iconographic Chamberlain Clock which stands at the entrance to the Quarter (Mason, 1998).

The Association brought a sense of greater importance to what had been a large body of co-existing trades. The collective thinking and image, heralded a new era in the history of the Quarter. The Association worked tirelessly to transform the image of the industry and the inhibitors to business success. One of their main concerns was that of criminal activity, both from outside the industry and on the inside (Mason, 1998). Interesting anecdotes arise from the many incidents which were revealed through closer examination. Alison Gledhill (1987) retells one such tale:

"Nevertheless there is a delightful story recorded at the turn of the century about a gold worker who was noted for continually rubbing his fingers through his greasy hair. When watched it was discovered that his nightly hair wash would involve allowing the dirty water to run through a flannel, thus catching all the gold dust."

The Jewellery Quarter rose again and by 1906 there was excellent demand for the goods on offer, but as these things cycle another unforeseen international downturn came, this time caused through an American market collapse, eventually by 1908 that had brought recession to the UK once more. This was a short-lived downturn and there followed a period of partial recovery, but this stalled because of the death of Edward VII in 1910. However, the death of one monarch leads to the accession of another, and the Coronation year for George V and Queen Mary, brought the much-needed relief, as the public clamoured for all-things commemorative (Allen, 1929).

During the previous decade the value of precious metals had changed significantly. Silver had fallen in value, as a consequence, articles such as silver jewellery were no longer profitable to manufacture as luxury items: the hours needed to produce one piece, proved prohibitive in recovering costs and turning a profit. Gold jewellery became the norm, and silverware manufacturers branched out into cheaper items such as toilet ware; brush-backs and mirrors, tableware, and cigarette cases. Some of these items could be made considerably cheaper using the methods of electroplating, and there was stiff competition between the two arms of the industry.

The changes in culture and local government did open up new markets for the silverware manufacturers. As I have already discussed, with many new municipal authorities requiring mayoral regalia and insignia for other organisations such as the Masons, this promoted a growth in local companies who now concentrated on the production of ceremonial items. There was a greater demand for medals and sports trophies in general, as more people took the opportunity to be able to undertake organised sports and pastimes (Allen, 1929).

Fashion changes dictated peaks and troughs as they always had, and in the same way that silver buckles had died and been replaced by laces, so watches on chains with fobs became a thing of the past. Manufacturers responded by moving into studs and links (collar studs and cufflinks), women's fashions demanded brooches which were on the increase. One dramatic change brought a trade back which had almost died, that of precious stones. There had been so little demand for them in the previous two decades, that any skills that had been in the Quarter had almost died out. Additionally, the price of stones was unstable and many jewellers had turned away from this, concentrating on more reliable methods of deriving income. However, the De Beers Combine was formed in 1889, which stabilised the precious stone price, by 1912 the trade had begun to consolidate in the Quarter once more (Allen, 1929).

As the motor car increased in availability along with the increase in other expensive items of luxury, it became noticeable to the industry that demand for jewellery slowed significantly. Also, foreign products of a much poorer quality had begun to flood the international markets, that combined with protectionist tariffs, created great difficulty for the export market (Allen, 1929); hence the campaign for 'honest' wares produced by the Jewellery Quarter. Despite all the adverse problems, the jewellery trade continued to expand and by 1913 it reached a peak of employment with an estimated 70,000 workers employed in the Quarter; although this may the collective figure of all of the associated trades, the actual figure probably being in the region of 50,000 (English Heritage, 2002).

It was the highest point in terms of people employed, but it has to be remembered that although the trade has always been labour intensive (a handcrafted object of supreme quality), some methods of production would have a few technological developments, and it would be a more accurate scale, to measure the income derived (if that figure could be assessed) rather than numbers of people employed. In those years before the First World War, there was a glut of female labour which was still poorly paid (and would remain so till the end of WW2), consequently, many more 'hands' could be employed profitably by the small factory owners by utilising female labour.

The Great War brought monumental changes to the Quarter, many of the more senior men, those businessmen and owners, enlisted, many general workers too, it was only when conscription came into force that those left were designated as 'reserved occupations' (those possessing essential skills for the economy). As was the same with many Birmingham industries, male workers that were skilled in metal were necessary for the engineering tasks, or essential to maintain the munition production lines that became staffed by armies of women workers (Debney, 2011). The Birmingham Jewellers' and Silversmiths' Association appealed to their members from the outset, not to dismiss any men with dependants from their workforce who had enlisted or were called up, and to ensure that these positions were held open.

Many of the firms in the Quarter were absorbed into the national munitions production because of their access to skilled operators and machinery. A Jewellery Munition Committee was formed to supervise work, however, according to Gledhill (1987) Birmingham was able to capitalise on the South African jewellery market which the Germans had been supplying. The first attempt to ship a large quantity of finished articles, was sunk by a German torpedo, the second ship made it and the exhibition proved successful during a difficult time for the trade.

Not every company could get Government work and the Jewellery Quarter became desolate in places and this was reported in the local newspapers of the time. There were a few firms that were brought to their knees and were forced to close during that period. The ones that survived were those that had turned their production to military regalia, cap badges and medals, and in the earlier years of the war, those that made silver photograph frames and 'keepsakes' such as lockets, did well (Mason, 1998).

As is evident throughout this history of the Quarter, whenever there is a war, a small boom immediately comes after. Post WWI was no exception and for eighteen months a partial recovery ensued. The Depression of the 1920's and 1930's hit the trade before most others, as luxury goods are the first things to be go when people are making economies; this and the difficulty in obtaining raw materials and the poor export trade, meant that once again the area suffered a severe economic downturn.

The Association responded through a variety of marketing activities including a Christmas campaign for 1927 'Gifts that last' (Gledhill, 1987). The Government of that time were introducing numerous Bills which hindered production in precious metals, to counteract this the B.J.S.A. supported the Merchandising Marks Act of 1926. Following this legislation, all products of silver or electroplate had to be stamped with their country of origin (The British Jewellers' Association – 1987). In 1933 they expanded their trade advertising from what had been a monthly bulletin in 1925, to a full trade magazine the 'British Jeweller'. They used this journal to discuss every aspect of the trade, and the national and international politics affecting it. The 1930's portrays the industry's fight to establish a better national economic climate in order to undertake exports. Interspersed between reports on the Berlin Trade Exhibition of 1935 are adverts for many of the local manufacturers of that time.

The journal was also used to educate others on the origins of various aspects of the trade, such the Swiss Watch industry (British Jeweller – October 1935). There was a considerable amount of anti-German debate stimulated in 1935, as many of those that had visited Germany, had witnessed a re-generated German economy that was considered to be 'stealing' the trade away, yet, the UK had two million unemployed. The magazine was also used to showcase local manufacturers under the sub-section 'Notable Birmingham Firms'; Pickering & Mayell Ltd, 'Well Displayed Goods Are Half Sold – the slogan of a progressive firm' (British Jeweller – September 1935).

The Association would honour those who had supported their society through the journal, such as the death of Sir Austen Chamberlain (British Jeweller – April 1937). They would endeavour to display their most celebrated connections, an article from the same year lists notable speakers; Winston Churchill, David Lloyd-George, Stanley Baldwin and Neville Chamberlain to name a few. Their efforts to promote the trade bore fruit and by 1934 there was a rise in trade, which seems to be reflected through the many more advertisements placed by members throughout those years. However, WW2 came and the B.J.S.A. was faced with another war, that of Purchase Tax which was levelled in 1940; they would have to fight this one for a further thirty years (The British Jewellers' Association – 1987).

In many ways, WW2 was far more detrimental on the Quarter than the First World War had been. Ernest Bevin had charged the Government with a need to turn over to a Total War Economy, meaning that all production must serve the war effort (Debney, 2011). The consequence of this, was the few that were left in reserved occupations could only make munitions or parts for planes; only with a Government contract could a firm have any hope of survival. The only exemptions given from the production of utility wares, was that of wedding rings, which demand grew for, yet supply was low (Gledhill, 1987). There was much bomb damage throughout the area, and those that did return to production after the cessation of hostilities were faced with a huge reconstruction programme; much of this was organised by a special committee which was set up in 1943.

The British Jeweller continued to print throughout the war, much in the same style as it had in previous times. Production of anything other than munitions was a novelty, but there were those firms, such as Gladman and Norman and Fattorini's who turned their staff to making pins for the Spitfire campaign and of course military cap badges and honours. In the October 1940 edition there is good article about fashion and regimental jewellery, which shows the military badges and fine items for women. Propaganda was rife throughout the war years in the journal, anti-German rhetoric was patriotically published at all given opportunities ('It Must Not Happen Again' – British Jeweller – February – 1941).

As with most trade journals during that time, the British Jeweller carried this message issued by The Board of Trade:

"The Pebble in the Pool.

A manufacturer changes from peace to war production – more for the Services and less for the civilian. A wholesaler gets less to distribute to the shops. A shopkeeper gets less to serve from his counters. A customer must buy less. When the pebble is dropped in the pool, the effects are felt to the very edge.

When a lifetime has been spent building up trade, it is hard to believe that some of that hard-won trade must be sacrificed for the common good. For accepting the necessity without complaining; for playing the game fairly; for explaining and easing the situation for their customers; for starting all over again to learn vital new jobs, the men who man the home supply services – manufacturers, wholesalers, representatives, and retailers alike – may well feel proud of the part they are playing to bring the day of victory closer yet."

(British Jeweller – 1941)

In 1943, the B.J.S.A. was gathering more and more members from out of the City, and the decision was taken to make it more reflective of its national membership by giving it a national identity, it now took the title the British Jewellers' and Silversmiths' Association, In 1947 a total unification of the trade associations nationally ensued, and the title transformed once more to the British Jewellers' Association (The British Jewellers' Association – 1987). The final accolade for the Association was the granting of Letters Patent in 1950.

The aftermath of the war and the period of austerity and reconstruction was lifted once more with royal connections. The present Queen acceded to the throne in 1953 and not only did this drive a boom for the area but the Association was able to place a monopoly on British goods being the only products to be sold as souvenirs. Many cities would demand commemorative emblems; chains of office and medals. Villages commissioned enamelled signs to honour the coronation. This was the time the Quarter began to boom once more, where many of the stories contained in this book start. A time when parking became a problem, with workers double parked the whole length of streets, and factories still had works canteens. There was a gradual clearance of the slums in Camden Street, and no one lived there anymore, it was truly a working Quarter.

Part II

GIVEN VOICE

"But as for me, I can never forget those bug-infested back-to-back hovels where I was born in 1903 and lived twenty-nine years in poverty and hardship, until I made heart-breaking decisions to leave all this behind me and to begin a new life for the better, for myself and my young family.

Often today, in my late years, I still find myself wandering around these old haunts, around the Jewellery Quarter, and recalling those once cobbled horse-roads and back alleyways, where I used to run to school with bare feet, in rags, with many other poor, half-starved kids, begging for food outside factory gates. Many parents had no time to give us love or affection, which we needed, only strong discipline with the bamboo cane at the ready. Many times, too, old Vicar Smith would chase us with his walking-stick if he caught us playing in the church-yard of St Paul's, or Titty-Bottle Park as we called it.

And as I stroll along today, in 1991, I notice how clean this church and the surrounding district are. There are no more of those dilapidated back-to-back hovels where, I remember, people often begged and scratched for a crust of bread. Today you can see lovely flats and restaurants, where people live and dine in comfort, yet many of these surrounding buildings have only had a facelift. Many famous landmarks have gone now to make way for progress – but let us not forget our history and who we are…"

"I recall the stories my granny used to tell me: how this district was called the Jewellery Quarter. Many people with large families – like my mother and father, and their families – who once lived in these hovels had no prospects, just living hand to mouth, and many who could not afford their rent let off their living-room to people who wanted to start a small business. They themselves moved to the upper floor to live. But granny said as soon as the landlords or the agents found out, they raised the rent to a level they knew the tenants couldn't afford. So they were either turned out on the streets or sent to the workhouse. This left entire old houses to be let or sold to people who wanted to start up making jewellery. From then on, it grew to what is still called the Jewellery Quarter today. There are many more alterations to be done to these buildings, yet many have only had a fresh coat of paint. There are still the back yards,

55

brew-houses, and even old brick sheds where people used to keep pigeons, and did their washing ready for the pawnshops, yet people still ply their trades there...”

"It was a sad time for us all the night that the bombs came without warning. Many of us lost loved ones, some to be buried in a communal grave in Warstone Lane Cemetery, just a few yards from where we once had lived. This cemetery is neglected too, and I hope that one day it will have a facelift, to remind us not to forget our loved ones.

Just a few more yards I walk, and I come to the junction of Warstone Lane, Vyse Street and Frederick Street, where one of our famous landmarks, 'Joseph Chamberlain's clock', stood with its ironwork painted dark green and gold, all faded and rusty. It has now been removed to be repaired and have a facelift too, but I'm told it will soon be restored to its original place. As I stand on the corner and look at that empty space, I remember the day my mother told me that when I was twelve months old she carried me to see that clock – which was erected in 1903, the year I was born – and to hear its chimes...”

(The Girl from Hockley – Kathleen Dayus, 2006)

Chapter 5

UNDER HER SKIN AND IN HER SOUL

Marie Haddleton

Kathleen Dayus wrote one of the most evocative books ever published – The Girl from Hockley, about what it was like to be born and grow up in the area of the Jewellery Quarter. She described in tear-jerking detail, the grinding poverty, disease and cruelty, that inhabited many of the back-to-backs that still existed there before and after the Great War. She lived on Camden Street, a stone's throw from where some of the businesses that I have researched for this book now operate. Many around the Quarter, knew her, and remember her with fond affection, as her book does not necessarily evoke the lively character that she became, more the reminiscences of an elderly woman reflecting in hindsight.

However, there is one other who can claim to the heritage coming into existence there as Kathleen did and spending many years in determined advocacy for the Quarter, her name is Marie Elizabeth Haddleton. I knew of Mrs Haddleton before I had managed to make contact with her, for she is a force to be reckoned with; her principled battles to save and conserve what she knows, have brought her much admiration, but also much criticism from those who may consider her approach an inhibitor to 'their' progress. Although, she has never handled the materials and tools as Kathleen did, her passion for the place she calls home is unrivalled.

She has for many years been the 'voice' of the Quarter, through her published monthly journal – The Hockley Flyer – which seeks to promote all aspects of the area; business, museums and conservation. She is not shy from tackling the more thorny political issues, such as; development and re-development, access and parking, both being much debated topics. Marie will stand on the toes of those detractors who seek to damage, what she considers the integrity and value of the Quarter, and if there is a project that needs funding, that no one else can find support for, she will press the need home until she has found a backer; the case of the Chamberlain Clock, and now the Key Hill and Warstone Cemeteries.

She is a 'grand dame' having achieved eighty-two years of age, and despite being challenged by her personal mobility in recent times, she continues to work and put many hours into her selfless quest to promote Birmingham's jewel. She is ably abetted by her son Mark, and they work as a team in their top floor offices in an old, grade 2 listed building in Frederick Street. She may no longer be quite as energetic and able to get around as she once did, but the respect and reputation that she commands now bring many to her door. I had heard so much about her before seeking an interview, I have to admit to certain trepidation as I climbed the steep stairs to seek admittance. But I need not have feared, for as with all of my experiences of the Quarter, I was received with warmth and hospitality and made to feel very welcome.

She was born in the Great Depression of 1929 at 12 Tenby Street, her father was the local 'copper' PC77 Richard Evans Jones. In her book 'The Jewellery Quarter', Marie describes the hard life that her parents had through the words of her own mother – Jessie Tease Fryer:

"There was no water to the houses so it had to be carried from a tap in the centre of the yard. There was no bathroom, and the kitchen

Rear of No. 12 Tenby Street, 1929, Marie in her mother's arms
(by the kind courtesy of the Hockley Flyer Collection).

comprised of a table in the corner of the room and all dirty water was carried out to a drain (known as the 'suff'). Bath water had to be heated in kettles on the open fire and a galvanised bath carried in from where it hung on a nail out in the yard, placed in front of the fire and filled with water from the kettles. Naturally, this was very laborious, and precious hot water could not be wasted so the whole family took a bath in the same water, dad first, then mom and so on down to the smallest child, then the water had to be ladled out again."

Her family were fortunate to be moved out of these crippling conditions, to what was termed as a three/quarter house in Well Street in Hockley, where her younger brother was born, making three children; quite a moderate sized family compared to many who had lived in the back-to-backs of Tenby Street. By then the 'City Fathers', as Marie refers to them, had decided it was time to clear the slums and offer all the residents a chance to basic amenities, such as a kitchen, a bathroom, running water and 'a bit of a garden'. However, these clearances were delayed by the outbreak of World War Two and were not completed until after.

She remembers her subsequent evacuation fondly, although as she says it was not the same for some poor children, whose parents 'forgot' to write their personal details on the brown luggage tag labels, making them unidentified and lost, never to be repatriated. For Marie it was a very different experience, for it was because of her fortunate evacuation to a small village near Nottingham that she discovered her love for education, in particular, the written word. She had found her previous experience in Birmingham daunting, always in the bottom of the C grade. During that time she had contracted tuberculosis and had had to convalesce in an inhumane TB hospital in Rhyl, where she described the nurses as being 'cruel'.

As she was a sickly child, she was housed in a hostel in Nottingham rather than a family home, along with some of the 'nameless' evacuees, many from London. Here she found herself under the watchful and caring eye of the matron, who took a liking to her and began her encouragement towards learning. It was a small village school, that had suddenly had the pupil numbers drastically increased, so the school hall was divided by curtains, enabling several classes to operate in situ. She was 'well taken care of' by the Headteacher and the local vicar; for whom Marie developed quite a crush. However, she was not to stay for the duration of the war, although she was achieving excellent marks at the age of 12, her mother 'fetched her back', fearing that her developing daughter may fall pregnant. Not that young people then had much understanding of any of the processes involved, with rudimentary, diagrammatic drawings appended to blackboards, of disconnected animal genitalia.

Initially, her receiving school in Birmingham put her back into the bottom of C grade, but with much perseverance and persistence, Marie climbed the ladder, and by the end of the following year she was top of the A grade. This brought her to the attention of the Headmaster, who considered that she must sit the entrance exams for Aston Commercial School; her mother was not so jubilant at the prospect because of the fees that would have to be paid. But fortune smiled on Marie, for having passed the examination she was offered a free place as her father's wage as a policemen was considered so low that the fees could be waived. She loved her experiences there and she was able to study a complete range of subjects, from the obvious commercial skills of shorthand and typing, to English, French, singing and music; she

Rear of No. 12 Tenby Street, 1929, Marie and her brother Ivor (by the kind courtesy of the Hockley Flyer Collection).

matriculated at fifteen and a half, 'which was old in them days'.

Her first position was at Tubes Ltd on Rocky Lane as a junior shorthand typist, Marie was not to remain at the bottom for long and having worked her way up through the ranks, she eventually ended up as a secretary in the drawing office, which was situated on Chester Road. It was during this time that she had met her future husband, and as most young couples of that time, money became the driver and Marie changed her job in order to earn more. She married and moved in with her in-laws, she describes the place as 'insanitary' where babies were 'not welcome' and by this stage Marie was pregnant. She was, as many of her generation were, completely ignorant of the mechanics, and found herself carrying her first child, jobless, and with the prospect of becoming homeless.

These were the years of the marriage bar, and no self-respecting employer would employ a young mother with children and it required a lot of deception on the part of honest young women to maintain an income. Marie was troubled in the position that she found herself in, working for two devoutly, religious brothers, who she admits, 'were very nice to her', but she managed to conceal the truth of her pregnancy until she was almost eight months gone, she says that she felt terrible lying to them but she had to help pay the rent and save towards a house of her own. However, a number of circumstances came together all at the same time, her father died just after she had given birth to her daughter, and one of her brothers had joined the army, the other was away to be married, so Marie, her husband, and her newborn daughter found themselves living under her mother's 'roof' in Great Barr. She managed this arrangement, with her daughter sharing their one room, for four years, then she pressed to buy her own home, which became her home of the past fifty-four years.

She had struggled to find the one hundred pounds deposit required, and then been beside herself when the solicitor informed her that he needed a further thirty pounds for his fees. She broke down in front of him, and because he was a kindly soul, he told her to pay when she could.

Those were hard years for Marie when she knew that with raising a family any aspirations had to be firmly held in check, and she had to take whatever employment that she could. She became an usherette in a cinema, which taught her some lessons, she suddenly became 'invisible' when she had been so highly appreciated; it was a humbling experience, and made her value even more any future appreciation. She had been away from shorthand and typing for seven years by that stage, and as many returning mothers feel when resuming their past lives, she considered that her skills would no longer be of value. However, a friend convinced her to try again as a temp. She had her own doubts that she could actually do it, but found herself very quickly employed, earning four times the salary that she had commanded seven years previously. In fact, she was so successful with the temping agency that had employed her, that she became their 'trouble shooter'; particularly in the cases where younger girls and women who had returned to the office in tears. Marie would be sent to these places where they had been temping to 'sort out' the problems.

It was at this point that she began to pick up private clients, including Aston University, also a barrister who worked for the council. She realised that she had enough ability and experience to go out on her own, and by 1963, she was officially self-employed. She would take on her own self-employed temping work, which because there was no intermediary agency taking commission, increased her salary yet again. However, this did involve a considerable amount of travelling and many additional hours. This prompted her to open her own office, so that clients might visit her for her services.

She opened her office in York Terrace, her first major investment being a photocopier; as she respectfully remarks, 'put many a good copy typist out of work'. Essentially, she ran an 'accommodation and telephone-answering service', open to all. Her business grew substantially, from all quarters, to the extent that she had to sign the Official Secrets Act and her address had to be registered with the police, as she was now handling Government work.

Her business arrived in the Quarter at an opportune time for many who were suffering under the new demands of accountancy regulation, especially with the advent of VAT. Many small business, who had survived on a hand-to-mouth existence, were simply lost in the mire of paperwork and book keeping that they now found themselves under; Marie became the 'girl Friday' and not just to those in the Quarter, but many around the city, who were being viewed by the Chamber of Commerce as the 'lame ducks'. Many such were passed onto Marie to 'sort out'. Marie remembers one such case, of an orange box arriving with three years of receipts, and other such detritus, including half eaten sandwiches, which all had to be waded through and put into an order for those auditing. In some cases, she was given months of dispensation by those in authority to make sense of the chaos that was landing daily. Marie and her husband, became so efficient in these processes that they were given special recognition by the VAT office, her husband being awarded a special merit, which was accompanied by an official tie to wear; on at least one occasion the wearing of this tie enabled Marie to alleviate problems with an over-zealous VAT inspector. Officially, she managed over thirty sets of books, this did not include all of those other companies that she would set up headings for their books to enable them to keep their own accounts.

She describes the Quarter of those days, as very different to the one that now exists. She has seen the worst of depression and poverty there, followed by the damage that WWII brought, and then time of plenty of the 1960's when busloads of people arrived to work in a thriving place. But as she points out, the current downswing in the economy is nothing new, and indeed the history of the Quarter much further back than that could show the same, peaks and troughs, it is another dip, and much as before, reviving, re-branding, better marketing, all would serve to better the fortunes of the business that still exist there. As in previous bad times, the Royal Family have been sought to help in these promotion activities; Princess Alexandra wearing jewellery from the

Quarter, the present Queen and her Father George VI have done much, and now Prince Charles is seen as an advocate for the Quarter, particularly, for the conservation of the buildings.

Marie is well known in the Quarter and generally loved by all for the colourful character that she is, and she is the first to admit that she is either 'liked or disliked' for her perceived interference; it is her belief that there are times that this interference is necessary in order to protect the integrity of the Quarter. One particular incident she feels has caused some to bulk at the objections that she raised at a timely moment.

At one point, a group of businessmen proposed an 'Urban Village' to be developed on the site of the Quarter, Marie was only made aware of these discussions by a mutual business friend, and attended the meeting, uninvited. At this meeting, she very quickly understood the real impact of these proposals, at this time there was no conservation of the Jewellery Quarter in place as an intact entity, which meant that much of the area was open to

PC 77 Richard Evan Jones – Marie's father – policeman in the Jewellery Quarter between the two World Wars – merit stripe for saving nine lives during the Hockley Brook Flood (by the kind courtesy of the Hockley Flyer Collection).

exploitative land developers, who could see that there was some large sums of money to be generated by buying up the older properties and selling the land. Much of this speculative land dealing had already been having a large impact on the smaller businesses, who were finding themselves pushed out by landlords demanding higher and higher rents, or elderly neighbouring workers selling off; L J Millington experienced much of this when they were in Pitsford Street.

Marie listened to her horror, to hear the proposals that all remaining planning restrictions – which had been carefully put in place by the Victorian Society some thirty or so years beforehand – be lifted to enable these developers to move in. She could foresee, that with this open-access policy that the Jewellery Quarter would vanish, as more and more, would be forced out, unable to meet the escalating costs of trying to do business there, effectively pushing the life blood out; and all that would remain would be the proposed bijou apartments and wine bars.

Marie decided enough was enough, and brought to their attention then that their plans had not correctly considered the geography of the Quarter, particularly traffic flow. It was obvious that she had a valid position to contribute and her opinion was sought. She used her intrinsic knowledge and forceful personality to the maximum; she identified the issues of 'living in a working Quarter'; the noise, the smells, the parking. Had they thought about the odour of boiling acids? Had they considered the

No. 12 Tenby Street – about 1940 – windows added to Attic for extra jeweller's workspace shop. The façade is Grade 2 listed (by the kind courtesy of the Hockley Flyer Collection).

noise and disruption a large stamping press could impose at all times of the night and day, particularly during the Christmas rush? It was not quite as simple as any of the 'great and the good' of the city had considered it might be.

After some initial debate and consultation the proposals were shelved and an alternative plan to conserve the Quarter – the 3,000 businesses and the 6,000 jobs – were suggested in various forum. Paul Spooner was given the task of 'picking Marie's brains' as to the best way of designating the Quarter; she insisted that the inner part should be protected at all costs. It took two years to have a final area planned and protected, within that period of time there was still some unfortunate property speculation which got under the wire. There had previously existed three areas of conservation; St Paul's, The Jewellery Quarter and Key Hill. The wide corridors which had bisected these areas were exploited during the interregnum, however, now the three areas are united as one, thanks to Marie's tenacity and determination.

As she admits, it is a fragile peace that exists, and is only held in place by the auspices of the Jewellery Quarter Association, she says there are those who would be quite happy to see all of the regulations overturned. Whatever arguments are proposed for and against the area now outlined, one fact remains, had that area not been designated, the developers would have moved in and there would be little if any business activity now ongoing in the Quarter, for the same arguments that were given by Marie at that consultation meeting as to why there should not be residential developments are now being given by the new residents, and softer businesses, that have moved in, in an effort to stop business activity interfering with their peace.

In her opinion, businesses are 'dying off', simply because the older workers are leaving, and others are being offered five times what their businesses are worth. Mark relayed to me the story of one old gentleman (40 years in the trade), who had come in to ask Marie's opinion of what he should do, when he had been offered a suitcase full of money, Mark and Marie honestly replied, 'take the money'. The old gentleman was somewhat taken aback by their candid response and said:

"But I don't want to let you down Marie."

The Jewellery Quarter Association and Marie Haddleton's name are synonymous. As a founder member President and Honorary Secretary she has done much to promote and fight for all that she believes in there. Whether, it has been raising the much needed £130,000 of funding from Mr Sanjiv Shah for the restoration of the much-loved Chamberlain Clock, which had fallen into dreadful disrepair, which now is fully restored and remains the icon of the Quarter; or pushing for a ramp for wheelchair access, by 'ripping a strip off' a senior council official. It is the fight for the smaller issues that Marie insists keeps the Quarter 'on top of the list'. The new battles being waged now are for

Marie Elizabeth Haddleton – JQA (by the kind courtesy of the Hockley Flyer Collection).

the restoration of the two cemeteries at Warstone Lane and Key Hill, and continued acknowledgement of the museums which commemorate the heritage; The Jewellery Museum and The Pen Room.

Not all changes have been necessarily progressive for the Quarter. Marie remembers the days when there existed a 'closed shop' on sales to the public; to some this was about protecting business interests in the Quarter by keeping the speculative retailing out, and any small independent indulging in retail was frowned upon. However, there were those small enterprising businesses who were not as content with this state of affairs, and took to placing a table just inside their premises, or knocking a few nails in the walls to hang their wares on. A time before security measures were necessary, when mutual trust abounded around the Quarter. In those days, Marie would make regular visits around

The Chamberlain Clock after restoration by the JQA (by the kind courtesy of the Hockley Flyer Collection).

the place with 'The Hockley Flyer', and would mischievously cause alarm by jokingly threatening 'to shop' the offenders to the local police station. There is no doubt that this small amount of retail did eventually open the flood gates, to other retailers, who have since moved in to speculate on the Quarter's prestige and demography; and only thirty percent of what is now on retail there is probably made in the Quarter itself.

Marie has developed a very effective network that keeps the Jewellery Quarter (and all that it stands for) in the focus of Birmingham Council. Her heart and soul are intrinsically part of the area and whether she is seen as an advocate or an inhibitor, she has done much good for the place and the conservation of its heart. There are many who have benefited from her hard work and energy and respect her for her determination to carry on; to such an extent that she was honoured with an invitation to a Buckingham Palace Garden Party. Unfortunately, in the same year that she was due to have her hip replacement, after much agonising she was forced to decline the invitation, but keeps her hat and shoes just in case the opportunity comes again. However, as a mark of how high she is held in the esteem of many within the Quarter, a sizeable fund had been raised on her behalf to facilitate her trip. All was not lost; it was decided to divert the funds into the purchase of a mobility scooter for her.

Marie is a very careful driver, this I know for she had to leave our interview earlier than expected, to feed the parking meter (the bane of all those that live and work in the Quarter), but a mobility scooter is a very different experience. On her first attempt, she went into reverse at speed by accident, narrowly missing a group of young female pedestrians, who suggested that she needed driving lessons. Undaunted, Marie tried again moments later, and had 'a small collision' with a police officer. So the scooter will have to wait a little while longer until her confidence is fully restored.

This sums Marie Haddleton up, she is not a person to give up on anything that she has set her mind to doing, even if all seems hopeless and without a solution, Marie will make something happen to change that. She is a cheerful character, who has many colourful stories to tell, she has seen the good times and the bad times in the Quarter and remains optimistic that despite all of the changes it will survive as a working place. She knows that it has a history of redeveloping and reinventing itself, in the most part due to the many hardworking and dedicated individuals and companies that operate there. It is after all the people that make the place, not the buildings or the streets; those people have to remain in order to keep the Quarter thriving, but it has to be affordable and practical to do so; it is those battles that Marie has fought for and will continue to fight for.

Chapter 6

SOCIAL NETWORKING
AND SMOOTH TALKING

Deakin and Francis

This chapter is the tale of a company which in all the conversations that I have had in the Quarter, is always spoken about with the greatest of respect. Deakin and Francis have a fine pedigree, they have seen the best of things, and worst, several times over, but always come through it with smiling charm. The new custodians are no different, James and Henry; they are both elegant, refined and extremely hard-working, like the leaders of the other long standing companies, there is just one thing that sets them apart, and by which they have an edge, they have youth on their side. James is 34 and Henry is 27, and their energy levels are incredible, their younger vision is highly creative, and it needs to be in this present economic downturn.

When I met with James we sat in the boardroom, which used to be part of the Harper's Hill in Regents Place where James Watt lived. It was a very moving moment for me, to have done so much research into the significance of Matthew Boulton and James Watt to the development of the Jewellery Quarter, to be sitting in a place where the inventor probably sat. James told me that they have a very long heritage as a company, as far back as 1786. He believes they are possibly the oldest firm of family jewellers in existence; Garrard's are older, but have changed owners many times. They have just unearthed a tremendous archive in another part of the building, which takes the family even further back to the 16th Century. During these times they were listed as sword makers and tanners producing harness for the military, both enterprises ended in disaster; the sword makers for refusing to bribe the Proof House and attempting to sue the Crown; the harness makers being sued and bankrupted for producing leather that stretched when wet.

Deakin and Francis have a very complex history, of family trauma and tragedy. Some of their forebears were more astute businessmen than

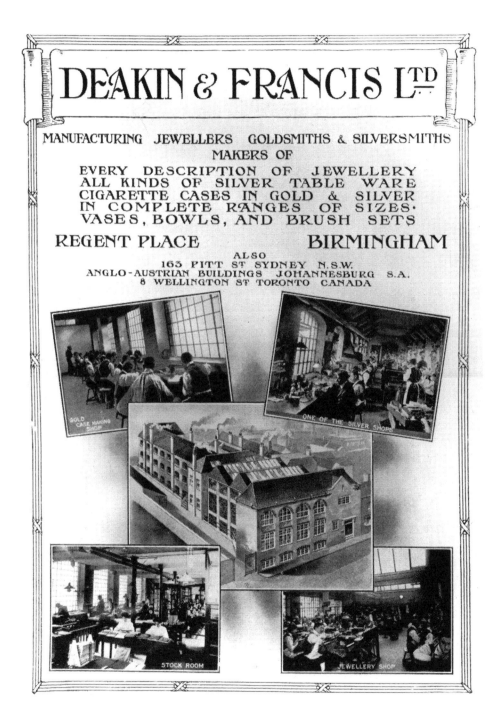

Deakin and Francis Ltd, in times gone by (by the kind courtesy of Deakin and Francis).

others, often it was the down to unrelated members of the management to bring the company round, when combinations of bad luck and poor judgement led the firm into difficulties. These times of internecine rivalry often left individuals resentful of their positions. I have been given two written narratives by previous incumbents in the senior positions, their given opinions of aspects of the company's history, contrast and conflict, which is a consequence of the diversity of views supplied by different people as to where the problems originated.

The first narrative was supplied by J. R. Green – a cousin of the actual family – who took over as MD during a particularly difficult time. The second is given by James' and Henry's father, David, when he assumed control from J. R. Green and subsequently brought the company back into the main stem of the family. Rather than discuss the micro-political nature of these narratives I have extracted the considered information which is informative, as regards the history and business experiences of a very complex situation.

Deakin and Francis was founded in 1786 by two men Turnball and Woolfield. Shortly, after the Napoleonic Wars and probably as a result in the slump in trade that was experienced nationally, Charles Washington Shirley

18ct White Gold Skull Cufflinks Pave set in Black Diamonds with moving jaw and White Diamond eyes (by the kind courtesy of Deakin and Francis).

Deakin bought the company for £4000 and operated it as a factor, trading as Deakin and Moore. The firm became listed as Deakin and Francis, two generations later in 1881, due to intermarriage between the two families, and were still operating as factors. The partners were Stephen Henry Deakin and his brother-in-law John Horace Francis. By the 1890's they had decided to build their factory in Regents Place at the back of their pre-existing warehouse. J. H. Francis ran the factory and S. H. Deakin was the one who travelled, mainly to the north, to create customers and sales. There is some assumption by Mr Green that this was not an easy partnership. By the 1900's Deakin was forced to take retirement on the grounds of ill health, but remained as Chairman. This meant that external partners had to be brought in to run the company, for the most part they were not considered to be successful businessmen. Additionally, Francis is credited with paying lower than average wages to his employees, which set the standard for the amount and quality of work produced.

Francis, had only one son, Jack Francis who was tragically killed in 1916 while serving somewhere in the trenches, this must have had a huge impact on Francis senior, who threw himself into working for various ex-servicemen societies and rather neglected his business interests. To counteract this, the private company was wound up and staff were encourage to buy shares in 1919. Despite this measure, the company fortunes began to dwindle and it was left to the Works Manager Mr K. J. Vann to assume control, when Francis suffered a stroke in 1930. Mr Vann did not have a particularly easy job to do; the post-war slump was catastrophic, followed shortly thereafter, by the worst depression in history. Somehow, he managed to turn the company around and by 1935, they were once again turning a profit. Shortly, before Francis senior died in 1932, J. R. Green joined the company and was able to witness the next momentous events in the company's history.

The Second World War had a devastating effect on the Quarter, not just through physical bomb damage, but through the loss of trade, as all available personnel not of serving age were turned to the Total War Production protocol of Mr Bevin's plan. Deakin and Francis lost all of their staff to war production. When Green returned in 1945, all he found were two girls working in the stockroom, Mr Vann and one other. Trade had been damaged further by the escalating purchase tax levies that were imposed at extremely high rates. In his narrative, Mr Green points out that in his opinion it was because Deakin and Francis did not try to cheat the system, and failed to benefit from the bullion fiddles of the post-war era as most did, that they suffered, as he writes:

18ct White Gold Octagonal Cufflinks with Onyx and Diamonds (by the kind courtesy of Deakin and Francis).

"The firm was the most honest that could be imagined."
Two structural effects had been felt by the impact of the war, an incendiary bomb which had been difficult to extinguish, coming through the office roof. Secondly, a disused air shelter, which had to be constructed when they were trying to expand the factory, but were stopped by subsequent changes to the building regulations. It is feared that this air raid shelter (which is under where their current car park is situated) will one day collapse due to the corrosion of the reinforced concrete structure that supports it. Green assumed the role of MD in the 1960's, this he confesses was an extremely difficult time, due to the national political structure. He blames the Labour Government's policies of the time for over-taxation of the middle class, thus, removing most of the Deakin and Francis customer base. Things became so acute for the firm, that Francis Deakin and J. R.

Green conjointly invested personal funds of £20,000 to try to keep the business afloat.

This is where David Deakin's narrative commences; his first task was to demolish the air raid shelter. He had been brought into the company during the 60's and appears to have had an uncomfortable time under that regime. Fortunately, for David, J. R. Green came into a substantial inheritance in 1970 and made David Deakin and K. J. Vann joint MD's. It was at this point that David discovered how indebted the company was to the previous management and decided to make it his first priority to ensure the debt was repaid. It took hard work and determination, but after a few years he paid it back in full, and impressed Green and Francis who rewarded him by placing all of their company shares with him. This probably irritated Vann, who did not work well with David, and after a difficult dispute with Mr Green he left, leaving David in sole charge.

These were good years for the company, David was able to focus the company's offering to the market, through inspirations taken from the work of Andrew Grima, they were able to emulate this feel, as David describes, by producing:

"very modern pieces featuring uncut gems and mineral specimens."

They became 'very much leaders of style and would always sell out on the first day of trade shows'. David was very hands-on in his approach to the business and actually designed all the pieces, which as a result, he particularly enjoyed selling. But he was also extremely driven, determined to established new clients and customers, and as a consequence, always travelling up and down the UK in his endeavours to sell. When he did venture into the factory, it seems he was honoured with the awful jobs, which would make him yearn to be back on the road again.

The advent of the new decade brought the biggest calamity that the manufacturers of silverware have ever experienced, that of the Bunker Hunt brothers attempting to corner the whole market. David explained the consequences:

"They forced the price from 0.25p per ounce to £20 per ounce over a period of 18 months, this made our hollowware unsaleable so we ended up melting the stock for cash and paying off silversmiths, engine turners, spinners, stampers and polishers."

The calamity that befell the Quarter then is quite unimaginable. Many of the outworkers and small companies depended on their trade in silver and the processes of working silver for their livelihoods. Deakin and Francis like all of the other larger concerns, used many of the outworking silversmiths

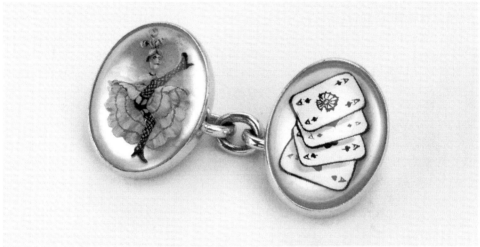

18ct Yellow Gold "Road to Ruin" or "4-Vices" Hand-painted Reverse Intaglio Crystal Cufflinks (by the kind courtesy of Deakin and Francis).

in the production of their wares. A considerable amount of these smaller concerns suffered total collapse, finding their incomes decimated over night, and left the industry. The description of the 'ghost town' that has been given to me by others of the area during the 1980's stems from this hideous action. Only the strongest could survive; those who worked in gold, or had a niche market; but even they found their firms stripped of personnel and working short weeks as a consequence. James told me that during that time and subsequently, Deakin and Francis have gone from at its height employing 300 (including outworkers) to 30.

Their only saving grace from the disaster was down to David's quick-thinking and astute business acumen. By paying everything off and downsizing to the most essential needs, they had become rich in capital. They were able to exploit their business in gold, combined with the keen Arab interest in 'London retail' by falling back on their trade in gold photograph frames among other things, such as; mobile phones, video cameras, gold enamel and gem set object d'art table centres, pot pourri, lamps and Kleenex boxes, all for Middle Eastern palaces. David also, focused his efforts on trade overseas, particularly the old Imperial concerns, and oil-rich economies. He expanded the worldwide markets considerably, breaking into the very American dominated USA markets. The most significant strategy for the company was to move away from the 'provincial thinking' of the Quarter – to place itself above London – and to actively seek clients in the capital. This opened new aspects for him such as dealing in precious gemstones from Thailand; he would seek out multi-coloured sapphires in particular, which could not be found in the UK.

He had a young family at the time, and worked himself extremely hard to make back the ground which had been lost by previous generations and poor management. David Deakin has built up considerable respect from many I have spoken to in the area, who see him as a very shrewd and hard working individual, with a personable character. His influence upon his sons is obvious and he must have inspired a keenness in them to become involved in the business when they were quite young. Eventually, James trained as a gemmologist at the Gemmological Institute in the USA, and then had his first serious commercial experience working for a few years at Asprey's in New York. There he learned the importance of image and customer service, which have formed part of his pre-requisite principles of business thinking. He told me that while he was at Asprey's, that he had to clean the window displays (even all of the gift boxes) every night, which set the tone of the quality of service that they give at every level. Henry trained as a gemmologist at the GIA branch in Vicenza in Italy, and he too moved to Asprey's in New York before joining Deakin and Francis.

When James returned from the USA his first instinct was to go to his bench, but David soon pointed out the error of his ways, telling him firmly:

"Craftsmen don't make money; businessmen make money."

A truism that I have found much supported from all of the evidence that I have gathered in this book. It is a sad fact, that those who have the gifts and talents, who have been trained to the highest level of skill, are often poorly rewarded for all of their hard work and efforts. I have analysed elsewhere, that I believe this is as much due to their own total devotion to the love of their craft, as to any active over-exploitation, by their masters.

The keen young men also absorbed a considerable amount of their father's business strategy, such as the focus of overseas markets, particularly America, and the broadening of their aspirations within London. James told me, that Deakin and Francis have been actively selling to America for over 20 years. They have managed to break into retail outlets which are known for their inscrutable buyers, who can be extremely difficult to build associations with. The constant approaches to these outlets by Deakin and Francis have paid large dividends, and they are now able to boast the likes

Silver and Vitreous Enamel Cufflinks showing the die-struck pattern through the translucent enamel (by the kind courtesy of Deakin and Francis).

of Bergdorf Goodman in their client list. Interestingly, Deakin and Francis refused approaches made by Neiman Marcus to them in the first instance, until they agreed to pay for the products supplied upfront; Neiman Marcus conceded, although they normally operate a policy of sale or return.

David's incessant travelling and over-work for forty years had detrimental effects on his health, James and Henry persuaded him that it was time for him to take a rest and allow them to show him what they could do. Not knowing of course that this present global recession was threatening, James jokingly laughs:

"Dad got out at the right time."

His sons made a conscious decision to leave as much intact as they could from David's time, that he had obviously worked so hard to conserve. As a consequence, they have changed very little, and have waited for the present turn of events economically to play itself out.

They have desires to expand the business, but for now they are in a period of contraction, as all are in the Quarter. When this new downturn occurred, their turnover dropped by one million overnight. They consider themselves to have been lucky, certainly luckier than many others. They closed a few accounts and culled where necessary; they have ridden the storm, so far. Their main strategy of managing this recession is to assume 'natural wastage' in order to lose personnel. Their eldest member in the employed staff at this time is in his mid-fifties, they are in no position to take anyone on in this present climate; apprenticeships are a consideration for the future. Through all of this, James maintains that there is lot of self-belief in the building, despite (when the greatest effects were felt) being reduced to a three-day week for a few months. He is very positive about the general morale of the workforce and like many glad to be still doing business, and doing it very well.

The young men have identified two areas of focus that they believe will capitalise on all of their combined skills and talents. Their first is 'to do what they do best as individuals'. James views himself very much as the man at the coal face, in the factory dealing with operations on the shop floor level, he loves the 'hustle and bustle' and design. Henry is brilliant in public relations, and is the one who is primarily credited with taking Deakin and Francis into the new age of Social Networking as a marketing force; which as proved elsewhere is an extremely effective channel for putting a message 'out there'. However, they both do the selling, which with the vastness of their markets geographically is necessary, but as James admits, not necessarily ideal for the day-to-day operations that must continue in the factory. The two are extremely adaptable and responsive to their business

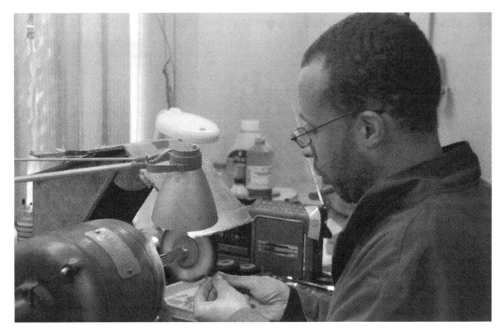

A fine finish (J. Debney).

situation. In these lean times they need to be, James explained that when they are pressed by 'rushed orders' that 'everyone mucks in'.

The second focus that they have set themselves is their product offering. Gone are the days when Deakin and Francis were employing 300 people and producing a wealth of goods in silverware and jewellery. Like everyone else that has a large enterprise in the area, a considerable amount of contraction has taken place, and the loss of manpower and processes means a degree of specialisation must ensue, and product identification is all part and parcel of that critical process. As with many, Deakin and Francis have focused themselves on a particular niche market; theirs is high-end, particularly exclusive cufflinks – the world's finest. They also concentrate on many of these being bespoke commissions.

They will produce almost anything that can be thought of as a pair of fabulous cufflinks, from a pair of diamond encrusted skulls, with articulated jaws, to beautiful racing yachts, finely crafted in high quality gold with mother of pearl sails. All these items completely to the customer's specification and approval, from photographs and sketches provided, or discussions, to produce copious design drawings, revised, until they have total client satisfaction.

This very modern approach to design is further emphasised by their presence on the Social Networking sites of Facebook and Twitter, and their ever-present Deakin and Francis blog. Through these regularly updated medium they advertise and promote all of their products past and present, at the same time, exposing their readers to interesting facts about the company. For instance, I learnt from Facebook that Cary Grant had been a frequent customer of the company during his visits to the United Kingdom to see his mother. This is where Henry's forte in all things cyberspace come to the fore. He makes sure that every activity, whether it be a commission, a trade show, a recent exhibition, or even the motorcycle trip that these guys took round America, are constantly high in the public profile and perception.

It is an interesting note to make here, that Deakin and Francis are probably the oldest company in the Quarter, yet by far, they are using the most up to date methods to market all that they have. This force to market, does not stop here, they are constantly on the look out for other opportunities to extract public relations potential from. They are particularly keen to make an intrinsic analysis of their own pedigree as a family, from the jumbled collection of memorabilia of letters and deeds, diaries and photographs, which has recently come to light in their rooms.

The old gas engine at the rear of Deakin and Francis (J. Debney).

To them any piece of data is essentially 'a treasure-trove' of potential for their marketing drive; they have recently employed a member of staff directly for this purpose. There is no doubt that in the boardroom alone, they have a selection of archived photographs from times gone by, which most companies would give their back teeth to own; including most notably, a picture of the original rectory, of which their boardroom used to form a part of. The factory's original engine still survives but is in need of some serious restoration, in the back car park; a photograph of which hangs in the boardroom from more pristine times.

They are very astute to perceptions across their markets of a Birmingham brand; they know that in London only a London stamp works, whereas in the USA the stamp of Birmingham, England is much appreciated. They have recently exhibited in Florence, they are beginning to open up in Paris, they have established good connections in Russia and are seeking to expand their eastern European potential. They have broken into the new Chinese economy, with its boom for ownership of special things for which the regime so long excluded the masses from. There seems no limit to where they will stop constantly seeking untapped potential and creating new client streams. The only downside of course, is the travel which is both long and costly, James told me, that in the first few months of that year they had notched up an astonishing 136 hours of flight time between them, at an average airfare of £4,000. Despite what seems like an inordinate investment in both time and money, their high-energy activities are paying off, as their profits accrue daily.

Of the Quarter itself, James feels that there is a place for identifying with the Quarter and all of the history that comes by association. He believes that there is a collective strength through the companies who now wish to exploit the joint marketing potential, that is very beneficial to Deakin and Francis. He also feels that is important to value the individuality of each firm, and that consequently, this drives the need for a balance between the two perspectives. He loves the 'red brick' feel of the Quarter and to him the retention of many of the old buildings through conservation is to praised:

"It has a charm all of its own."

However, he does speculate with all of the recent economic woes, how some businesses have survived and are still in operation.

I was able to walk around the factory as James took me on a brief guided tour. As has so often happened to me around the area, in the various places, large and small, that I have been in; the smell took me back immediately, to my own days of working in metal shop, and that feeling of 'coming home'

Scenes from Deakin and Francis (J. Debney).

washed over me. I was able to see the engine, which definitely needs 'a can of diesel' to clean it up. Even the original driveshaft and belt mechanism that is just inside the factory that transmitted the power to the engine shop, is still in situ.

I talked briefly with Trevor Batchelor who is 52 and has worked as a polisher for 34 years, 12 of those with Deakin and Francis. He was cheerful and full of stories, it seems that the enthusiasm and optimism that James and Henry exude rubs off on the staff. I asked Trevor primarily about the Quarter, he shares the opinions of many, the feeling of family, the fact that everyone knows everyone. He remembers when it was 'four times the size that it is now' and he feels that despite the shrinking it has still retained a lot of the atmosphere. He was one of the few that I have chatted to that believes the coming of the apartments, and by that fact, the residents, 'may be a good thing'. His only concern is another that is often expressed, 'the lack of training', he is worried that the area could go as the trades die off, through an inability to find new people to work in the various processes needed.

I spent the rest of that afternoon, leafing through the wealth of un-archived family memorabilia in an old wooden box. The stories came alive, as I read the minute books from the 1920's and before that charted the haphazard decline of the company. My heart went out to J. H. Francis as I found the picture of his son Jack who had been killed serving in the Great War, and the collection of obituaries of many of the names that have been woven into this story. But then I found a diary, probably from the evidence enclosed within, written by a John Francis dated in the 1880's, which told of visits and holidays made. That is when history becomes real, not the facts, dates and places, it is the written thoughts and emotions of the individual that gives a sense of feeling and relating. I hope that they put this archive to good use in their campaign to market their heritage. I make a toast to two fine young men, who in very challenging times are working their socks off to build a highly successful company to pass on to the next generation; to the 'Cufflink Boys' and long may you remain, a company that has put the Quarter on the map of the United Kingdom.

Chapter 7

CUSTODIANS OF
THE FAMILY CONCERN

Charles Green

Charles Green is another company with a very long heritage in the Jewellery Quarter. It has a history of strong family tradition, and at times became a victim of its own success in producing a large family, with a numbers of sons, all with the same driving ambition to succeed. It has suffered the worst calamities of war, which for a while impeded its progress, but from all this the company has been passed to the sixth generation of the same family, Tom Green, who values all that has come before and modestly views his position as the custodian.

Tom has an air of unruffled sophistication. He knows the business that he is in, back to front and inside out. Every aspect of the firm is in his blood, however, it was not an automatic assumption that he would be in the role that he is now, as he wryly notes, he joined the family business merely as a summer job 38 years ago:

"Once you get in you never leave – you either love it, or you hate it."

That is not to say that all things are as they used to be in the Jewellery Quarter. In that 38 years, Tom has witnessed some significant changes, both in the decline in prosperity and the general deterioration of the area. One of the greatest problems to have developed in recent years, is caused by the ease at which gold and jewellery can be exchanged for money. This has meant that those with criminal intent, now skulk in the shadows of the Quarter waiting for careless victims, who are not as security conscious as they might be. Tom never tells anyone where he works now, just for security reasons of safety, as he tells me, a gentleman had petrol poured over him recently and was mugged for what he had; in these times it is not the best of ideas to advertise where you come from and what you do. Tom remains very relaxed and secure in his own self, he just thinks twice when walking the streets, a sensible strategy.

All images by the kind courtesy of Charles Green.

Charles Green has a pedigree that goes back over two hundred years. It may even go back further, as along with his cousin Steven Green, they are at this moment conducting significant family research, which has revealed that there may have been a 'Charles Green' connection on one of Captain Cook's voyages; certainly, this 'Charles Green' was able to repair the sextant when it was man-handled by natives. That is not a general skill that most possess, unless they have some close experience in mathematical instrumentation.

Charles Green has in its possession a copy of an indenture of one George Coley who was apprenticed to a Charles Green in 1824 to 'train as a gold worker'. By that measure, that particular Charles Green would have become established as a jeweller before the turn of the century, and obviously, learnt his craft from another (a father maybe). However, one can confidently assume that the family have strong connections to the area for over two hundred years. The same year as George Coley was apprenticed, Charles Green established his business. From my own personal research about the rise of industry in Birmingham, these years were some of the most significant in its development and rise, certainly, Charles Green senior managed to start his business at just the right time to capitalise on the surge and upswing, economically, post the Napoleonic Wars.

He is recorded 'as a manufacturer of signet rings', and his first premises were in Brearley Street West. He stayed there for over two decades before moving to Augusta Street sometime after 1851. By 1863, the title of the firm had changed to Charles Green and Son, as the next generation Charles Green junior, joined his father in his enterprise. This continued as such, until the patriarch died, whereupon both of his sons, Charles junior and George operated the business together for some years.

In 1876, George Green left the business and the partnership was dissolved, it once more became a one-man concern. Prince Albert the consort to Queen Victoria, had died young in 1861. Queen Victoria never really recovered from the death of her 'beloved Albert', and went into deep mourning; only wearing black, no adornments of lace, or buckles, or buttons, and certainly no jewellery. The Queen set the fashion for the rest of the country, particularly, those in society and although they did not wear black necessarily, the fashion for wearing jewellery had declined dramatically. This dissolution of the brothers' partnership may have been precipitated because the business at that time could no longer support two families. Certainly, Charles Green junior decided to take action to change the present state of affairs which was pushing the jewellery industry, and subsequently, the Jewellery Quarter into rapid decline.

An approach in the form of an appeal was made to the Princess of Wales (Alexandra of Denmark). She met with Charles Green and another influential figure from the Jewellery Quarter, a gentleman called Jacob Jacobs at her London home Marlborough House. She was sensitive to the needs of promoting commerce and on seeing some of the pieces that the two had brought with them, purchased those that she considered most appealing. She then made a point of wearing them at many occasions, regenerating the fashionable demand for jewellery, and encouraging many of those fashion conscious members of society to visit Birmingham, in order that they might emulate the Princess of Wales.

Charles Green junior, was instrumental in starting the British Jewellers' Association, or as it was then, The Birmingham Jewellers' and Silversmiths' Association. Charles had realised the necessity for the trade to raise the profile of the industry by forming a professional association and network, he also realised the need to invest in an underpinning of education and training, this led to the eventual foundation of the Birmingham School of Jewellery. Charles was elected as the first chairman of the Birmingham Jewellers' and Silversmiths' Association and gave the organisation a temporary home on his premises, 'The British Jewellers' Association – 100 Years of Service':

> "In 1897 it was resolved that the time had come for the Association to have its own permanent secretary and offices in the Jewellery Quarter. Mr H. C. Lowe was appointed clerk to the Association on 8th March 1897 at a starting salary of £100 per year commencing 29th March 1897 and the association rented offices at 50 Augusta Street. The rooms were offered by Charles Green at a rental of £20 per year including rent, rates, taxes, coal, gas and cleaning."

Another great-grandfather to Tom, Mr J Millward Banks, was subsequently a chairman of same trade association in 1890; this emphasises the tight-knit nature of the business community at that time, which through their working relations led to more familiar connections.

The first family rift occurred between Charles Green junior and his eldest son, Charles Green. Although the company was profitable once more, there were three sons and it is unlikely that the firm could support that number. The young Charles felt that it was time to establish his own concern, and in 1903 he was given £100 by his father to set up in business on his own, this story is explained further in the chapter regarding Steven Green, as he was Steven's grandfather. This left the two younger sons, Lionel and Roland to assist their father until he died 3rd January 1906, whereupon they assumed control.

The following generation was controlled by Simon Green, the son of Lionel, and Martin Green the son of Roland. The cousins held the company together through some of the most difficult years of World War II. During that time with most of the men away including the owners, the premises in Augusta Street were totally destroyed by a German bomb. A shell of a company remained, with two or three workers, left in other premises, Simon's wife doing what she could to hold things together. Tom's father was captured at Dunkirk and interned as a prisoner of war, until he was repatriated in 1943 due to the extent of his injuries, which were quite severe.

Once he had fully convalesced, he became the driving force that rebuilt the company from the tatters that remained. For a number of years till the 1960's the firm had to rent premises, unfortunately all of their pre-war records had been lost in the blitz, so much of the company history had been destroyed. Eventually, Simon Green was able to commission the building of new premises in Tenby Street.

These premises are of their time, and are designed as a manufacturing establishment. With the new drive to 'open doors' and make companies more accessible, this place may seem austere and faces similar challenges to that of

Mr Tom Green – Managing Director.

Toye, Kenning & Spencer, of trying to create a more welcoming environment to those that may visit. What they may lose in the severity of the building is gained back by the youth and enthusiasm of the staff now employed.

Tom and his brother Adam, assumed control from their father, eventually full control passing to Tom in 2005. Since then Tom has worked hard to generate the new face of Charles Green. His philosophy is to encourage fresh blood and innovative thinking rather than living with the old traditional dogma. He proudly notes, that they now have a very young team, which is a slightly different profile to many of their competitors; even the Sales Director at this time is under 30, 'they see things differently'.

Charles Green have changed their products to suit the times over the years since they commenced in business and much of that foresight to visualise new trends and understand the current markets, have made them proactive in their decision making as to which products to promote, and at what time. Their original trade was in signet rings. They have a fine example of a pearl and diamond ring manufactured in the 1860's conserved within their archive. What has changed is the time factor that used to allow for the quality of production. They produce a range of items from; signet rings, gem set rings, chains, bracelets, crosses, bangles, cufflinks and lockets, however, some things go in and out of fashion and are held back for markets to change. No longer are they producing heavy gold chains and bracelets, for the trends are towards fine jewellery, but they retain a simple moto: 'Discontinue Nothing'; for they know these fashions will return again.

These days wedding rings have become diamond set wedding rings; heavy 18ct charm bracelets have faded due to the extremely high price of gold. They have responded to these changes by a contraction to the product offering, they no longer offer cameos for instance. They have found their niche in finely crafted 18ct gold, with a service 'second to none', as Tom emphasises, this approach combined with 'the personnel which bring a modern twist, not so nineteenth century as other companies':

"The hardest thing that a company faces is not evolving, not moving on."

Their stock books from previous times, carefully record, 'mounting 35 hours, 7 hours to set a stone'. Nowadays times are reduced to the mere essence with two hours as a set time on a similar piece, it is an indictment of the general public's lack of understanding of what it takes to fabricate a finally crafted piece, as Tom acknowledges 'people will not pay for the labour'.

Tom is concerned with the current state of the market, as most other producers are, as he points out '85% of jewellery sold in the UK is made

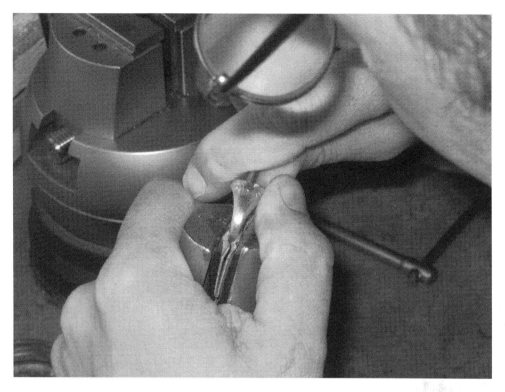

In the workshop of Charles Green (by the kind courtesy of Charles Green).

abroad'. This is reflected in the current state of the Jewellery Quarter itself. Tom has a copy of a map of one hundred and fifty years ago, when the Quarter is clearly defined as a quarter of the city itself. It emphasises the great importance that it played to the development of Birmingham, by contrast now, most of that same area is not involved in the manufacture of items that it was once famed for, and is now but a dot on the map of the greater extent of the city.

He believes that the discussions towards the Assay Office deregulation is the 'start of the slippery slope', he elaborates further:

"No one will miss it from week one, but in ten years time they will wonder why they let it happen."

This is a point shared by others who I have talked to in the area. There is a move to stop the removal of the hallmark, a point which Tom confirms, and he stresses that if the alternative is that it becomes a voluntary process, they will insist on keeping it – the company values the importance of keeping this quality standard even if it is by self-regulation.

Tom is aware that things are shifting significantly at the moment and can perceive a groundswell of change that is encompassing the industry as a whole:

'We are in for a change, we are going to see more change in the next two years than we have seen in the last thirty. And the following two years after that change will continue, this 'change' is happening at a pace that we have not seen the like of before."

The first marks of this evolution have been witnessed with the advent of ecommerce, which has forced a cultural shift within the Quarter, which has made companies adapt to these new developments in retail; L J Millington talk extensively of how they adopted these methods and capitalised on the new ways of retail.

Tom too, has witnessed this shift in people's buying habits, but he fears that this accessibility has extreme shortcomings, as far as the jewellery trade is concerned. He considers that the advent of 24 hour shopping which has been driven by the development of the internet has made people more aware of availability and some limited perception of price, but this is all too often based on inaccurate and abstract information. This leads to great

The workshop of Charles Green in earlier times (by the kind courtesy of Charles Green).

The workshop of Charles Green in earlier times (by the kind courtesy of Charles Green).

misunderstandings of what is, and what is not quality. Consequently, when many do venture into the shops to buy, they have a very false perception of what they can actually afford, because of the incorrect knowledge that the internet is feeding them.

He gave an example which he commonly experiences from the customers who come to Charles Green expecting to commission the manufacture of a diamond engagement ring. Tom's first premise is to start with the diamond itself, and select the right stone for the individual pocket. Tom says that all too often:

> "They have some knowledge of the four 'C's but have very little understanding of all of the other variables. With a diamond you may start at 6K and move up to 30K, when the person buying only has 4K in total… right a bit of coal then, no problem."

He believes that the person's priority when buying is ultimately the price, which they have only considered with only a fractional notion of the intrinsic value of the item, and very rarely do they consider the quality of the product

The indenture of George Coley to Charles Green (gold worker) in 1824 (by the kind courtesy of Charles Green).

that lasts a lifetime. As a consequence, when they do get a 'real' cost-to-value of the product they are very often not prepared for it.

That is not to say as a company that they do not benefit greatly from their internet revolution, in fact, it is safe to say that Charles Green are very 'hip' in current trends and usage of computers to enhance their sales and marketing. Their very young sales team, are 'tooled up' with the latest Ipads, complete with all of the company information and catalogue to hand instantly for clients and customers. Tom and his staff view trade shows, very much as a thing of the past. These events did work in the years before computers to provide a shop window and an excellent networking opportunity, but now it is far more efficient to be more focused on how products are promoted to their potential audience. This is a change that Tom feels most comfortable with that has been swept in by his young dynamic team. He likes to give his staff their head to make transformations that are necessary to modernise the company. This brought results that surprised him once, when he returned from a business trip to find that they had changed the company image from British Racing Green colours, to a rather sexy black.

The other major challenge that faces the Quarter is that of education and the development of the next generation of workers within the area. He is conscious that his own great-grandfather played a significant role in the development of the School of Jewellery, and that was very much a response to the needs and of that time, it was established to provide a throughput of good quality workers who were trained in good skills. He has witnessed the change in ethos of the School which now attracts a very different type of student, one who is more esoteric and less informed about the reality of production. These students are ones who attract funding to subsidise the high cost of tuition fees, most have absolutely no connection to the Quarter and will have very little interest in remaining in the Quarter in the long run, unless something is done to change their perceptions.

Charles Green is very active in trying to work with the School to inject reality into the students' experience of working within the production constraints of commercial jewellery manufacture. This is partly due to fact that Tom has employed a young man – Phillip Beale – who is an ex-design student of the School. He is now responsible for web design and product design within the firm He comments that the School has excellent facilities, however, the experience can be unrealistic; he undertook mainly conceptual work when he was there. As such, Charles Green now promotes a sponsored competition within the school to encourage students to work towards designing marketable products.

The outcome of last year's project involved 13 of the School's students being involved. Charles Green chose the stones and donated the metal that was used, the students were then given a design brief to fulfil using Computer Aided Design. Each of the students worked with an individual stone which followed the brief:

"This is a stone from my grandmother. Please design and make a piece for me..."

Within the given specification, they had to consider that product had to both be saleable, and profitable, and be made within a reasonable period of time. Tom views this strategy as a way to inject a sense of realism into the students' design vocabulary, as he comments:

"We live in the real world where you have got to take ownership of the piece... you can design some wonderful things, but they might never happen."

There are some positive movements within this higher level of education; the HND is now moving towards a BA course. There are at least five or so of the past students, who are still working in and around the Quarter. Further to this, many of the manufacturers are becoming more pro-active towards the encouragement of the retention of this talent that has in recent years been transient. This is being achieved by allowing the students to work in-house two or three days a week, and using the remainder of that time to work freelance:

"We have to keep them; they are the life-blood of the Quarter."

In opposition to this position, Charles Green do have issues about the large amount of municipal funding which is being poured into the museum and conservation projects in and around the area. They consider that the minimum amount of income generated by such places combined with the low employment opportunities, do not justify that level of support that they can attract. It is the businesses that generate the wealth and offer a high proportion of paid employment, as such, the City Council should be diverting this funding towards large marketing campaigns 'to promote the industry that is making the name for Birmingham'. As Tom highlights, after the war the Corporation realised the importance of the Quarter towards reconstruction and wealth generation, and actively supported this by laying on additional buses just to meet the demand for transportation. It is a very different tale now with the workers who struggle to find places to park, which cost a considerable amount of money and needs attention at least twice a day (as the maximum period of parking is four hours).

"What we sell here is unique and handcrafted. It is what gives the Quarter a steal! It needs to be promoted!"

He does worry that this short-termism towards economic development that pervades the thinking of those of influence, could strike a blow against all that is there. However, he is hopeful that those with the long-standing tradition will carry on against all of the odds, but those without that heritage with succumb eventually and leave.

Phillip has worked for Charles Green for six years. He started after he left the School of Jewellery. He has made some very interesting observations since coming into the commercial side of jewellery manufacture, he sees the differences between the more conservative UK market and the less traditional European and American markets. He tells me that people are often amazed to see how 'hands on and individual' the work is. There is some use of CAD and CAM in the design and production, but they have tended to revert to the traditional handcraft methods for two reasons. Firstly, a machine is dependent on software and the size/shape of the piece to be held, consequently, this has the tendency to limit the outcomes to a 'sameness' by all the manufacturers who adopt these processes. By returning to more manual methods, they are reintroducing the personal individuality. Which leads to the second reason, that of uniqueness, even if an item is

Many years of experience (J. Debney).

reproduced, it is still produced as an individual item, which gives the piece an intrinsic specialness, and thus, it can be valued higher. However, the investment that they have made in a more up-to-date CAD/CAM machine has been worthwhile, as it does have its uses, and with the price of such technology falling dramatically, it has paid for itself within one year.

This celebration of the art of the craft, continues throughout the factory. I was proudly informed that within one workshop, where three very skilled men were working, there was over one hundred years of experience. Charles Green has retained many of their good operatives over a number of years. In the polishing shop I met Christine Yates, who has been polishing for 35 years, and like many in the area, her mother had worked in Quarter as a solderer, she had died at the age of 75. On a good day, Christine polishes over one hundred items. She often sees her work elsewhere, and it fills her with a sense of pride. She is especially proud of the pair of cufflinks that she once helped to produce for the Queen.

Tom is the first to admit, that the Quarter has had a very sexist tradition of employment; with the various processes within the trade defined along gender lines; women tended to do presswork, enamelling and polishing, men were the silversmiths, the jewellers and setters. This is an historical situation due to who was considered to be the breadwinner. In other trades men were unionised, and thus, commanded higher wages, their wages in the Quarter reflected this. On the other hand, women could not join a union, they became victims of the employment system, very often condemned to do the tasks that the men would not do; the evidence of this exploitation was acute in the pen trade (Morgan 2001).

Charles Green still run a training system, they have noticed recently that the majority of trainees coming from the schools are girls. This is a concern that it is because of the lack of exposure to the metal trades in schools that is deterring many boys from seeking work there. They have recently acquired a new apprentice called Andy, who when I visited had literally just started and had spent two weeks on signet rings. I was told that he could now file a wedding ring competently and solder. The length of training time is always dependent on the individual concerned, but generally they would expect a trainee to 'go solo' within two years.

Within the same room, where Andy was working alongside his mentor, I met Tony Billings who is 59 and worked in the trade since he was 15. He has been with Charles Green for 19 of those years. He was very keen to explain the 'hold' that the Quarter has over the workers for the love of what they do:

"You sort of fall into it – once you are in it they sort of get their grip on you." Interestingly, although I know from my own professional experience that Tony is multi-skilled and could turn his hands to almost anything, he believes that he is 'too specialised to be much good at anything else'.

There too, I met Ish, he is the head setter of stones, a technique that I was hoping that I would witness on my visit to the Quarter. It always strikes me as such a dedicated process of absolute accuracy, and like most other skills requiring an eye to balance. I watched as he painstakingly set a stone, totally absorbed in what he was doing, and with considerable finesse. He has worked at Charles Green for 24 years, another mark of their longevity and tradition, and had been trained by the previous setter; to Ish precision and a keen eye sight are his defining capabilities.

Tom is very keen to stress that the one thing that Charles Green will not stint on is their service and aftercare. That means that all of the items that are returned for renovation, or service, are looked after in exactly the same manner as they were when they were first manufactured. With a handmade piece that is something that can be achieved with total success. They sometimes service badly made machined pieces, which are quite a different story to rectify.

My final memory of Charles Green was one of pure joy. Tom showed me some pieces of the finest and most delicately enamelled work that I have ever seen, that have recently found their way back to Charles Green. They know that they were manufactured by Charles Green, but for whom and why, remains a mystery, however, they are a tribute to the unique beauty of handcrafted pieces that is the essence of the company that continues.

The 'Setter' (J. Debney).

Chapter 8

ALL SMOKE AND MIRRORS, BELLS AND WHISTLES

ACME Whistles

Acme is a name to conjure with and always brings a smile to everyone who hears it, it evokes the memories to us of all of the old Wile E. Coyote scheming his plans to catch his prey, the nifty Road Runner; and it always ended the same way, with the coyote being launched into the air after an explosion, or down in some deep hole his body had made, on impact with the ground. It is certainly a trademark that does not lose its power to connect wherever it is seen.

The owner of Acme Whistles is Simon Topman, a man with copious amounts of disarming charm, who knows all there is to know about his company, its history and its products, in fact what Simon does not know is not worth knowing. He is the first to admit that since joining the company in 1982, he has made it his mission to gather as much information together and he jokingly analyses that he probably knows more about the Hudson family than he does about his own. Although Debbie, his wife, may know more about the present 'Hudson family' – the workers. When I conducted my interviews with his staff they all chimed the same tune, Simon is the public face, and Debbie knows us all as 'family'.

The citing of Acme – or the other name it uses – Hudson Whistles – in this book, may seem somewhat on the periphery being both on the edge of the Quarter in location and product, but it probably has a greater connection with what was made in that area two hundred years ago, the Birmingham 'toys'. A whistle used to be a small functional item fabricated in metal, that is exactly what the Birmingham 'toys' were. Also it is important to remember that the whole of that area was alive with many manufactories producing, pens and parts of all description, which were essentially the overspill from the Quarter. A third point to acknowledge is

Photograph of the three generations of the Hudson family who worked together and between them owned the company from 1870 to 1982 (by the kind courtesy of ACME Whistles).

the publicity that Acme constantly attracts, due to the hard work that Simon Topman does on a continual basis to promote his company and the product. This high-profile created by Simon draws the attention of the interested parties towards the Quarter; it is a mutually-beneficial partnership for the area to give credit to Acme, and Acme to emphasise its close connections to the area.

Simon was originally working in the steel industry in the late 1970's, his father was the manager at Hudson Whistles during this time. Simon was approaching 30, and realising that the future of the heavily subsidised steel industry was in jeopardy, 'It was probably not a great place to be'. He experienced an epiphany of seeing himself in his late forties, trying to find a new career as the industry went through its final death throws around him, and made up his mind to get out. That is when Simon began to show an active interest in Acme Whistles. By that stage the company was owned by the third generation of the Hudson family, with no heirs to inherit. The analogy of rags to rags, was playing through, as the present Mr Hudson of that time lacked any inspiration towards the company because he had enough money. The whole place had been in serious decline, the factory had not been painted in thirty years. There had been no new products put forward to the open market for thirty-five years, so much so, that after Simon did take the company over, customers complained because so many new products appeared regularly.

Simon came in as Sales Manager in 1982, in the same year, the last male member of the Hudson family died, Simon was able to acquire shares from the estate. By 1988 he had become the Managing Director, and by 1991 he had obtained the controlling share of 95% and became MD and owner outright.

Simon was fascinated to learn more about the original founder Joseph Hudson, and he describes him as 'an interesting fellow, a humble entrepreneur'. He hailed from the same vein as Joseph Lucas and Joseph Gillott who operated in and around the same area. His business interests commenced in a washroom that was located on the side of his house, which he rented 1s per week. There, he was undertaking a collection of trades from cobbling, to manufacturing corkscrews and whistles. In 1883 the London Metropolitan Police advertised for an inventor to produce an idea to replace the rattle, which had been used to summon help. The tale that is told, was that Joseph had been playing his violin and the instrument had fallen from the kitchen table breaking, and making a grating and irritating noise. This had been his inspiration to reproduce this discordant tone.

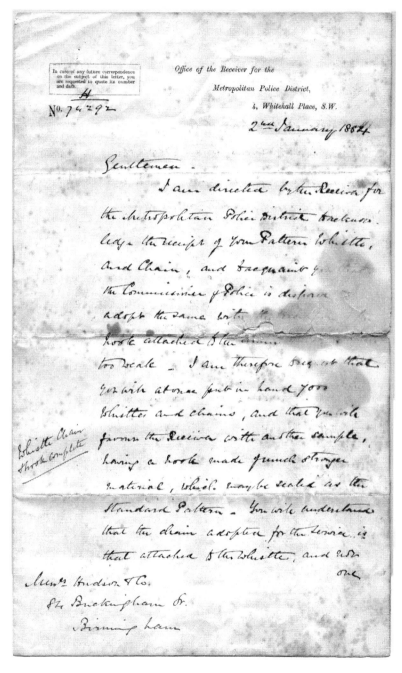

*Original order from the Metropolitan Police for police whistles, 1884
(by the kind courtesy of ACME Whistles).*

He submitted his ideas and the police force showed interest and invited him to a test on Clapham Common. The whistle performed brilliantly, at over a mile in distance, the Force were suitably impressed and promised an order. Joseph Hudson returned to Birmingham and waited. Months went by, and still he had heard nothing, somewhat disgruntled he returned to London, to be told that they had lost his address and had given his designs and the order to someone else.

Joseph Hudson was a canny man and had registered the patent on his whistle beforehand, as he did with camping stove in 1907, and his battery charger in 1912. He caught the alternative manufacturer for infringement of patent, and the police were left with no alternative but to place the order for 21,000 whistles with Joseph Hudson, not knowing that he had no company to produce them, and more than that, he was operating out of a washhouse rented for less than 5p per week.

Joseph Hudson was a particularly enterprising individual and asked the Metropolitan Police for a loan for £20, so that he could start his own business and fulfil his order; and whether it was through desperation for the item, or incredulity at his bare-faced cheek, the money was given to him. He delivered all of the 21,000 whistles complete, by the end of 1884.

However, all did not end there, the new whistle created quite a furore, there were even debates about it in the House of Commons. The fear was that the whistle could be used by criminals, to create diversion from the real crimes. This was tremendous advertising for Joseph Hudson, and he found that within one year everyone wanted the whistle. He then experienced a meteoric rise, and was employing 50 people in his new factory which was sited round the corner from where they are now, in Buckingham Street in the Jewellery Quarter. Since that date Acme have completed 460,000,000 of the whistles.

Joseph was a stickler for quality control and insisted on all of the whistles being properly tested, by being blown, before they left the factory, a practice that has persisted to this day. It is not a necessary procedure in these days with the advent of injection moulding of plastic, but they still do it. There are rejects from time-to-time, but the customer never sees them. They are particularly careful with the orders that have to travel a very long distance, because they do not wish the first whistle to be blown to be a dud and the whole batch to be rejected. Joseph Hudson was a driven man, and he did not stop work until three months before he died in 1928 at the age of 82; his bench still stands as a memorial to his hard work and determination.

Clifford Hudson succeeded his father and was very much the 'classic' second generation heir; as determined to carry the torch, as his father had been to get on. He attended King Edwards Grammar School and was endowed with clear-thinking, intellectualism. From the mid 1890's when he started working alongside his father to the mid 1940's he drove the business hard and grew the markets nationally, and internationally. There were difficult times during the Great Depression, but they offset this by bringing out a cheaper range of whistles, which they called Emca – an obvious anagram. His son Leon, 'liked the good life' too much and was willing to take the profits but wanted very little to do with the business itself. He was a bit of a spendthrift and by the time he died at the age of 76, his fortune was dwindling.

Simon revealed to me that he had a meeting with the Bank Manager shortly after he acquired control, who was very direct in asking him whether he was third generation, obviously following the 'rags to rags in three generations' analogy. Simon explained that he was fourth generation (or could be seen to be), the Bank Manager made it clear that had he been third generation it would have affected his decision.

The Silent Dog Whistle almost inaudible to the human ear but loud to dogs who respond to it over a mile distant (by the kind courtesy of ACME Whistles).

Left: The ACME Thunderer sports whistle, the first and still a classic. Right: The reproduction of the original mates whistle used on the Titanic in 1912, still made in the original workshop using original tools (by the kind courtesy of ACME Whistles).

The humorous trademark of Acme was something that the foresighted Joseph Hudson acquired while he still could, not that he would have envisaged an animated cartoon about a bird and a dog. In the late 1880's the word acme was incredibly popular as a trademark, because the translation from ancient Greek means the highest point in a planet's pathway. Joseph registered the trademark in 1884, when it was highly popular, but then it became common and many dropped the name. The Hudson's were simple folk and did not understand the snobbery of fashion

and continued with the mark. It is fortunate that they did, for a company is not allowed to register a laudatory name as trademark now, but if it pre-exists it cannot be removed.

By the time that the Time Warner Company adopted the 'Acme' brand in 1913, it was considered to be a joke of 'all things that were Acme'. However, no one forgets the magic of the Road Runner cartoon and to this day the name attracts a great deal of interest. Simon often finds at Trade Shows that many people, synonymise the cartoon and Acme Whistles as one; as if the cartoon was advertising for the company. Simon does not race to dispel these misconceptions, as it is always an opening for a conversation which may lead to a sale.

They have 83 products in total, which are registered, but only those that are required by the market are in production at any one time. Simon is a great believer that 'you should stick to your core market'. In his opinion, the demise of many successful companies has been due to their diversification into other things, which has sapped their business potency and potential.

Simon believes that the company straddles a fine line between pedigree and ingenuity; both are as important as one another, and it is often a very difficult balancing act for an innovative company that comes from a heritage. It is to him 'the essential conundrum', they are blessed with their pedigree, but they do not want people to think that is all there is. He has tried to balance the design of the website between the exploitation of the 'old' retro imagery of Acme, with a feeling of progressive 'newness'.

Simon Topman is the first to admit that he possesses no formal qualification, he is in every sense a natural entrepreneur, he has a 'feeling', an intuitive sense for business. That is not to presume that he does not read extensively and keep himself abreast of trends and developments in all of the markets. He is currently experiencing his third recession and sees himself as 'old lag', his business philosophy is:

"Look after the business and the business will look after you."
He follows simple business economics, when times are good 'conserve your cash, pay off your debts, be strong', as he says it is tempting then to acquire an Aston Martin, but it would be foolish to do so, for after every peak there is always a downturn; usually, in a cycle of 8 to 12 years. Then it is the time to invest, because you will never acquire assets more cheaply than you will then. He advises that as soon as the market becomes quiet, it is the best time to innovate; using the slack time for research and development. This means as soon as the markets return you have a new product, 'the feel good factor' for people to look forward to, to move them away from old thinking.

Following these principles, Simon does believe that there is still a need to drive the market forward; identify new groups in the market that new products can be designed for. It is surprising just how many design ideas for whistles can be produced, and the many different applications that they can be turned to. More importantly the whistle needs to be responsive to the needs of the individual using it, within the environment that it has to be used. The requirements for a whistle used at sea in very challenging acoustics caused by weather, are very different from those that are generated by the 'wall of sound' in the Ajax Stadium in Holland during a soccer match.

Simon tells me that product development is a highly technical process which relies on a clear understanding of auditory perception; it is important to appreciate how the human ear receives the sound in waves; the loudest whistle is not always the best. Consequently, much of their research and development is carried out conjointly with Birmingham University in the department of Engineering and Acoustics. The next main criteria for design, is the user themselves; a person who is fit with large lung capacity, has more ability to blow powerfully to create sound, than an elderly person in a situation of high stress. A life jacket whistle carries a completely different set of design requirements, needing much less lung pressure – when you are cold and wet and have less ability to blow – 80 dcbs of sound is required at low pressure. Whereas the Acme Tornado 2000, which is the latest offering to the market, is designed to be heard in the most challenging of football stadia, this produces 125 dcbs of sound, but is dependent on a good pair of lungs.

Much innovation comes from past ideas, they continually revisit past products for inspiration towards the new. The original police whistle from 1883, their famous Titanic whistle, their boson's pipes are a traditional offering which is still made, as there continues to be a high demand for the retro products. They do find that by merging the prospective and the retrospective, they can constantly re-energise the markets with novel whistles.

Simon believes that the possibility for new product ideas is endless because trends change, for instance, there was a diamond-encrusted, gold whistle designed in the 1940's which had no market then, but it has one now. He is an active researcher and, as the one closest to the market, he is always listening and looking for changes in trends. As he says:

"Do you allow the market to dictate to you, or do you lead the market?" He does accept that it has been the customer that has driven the markets since the 1980's, dictating product, cost and need, the producer had to be

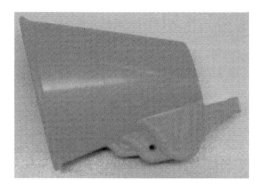

Left: The newest ACME whistle, the Hellova, a powerful Thunderer with a sound boosting and highly directional horn fitted. Projects over great distances. Right: The Cyclone – a modern pealess sports whistle used in FIFA Internationals, Champions League games; the world's most powerful whistle (by the kind courtesy of ACME Whistles).

reactive. Much of this has dictated the advent of ecommerce, where the buyer has a complete shop-window to visit and peruse. However, he feels that there maybe chance for the producer to be more pro-active once more, he suggests that it is time for:

"A bit of a wing or a prayer. Be prepared to go out on a limb, do something new, do something original, and say to the market this is what you need."

As a consequence of his focus to find the 'new', Simon always has something interesting to show and talk to people about. He has a natural feeling for business. He believes that although technical aspects of business can be taught, it comes down to the person who has a 'feel', especially, in the case of businesses that tend to be most successful. He has imbued a sense of 'pride in ownership' into his workforce and from my visit I can see that the staff are content and proud, they view Simon as a 'nice guy' to work for.

Simon places much of the credit for the energy in the company down to the young staff that he has intentionally sought out. Having acquired these energetic individuals with differing perceptions he realised the importance of letting them have a go, giving them their head:

"The biggest mistake is not to allow young people to step in where you were 20 years ago. There is always a generation gap. Don't fall down the gap."

Recently, his young team were put to the test by a challenge that stemmed from an order that been received from a company, that previously

Joseph Hudson's bench (J. Debney).

in the year had been sued by Acme for copyright infringement. This company had been forced to withdraw their products from the market and destroy all of their tooling. There was never any question that Hudson's would not win, and they were obviously quite shocked when they realised that Hudson's were not 'the easy touch' that they assumed they would be.

Simon put the questions to the team, firstly should they supply the order? One of his young protégées was adamant that the order should not be filled at all costs, the other said that it should be filled but with an increased cost. This was countered by the discussion that they may not proceed if the cost were increased. Simon then complicated the debate, for there was a fear that this company will establish a market share eventually, by designing their own product, and by being seen to have a cooperative relationship with Acme, might they exploit this image of close association in order to capitalise on it? By that fact, would Acme need them as another distributor at higher than factory prices?

These other considerations turned the argument further and some debate in this group ensued. The final decision was made to carefully draft a letter to the company, explaining clearly that they were no longer to have the privilege of being a direct distributor because of their past actions, but Acme were willing to supply them with a list of distributors in order that they could continue to stock the product. This action would cause the company buying to increase their costs by 40%, defusing any immediate threat that they posed to Acme.

Simon has a great confidence in his young team as he does in his general workforce as a whole. I was able to meet four of these people and talk to them. The first is Terry Wilkinson who is 53 years of age and has worked for the firm for 38 years. Terry is the Works Superintendent, and has worked his way up through the ranks and has seen much change in his years there. In the old days, he tells me, the orders were for 'dozens and grosses' now they are for 'thousands and thousands'. These days there are approximately 52 people employed, and 20 to 30 products being manufactured simultaneously. In times gone by Terry remembers that the managers were from 'the old school', they were, 'sticklers for what had to be done, there was no walking about'. It was a very formal atmosphere where the bosses were referred to as 'Mr so and so', if you were caught in another department you were given a severe reprimand.

He remembers 'Mr Leon' as a very stern and quite a tall man, who used to 'sneak around like a ghost'. The whisper used to go around the factory that 'the old man is in the building'. Terry was quite a shy young apprentice then, and all of sudden he would find 'Mr Leon' standing over him. In those times, workers were not allowed to make conversation with him, unless he started one. He was one to have favourites, and would come around at Christmas with calendars and diaries for the 'favourites'. Terry was known as 'the young man' and as he had not been there long enough, was never given a Christmas gift; Terry believes to this day, that Mr Leon had no idea what his name was. Eventually, Mr Leon died and his brother-in-law (Simon's father) took over the helm. Terry had an uncomfortable relationship with him in the beginning, he says that 'he used to jump down your throat, as soon as look at you, but he did mellow'.

Terry started with Hudson's the year after they had celebrated their centenary in 1972, in those days the firm employed many people. Terry had attended the same school as Debbie Topman. He loved school, but coming from a family of eight he had to leave 'to earn the pennies'. He decided to find his own job rather than being sent to one from the school. He went to Hudson's and met an elderly lady on the door as she went off on her lunch break, he is very grateful to that lady for:

"If it hadn't have been for her going back in and having a word with the management, I probably would not be here today."

But he was nearly thwarted by his careers teacher who had arranged an interview for him at a local firm of builders. Terry ignored that and went back for an interview with the works manager at Hudson's, Ken Kirkpatrick. Ken took him on and phoned the head of plastics 'a big, enormous, tall fellow' by the name of Bill Smart. After that Easter, Terry started in the plastics department, but his first year was not a successful one, he admits, that he did not take it as seriously as he should have and ended up leaving and building garages for a while for less money (he had been earning £12.50 at Hudson's). Terry soon realised the error of his ways and asked if he could come back. They decided to give him one more chance, he pulled up his socks up and set about leaning all the aspects of the business that he could. His endeavours paid off, and he was made up to charge hand, then foreman and then supervisor, following this he was put in charge of the soldering department.

The one thing that he really enjoyed from those times was the camaraderie of the old chaps. There was always banter and stories from their National Service days, which would make Terry laugh. He particularly liked working Saturdays as Ken Kirkpatrick was in and he had been a tank commander during the war, he always had plenty of tales to tell. Being the youngest by far, Terry reflects, that many of these older guys looked on him like a son that they had never had.

ACME Whistles (J. Debney).

There were other striking differences then too. More women worked there, only on the presses and guillotines and consequently, they were paid less. There were no unions in Hudson's, all the workers were scared of the unions and the trouble they could cause, it was the time of all the strikes at British Leyland. He misses all of the traditional outings that used to take place at Christmas, it used to be extremely elitist and sexist, but that was the time. Mr Leon would take the men for the foreman's meal 'up Soho Road for cigars and drinky poos'. Of course the only woman of that rank was not allowed to attend. Later it changed to a Christmas dinner and dance, which he loved – open to all. Now Debbie, who is very sensitive to the diversity of ethnicity employed, organises caterers to come, to ensure all tastes and traditions are accommodated and respected.

Terry believes that the continued success of the company is due to the product first and foremost, and to some extent the brand. The products have a good lineage, with the Titanic whistles, the silent-dog whistles and

ACME Whistles (J. Debney).

the Thunderer. His opinion is that Simon would like to promote the authenticity and the heritage primarily, but he believes that there needs to be a balance between volume and heritage. He is concerned with the rising costs of the overheads and wages, that there needs to be an increase in volume, but he 'does not want to lose' the hand-made product. Terry points out that there are between 7,000 and 8,000 guillotine caps produced a day, which he believes is too slow and not enough, 'we are changing our ways and moving with the times with machines'; an item that used take five or six different processes is being streamlined.

Terry admits that although there are companies out there producing things in quantity, that their quality is not as finished. That is the one thing that he is proud of more than anything else, the adherence to quality which was laid down by Joseph Hudson from the very beginning:

"If it doesn't come up to scratch, it gets scrapped straight away. Everything is tested, nothing is allowed out that is scrap or second."

This may not have changed, but the management style has, and Terry has a great deal of time for Simon who he sees as a 'really good bloke'. It is certainly a much more relaxed atmosphere to the one that he started in.

Terry views himself as 'the Jack of all trades' and he is the one who is called in to 'troubleshoot all day'. He is very concerned that he does have to train someone up before his retirement in eleven years, with his thirty-eight years of skills, as a matter of some urgency. He is looking forward to retirement, but it does cause him to reflect back when he was first apprenticed on £7 per week and his mother used to take all of his money, until his foreman had a quiet word in his ear about 'overtime and keeping it quiet'.

Next I was introduced to Errol Flynn Mathis who has worked for Hudson's for thirty-six years in the polishing shop. Errol says that he thought he would come for a year or two, and see if he liked it, and then he stayed. When he started he earned £7 per week, he chose to give his family £2 or so of that. He remembers years gone by with great affection:

"Mr Leon was a nice, polite gentleman. At certain times of the year he would come round and shake your hand."

Errol found it easier to work then because there were more people and it meant there was less stress; there was between 8 and 10 working in the polishing shop. As a consequence, the pressure was not so intense and it made work interesting because there were others around and more people to have 'fun' with. He remembers the many girls that worked there who were a 'good laugh':

"There were lots of girls around – it made coming to work fun."

Particularly, at Christmas when they all used to go out for a drink and a get together, there was often a bit of mistletoe doing the rounds.

To Errol the quality of the product is good because of the skills in the workforce that Hudson's has managed to retain, which have been passed down generation to generation. It is his opinion, that with continued good management, the company will keep going another hundred years. He views that there are two distinct sides to the management now, 'Simon is in the background' he promotes the firm, and 'Debbie keeps the family together'.

I met with Linda Blackford afterwards, who has worked for Hudson's in the assembly shop for 40 years, she is the team leader. She has seen a considerable amount of change since she started as a trainee assembler all those years ago. In those days, there were a lot of women working there, and they were separated into different assembly shops, now they are amalgamated together.

When she first left school she started in an office, and she was not comfortable. A friend who worked for Hudson's introduced her to the company, she was given a job, but it was not her intention to stay long. At first she worked in the assembly shop for the Thunderer; she was with 12 other women, and she was paid £3 per week; they were never allowed to know what the men were earning. Initially, they were paid on a day rate, but as their skills improved and their speed increased they were moved over to piecework.

She tells me, that when it comes to assembly of the whistles that very little has changed since she started. There are many different parts to the whistles and it is very labour intensive; she can assemble between 600 and 800 per day. She used to be on the same one day, after day, she prefers the variety now, but it requires the assembler to be adaptable to change. The constant repetition can decrease quality, but it can be valuable to increase individual skill and knowledge.

She remembers the sternness of Mr Leon, she says that he very rarely spoke to anyone 'he was a proper superior boss – he was a gentleman', but if he saw anything on the floor he would make them pick it up with a tone of rebuke:

"This is money on the floor!"

She said that women never got the same 'perks' at Christmas with the 'do's' for the male employees. Women were not considered as important, and as a consequence, they would arrange things on their own; the older ones would take care of the younger ones.

Arthur Topman was thought of as quite an authoritarian, who was very rarely seen unless there was a problem, whereas, Simon is much more 'hands on' and approachable, sometimes that can be difficult because of the familiarity which makes it hard to say no.

Their staffing levels are reduced, causing everyone to have to work much harder, and the manufacturing methods mean that they are no longer manufacturing the volume. The 'demand' method of production, means that they have to be far more responsive to change, as they no longer carry stock. Linda has enjoyed her time at Hudson's, but she was looking forward to her retirement, however she has just heard she may have to work an extra year until she is 61. Then her intentions are to do lots of work for her local church and enjoy her gardening.

Finally, I talked to Kamla Maman who has worked for Hudson's for 34 years, she is 58 years of age. She used to live out towards Hockley and needed to find work, so she went 'knocking from door-to-door' to find vacancies. She was interviewed by Mr Kirkpatrick who gave her a job starting the very next day. Initially, her job was on the assembly for the Metropolitan Police whistle,

Kamla at ACME Whistles (J. Debney).

but after a short while she left to have a baby. She was taken on again afterwards, and this time because she had a good command of English she was set to work wiring-up whistles for plating. The next time she fell pregnant in 1980, she was able to take advantage of Maternity Leave and she was able to return to her old position. Then with her third child (a son who works upstairs) she was moved into the packaging department, that was 27 years ago.

She remembers that Mr Leon would come round once a month, but he would not stay very long; Mr Arthur was the same, but he did introduce his son (Simon) around; they knew he was being shown around because he was going to take over. Kamla views Debbie as 'more one of the family, she sorts everyone's problems out'. Kamla considers that product quality is so good, because of the working relationships there, 'everyone gets on with everyone'.

She admits that sometimes they do feel the pressure of work and they need an extra pair of hands, but she loves coming to work. At that point the rest of the packing shop shouted 'she'll be here till she's 90!' Kamla's secret is keeping in good health, she gave me some advice:

"You need your health and good people around you."

There is no doubt that Simon runs a very happy place, there are the normal moans and groans that you will always find in any firm that has survived so long, where change has been inevitable, and some who have been there throughout have had to adjust to. I asked Simon whether he has considered the future prospects of Acme, he made a very realistic assessment that it would all end one day, but he can envisage it will survive for a while yet. He would like to see it move on to someone who would allow it to change and not become too precious about it. For his own position, he told me that he considers himself in these terms:

"I am an itinerant here, a caretaker. I would like it to be stronger when I
leave than when I started."

Not that he has any intention of retiring. Simon wears many hats in the City, such as; the Chair of West Midlands Chamber of Commerce; Chair of Aston Prime New Deals for Communities; Chair of the Housing and Infrastructure Board (which has a 10 billion budget and is concerned with the growth of the city for the next decade), and he still does work for the Department of Business. He never considered that he would 'sit in Hockley' for the rest of his life, but others who know him argue the point, that it is too much in his blood, at that moment he gave a fabulous rendition of 'I've got you under my skin'.

This chapter has been an extensive and reflects the nature and size of the business. I had many funny anecdotes relayed to me on my visits to Acme but one is particularly amusing. Simon told me, that some years ago, probably in Mr Clifford's time, a group of lads were playing football in a street just inside the Quarter, somewhere near a clockmakers (which had just been taken over and was undergoing renovation works), next door to a local bullion dealers. They found themselves hampered through the lack of a whistle, so they knocked on the door of Hudson's. The foreman very kindly found them one from the scrap bin and sent them on their way, to resume their football game.

There was a lot of banging coming from the restoration work in the clockmakers. The boys played their game above the noise, after five minutes the banging stopped abruptly, and all of a sudden a number shifty figures high-tailed it, out of the shop. It turns out they had been a group of criminals, tunnelling their way into the bullion dealers, and the boys playing football had scared the wits out of them, because the whistle that they had been donated by the kindly chap at Hudson's was a Metropolitan Police whistle!

Chapter 9

THE WEAVER'S TALE

Toye, Kenning & Spencer

The wealth and affluence of the United Kingdom has often been enhanced over the years by successive waves of immigration, often with the migrants seeking sanctuary from oppression and persecution in their native lands. French Protestants, or Huguenots, had been able to follow their faith and their daily lives relatively unhindered in Catholic France due to the Edict of Nantes. In 1685 Louis XIV revoked the edict, and the Huguenots, who comprised a large portion of the skilled and professional classes, were forced to flee for their lives. Many came to England where the Reformation had taken firm hold after Henry VIII's break from Rome and the dissolution of the monasteries.

The Huguenots were renowned for fine craftsmanship and hard work, with a tradition of whole families devoting themselves to the nurture of particular trade skills. A prime example of this is the Toye family, whose family enterprise of weaving and embroidering silk and spun gold found them a place in the thriving metropolis of London. They arrived in London in 1685 by boat disguised as cattle dealers. The Catholic King James II was on the throne briefly; he was succeeded by William and Mary (a Dutch Protestant Prince and an English Protestant Princess – the daughter of James II) Parliament had invited them to rule in their name, marking the end of the absolute monarchy in the United Kingdom and the beginning of the Glorious Revolution.

The family settled to the east of London in aptly named Hopetown (now Bethnal Green) and re-established their traditional business of weaving and embroidery, lace-making and gold and silver wire drawing. The lavish fashions of the time that were dictated by the Court and Upper classes, for ornate military uniforms, combined with the popularity of the theatre, provided plenty of work for them, and trade flourished. Over the succeeding centuries the family exhibited a talent for adapting to changes in society, fashion and business. Over

Above and Opposite: The Birmingham Warstone site circa 1907 (all images by the kind courtesy of Toye, Kenning & Spencer).

time, they moved their homes and workplaces westwards to the Theobalds Road and Red Lion Square near Kingsway and Covent Garden. Also, they began to expand and diversify their craft repertoire to include; gold and silver smithing, medal and button making, vitreous enamelling, banner and flag making and bookbinding. Their markets now included; State, Civic and Masonic Regalia, Trade Unions and clubs. In so doing, the enterprise founded by the Toye family had evolved from merely creating adornment into defining identity and status.

Until the middle of the twentieth century Toye & Co. remained in London, but acquired manufacturing and retail satellites in other parts of the UK, sometimes through the merger and acquisition of other companies. Kenning and Spencer were major rivals in the Masonic market, who were subject to merger after World War Two. The company's presence in the Birmingham's Jewellery Quarter transpired through the acquisition of W. J. Dingley & Co, a firm that had been established there since the late nineteenth century specialising in; die and tool-making, stamping, plating, and mounting. Mr Bert Toye, the father of the present Chairman Bryan Toye made the decision in 1969 to transfer all of the Toye & Co. metal working to Birmingham; the London factory was increasingly difficult to sustain as all supporting trades had moved away, and it was expensive and difficult to maintain the workforce. In so doing, the textile operations were relocated to the old Kenning factory in Bedworth near Coventry (Toye's had a weaving house in Coventry that was lost during the blitz).

Bryan Toye served most of his apprenticeship in the jewellery trade in the Warstone Lane factory, and eventually became Manager of the site in the early sixties, so was witness to the days of humming factories and workshops, queues on the streets at lunch hour, and crowded pubs buzzing with 'trade gossip' at the end of every day. Even St Paul's Square was still hemmed with bright and busy workshops in the early sixties. Due to the wide range of craft skills that the company has always excelled in, it was a popular and a well-respected training ground for apprentices. Many stayed with the company, (and are still there to this day – the skilled masters of their trade), and others went on to

TOYE & COMPANY Ltd

PART OF OUR ENAMELLING ROOM IN
BIRMINGHAM

work elsewhere in the Quarter, in Hatton Garden in London, and beyond. Bryan rose to become Chairman and Managing Director of Toye & Co, and has worked for the company for over fifty years. This is an impressive link in the generational chain that has stretched from father to son since the family arrived in 1685. The unbroken lineage of family stewardship has continued with the appointment of Bryan's wife, Fiona, as Chief Executive in 2009.

Fiona is a fast-talking and very direct individual with a shrewd business sense, who intuitively understands that although her priority is the growth of Toye, Kenning & Spencer, to achieve this it is important to understand the contextual place of the company within the Quarter:

> "We need a clear vision of what we want the company to be in five years time, and working towards this involves consideration of the environment in which we operate. The businesses in the Quarter need to influence and have control over the changes for their own benefit, and for the benefit of the community at large."

She realises the need to exploit all of the 'mutually beneficial' assets that lie on the doorstep, and to promote the intrinsic wealth of skill and talent of other companies collaboratively, rather than operating in an exclusive way.

Part of the tool store at Toye, Kenning & Spencer.

Power presses at work in The Stamp Shop.

Toye, Kenning & Spencer's output includes both medals and buttons.

In Fiona's opinion, the heritage of the Quarter, and a reawakening to that history is an important part of the process of rejuvenation:

"You are never disconnected from your past, appreciation and pride in history is needed to revitalise the present."

Her shrewd analysis of the company history identifies that the policy to merge and acquire drove it into new markets and from that wealth was generated:

"Calculated risk taking is necessary for survival; everything has to pay for itself, there must be a pragmatic approach to retaining skills. Sometimes contraction is needed to ensure future growth."

Fiona is making reference to the deliberate policy of reducing high-volume, low-value production in the factory with the consequent reduction in staff. The large Design Studio on the top floor is now the driving force of the factory rather than the stamp shop, the shift in emphasis of production has now evolved to high-quality, low-volume work. The same attention to good design is being applied to the low-value work (as is applied to the high-value products) in order to achieve best price for the customer and best margins for the company.

A C.B.E. being enamelled.

Toye, Kenning & Spencer own a large premises on Warstone Lane; the original Victorian factory of W. J. Dingley is now totally hidden behind a typical early 1960's addition. When I arrived there, substantial work was taking place to make the entrance more welcoming to visitors and clients. This is very much part of the opening of doors that is going on throughout the Quarter in order to remove the closed shop atmosphere that has operated for many years. Not since the days of Matthew Boulton and the Soho Manufactory has there been such a policy to promote the activities of the Quarter through accessibility to all. The factory is quite a warren, and this is just one of the challenges in adapting to business in the 21st century. There are now about 55 people employed on site, with further sales staff at the Showroom in London and the large textile factory in Bedworth.

The factory is divided into 'shops', each with a lead-hand – the traditional mode of organisation. It is an elaborate hive of activity, with multiple working areas including; the Tool-making Shop in the basement; the Stamp Shop and Proofing room, the Mounting Shop and Finishing room and Despatch room on the ground floor; the Die-making Shop, the Enamelling Shop, the Plating Shop and the Polishing Shop on the first floor; and the Design Studio, administrative and sales offices combined with records on the top floor. This arrangement displays quite a complex web of activity, with innumerable other chambers in between.

Jeffrey David Hacker.

Left: Fiona Toye, with a copy of the banner originally supplied to the N.F.W.W. by Toye, Kenning & Spencer. Right: Products include banners, flags and medal ribbons (all images by the kind courtesy of Toye, Kenning & Spencer).

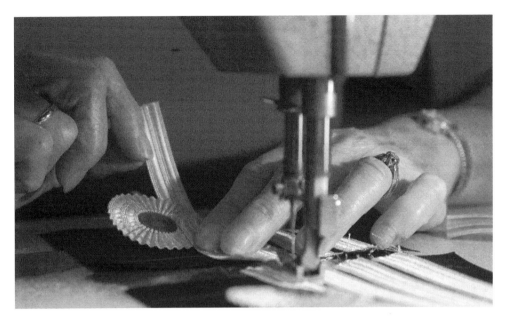

Sewing skills are as much in demand as metal working.

The products they produce are as diverse as the many craftsmen under their roof, in the many areas that they inhabit. From the intricacies of awards and Masonic regalia, to the opulence of medals and orders such as the C.B.E., each item requires fine engineering and skilled handwork to reach the highest quality of finish. This is not a manufacture that allows for seconds or substandard work. Each product is the result of multiple processes, and the combined skill and dexterity of a number of individuals. The contribution of each craftsperson is invaluable to achieving the final product – the quintessential team effort. But it is an aging team, not just at Toye & Co., but in the Jewellery Quarter and the trade in general. In Fiona's opinion, the members of this aging workforce are the teachers of the next generation of craftsmen, 'there should be an apprentice or more to every master'. She visualises this form of education as having been the backbone of manufacture in Europe since medieval times; the young learning their trade and life-skills alongside a master craftsmen; their standards of accomplishment and welfare governed by a trade guild.

Ron Jackson is a master craftsman, his skills in stamping are sought out by many in the Quarter. He fell on difficult times after the death of his partner in his previous business enterprise. His survival in the stamping trade was ensured by the support of Bryan Toye; who invited Ron to move his plant and equipment and workers into the factory. In Ron's opinion many of those in the Quarter owe their livelihoods to the involvement of Toye, Kenning & Spencer in the area:

"If you were Toye's trained it meant something. Most of the businesses of the last fifty years were due to training at Toye's. It was the best grounding for silversmiths and enamellers etc."

Fiona Toye values the skills of workers such as Ron and wishes to ensure the retention and development of such skills in young people, by utilising the enthusiasm of the older workers for their craft. She feels that it is not just a solution for the skills shortage in the Quarter but a much wider problem which has developed within society:

"It is not just a matter of sustaining production but sustaining the fabric of society. Everyone needs to feel their life has purpose and value. We need to provide opportunities for young people from all backgrounds and educational accomplishment to develop work and life skills that will enhance their self worth and give them the chance to be part of the working world. Education needs to be alongside and part of industry."

She visualises apprenticeship training that places young people alongside the skilled craftsmen that are still left. For her, the discipline and focus of the workplace, and the mentorship of the trade teacher fulfil the educational requirements of these young people better than any theoretical exercises in a classroom:

"Solving problems... finding solutions, communicating information accurately, our workforce are required to do this every day. Some are better at it than others, but this daily-exercise promotes mental agility, imagination and self-confidence."

Left: Royal Horse Artillery insignia. Right: Royal Air Force buttons.

How a modern day apprenticeship scheme in the Jewellery Quarter can be delivered has yet to be determined. But there is a concerted effort to bring the scheme to life supported not only by the local manufacturers, but by the Worshipful Company of Goldsmiths, The British Jewellery Association, The Birmingham Assay Office and the Birmingham City Council.

The community of the Quarter is very important to Fiona, and she has positioned herself strategically in many of the groups which operate to promote the Quarter and its development. For instance they are in the process of establishing a Community Development Trust. Through this initiative it is hoped to develop a greater sense of community and ownership in those who live and work in the area. Fiona is Chair of the recently formed Jewellery Quarter

The finishing of a C.B.E. award.

Trade Alliance. This is an association of all the manufacturers and allied trades in the Quarter, whether large companies or one-man businesses. The aims of the Alliance are to represent the interests of their members in the Jewellery Quarter and City community, to further the interests of skills training and business development initiatives for the benefit of their members and the community at large. Manufacturers in the Quarter have reached a critical mass and this has generated a greater awareness that it is better to work collegiately in order to secure the future of their businesses and their trade.

Although as an entity Toye Kenning & Spencer have only existed in the Quarter for a fraction of their three hundred year history, they have brought with them a wealth of knowledge and resources, an example of which is held in their large storeroom which Ron Jackson proudly showed to me. There in the cellars are thousands of dies, some more than a hundred years old, which are the stamps for all sorts of ceremonial medallions, medals and other pieces. Most have been hand made, there are even some French dies dating back to the 1780's.

Ron is 69 years old and started in the gun trade, in the gun Quarter which used to exist around Loveday Street. He began his working life as a stamper, and then came to Toye, Kenning & Spencer to work for them. In my opinion, he is one of the most enthusiastic promoters of the Quarter and all it stands for. He is extremely proud of what he does and the immense power of the awesome machines that he operates. He took great delight in exhibiting to me the 90lb hammer striking the metal from height, exerting one hundred tonnes of force as he operated a behemoth kick-stamper.

He went into his own stamping business with his friend thirty years ago (Jackson and Froggatt). He had sixteen stampers operating at the peak, and after the demise of the business, Toye, Kenning & Spencer acquired the business to secure the plant and skills. Ron is very grateful to the patronage that has been shown to him; the recessionary times which he has experienced in recent years almost wiped him out, and Bryan Toye was farsighted enough to realise that the loss of the wealth of skill and knowledge that Ron and his workers have, could have been extremely detrimental to the Quarter.

In some ways Ron shares many of Fiona's ideas for the Quarter. He too values the idea for a well-organised apprenticeship scheme with internationally recognised curricula and qualifications that would be of benefit not just to the Quarter, but to the multifarious small engineering businesses which comprise the manufacturing sector around the city. This is not to say that there is not a place for the School of Jewellery, but it is at a higher level of specialism and is not necessarily an education that considers the needs of production costs and processes. An apprenticeship scheme would cater for the technical skills essential to industrial replication and production.

Left: A finished award ready for Buckingham Palace. Right: Argyll and Sutherland Highlanders Regalia.

On my visit to the factory, I was able to speak to a number of people employed there, among them Jeffrey David Hacker, known as David. David comes from a long-line of relatives who have worked in the Quarter or allied metal trades. He originally hailed from Dudley Road; his mother was an enameller and his father a Rose Engine turner, his father climbed up in the trade but was always poorly paid. When he was young he remembers that there were very few living in the Quarter by then, but he had many relations who worked in and around there as jewellers, pewter smiths and gilders, they all lived close by and as with many hundreds of other workers, would walk to work.

He is now 65 years of age and has worked as an engraver, hand cutter and carver for 49 years, he was apprenticed to Toye, Kenning &

A display of finished badges.

Spencer and the room where he works used to have others undertaking the same activities, then the number declined to two, now he is last one. He is very conscious that he will have to pass his skills on with some urgency and train someone to take his place before he retires.

In the past the engraving shop was full of six engravers, feverishly engraving sports cups and shields. The advent of laser and computer technology finished the need for intensive hand-engraving and unfortunately, these engravers were not replaced. In recent years there has been somewhat of a renaissance towards hand engraving, as the quality of machine cut, and laser cut work is questioned, this makes the possession of a qualified skilled hand engraver a real asset to any company within the Quarter. Even though the process is much more expensive at between £1 to £2 per letter, the end results and the finish are second to none. As David points out, the machines are limited to the surface that they can cut and the size and shape of the object, an engraving machine lacks the objectivity of a well-trained eye. I have witnessed the care and the scrutiny that he gives each piece that comes before him on the bench, the precision with which he decides to make each mark to the finish that satisfies him; a machine will never have that capability.

Not far away from David, in the warren of workshops that make up the premises, is another brand, now a division of Toye, Kenning & Spencer, that is KJD Jewellers, the initials of the name of the man who established the company before it was acquired. KJD Jewellers manufacture exquisitely enamelled cufflinks. Keith Davies is now the Site Director, and his brother Neil is the Production Manager. Their mother Brenda, is the mainstay of the brand, she is a remarkably skilled enameller, and possess a very calm and peaceful nature. She attended St Chads School in Ladywood until the age of 15 in 1962, where upon the school found her an apprenticeship as a enameller within the commercial division of Fattorini.

She trained with thirty-five other enamellers in all aspects of working on silver and gold for £3 per week. As with others that I have spoken to, working as a factory enameller does tend to shelter them from the harder aspects of life and it was not until she decided that she was worth more and went into business on her own that she 'learnt speed' as she remembers:

"Apprenticeship is cosy and cushioned, piecework increases speed."

At 21 in 1968, she set up in business as an outworker, on her own in a back street enamelling shop, as many women had done before her. On meeting her husband, who was a jeweller, she was able to juggle her working life with having children, sometimes doing her own outwork and on other occasions, assisting her husband in his shop. In her opinion, the biggest drawback of working in the Quarter is trying to park and was always the cause of the greatest stress for her.

Like many others in Quarter, Brenda is conscious of the need to pass her skills onto new generations, she has had apprentices in the past and continues to take them on now. She still stands by her opinion that it is best to get them when they have come straight from school, however, that is becoming increasingly more difficult due to policy of the school's career service. On one occasion she

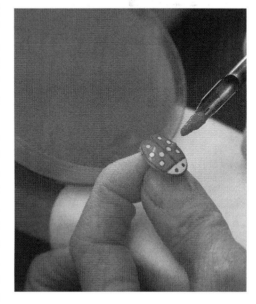

Enamelled cufflinks being finished.

resorted to taking a couple of much older girls from the School of Jewellery, but she found that many of the methods that they had been taught, were impractical and inhibited their work. They had been taught to use tweezers to handle their work, which meant that they had not got the sensitivity of work handling necessary or the speed, whereas, a person that comes from school can be taught good habits from scratch and not acquire any bad practices.

Like others, Brenda has no thoughts of retirement, she loves her work, she loves coming to work, for her the life that she would have without it would be pointless. Indeed, she will often be enamelling the next season's collection after she has served lunch on Christmas Day. When you witness the care with which she lovingly applies the many layers of colours to each piece (it maybe a piece that is a repeat of many, but each individual one is as important as the other) it is not hard to understand her devotion to her work. She finds the colours of home very drab in comparison to those that she handles on a daily basis:

"I have got all of these colours in my life, it is a joy. I am never going to retire."

This is a passion and a pride that I have encountered in all my interviews that I have conducted around the Jewellery Quarter for this book and it does not just concern those who handle the tools and materials, it applies to the back room ladies and gentleman, or front of house, however they wish to be seen. Christine and Janet who met me on my visit to Toye, Kenning & Spencer are as equally proud of all that their firm stands for. Christine has worked there since 1979, originally as a Designer when all the designs were hand drawn and painted, and remembers the quiet times 'but there were always posh cars parked outside'. She relishes the changes that have taken place and the inclusion of the farmers market, making the Quarter more of a community again. Janet has deeper roots, her grandmother who is now 94 having worked in the Quarter in the days that if you were late you were locked out until lunchtime.

Every person in the Quarter has a part to play in the survival of that area, and there is a whole network of 'others' who support the valuable craftsmanship that goes on in the warren of rooms that spreads out across the web of streets. More than ever the larger companies have a role to play in the growth and regeneration of the area, as much for their own pragmatic survival as for any philanthropic endeavour. Toye, Kenning & Spencer are one such company which is leading the vanguard to place the Jewellery Quarter on the map; they hold the Royal Warrant as few others do, the ultimate mark of quality, they are custodians of a long heritage and will endeavour to perpetuate their place in the market long into the future.

Platinum 'Oversize' (height of skull is 3cm) Skull Cufflinks Pave set Diamonds with moving jaw and Ruby eyes (by the kind courtesy of Deakin and Francis).

Rings of quality and distinction (by the kind courtesy of Charles Green).

Kamla at ACME Whistles (J. Debney).

Fine detail in every item (by the kind courtesy of Toye, Kenning & Spencer).

Sports medals, being cleaned by hand (by the kind courtesy of Toye, Kenning & Spencer).

Montenegro 'Order of Danilo' 3rd Class Commander – a sample of very high quality double sided vitreous enamelling in 2010 (by the kind courtesy of Thomas Fattorini Ltd.).

'Fabergé' style sterling silver and enamel egg surprise made for The Franklin Mint in 1977 called 'The Lily of the Valley' – this was technically very difficult, the egg shell was stamped from a flat blank and in 1977 the whole company was involved in making these eggs to a tight deadline to the detriment of all of their normal customers (by the kind courtesy of Thomas Fattorini Ltd.).

A group of MVO medals (by the kind courtesy of Gladman and Norman Ltd.).

Exceptional craftsmanship (by the kind courtesy of Gladman and Norman Ltd.).

A fine example of Mary Burden's handiwork (J. Debney).

A selection of fine medals (by the kind courtesy of W. H. Darby Ltd.).

One of Bill Haynes' commissioned classical pieces in H M Sterling Silver (by the kind courtesy of Mr William Haynes).

Displays from the Pen Room (J. Debney).

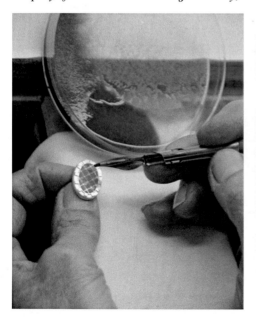

Left: Brenda Davies displays her incredible skill with a steady hand.
Right: Three hundred years of stamping history.

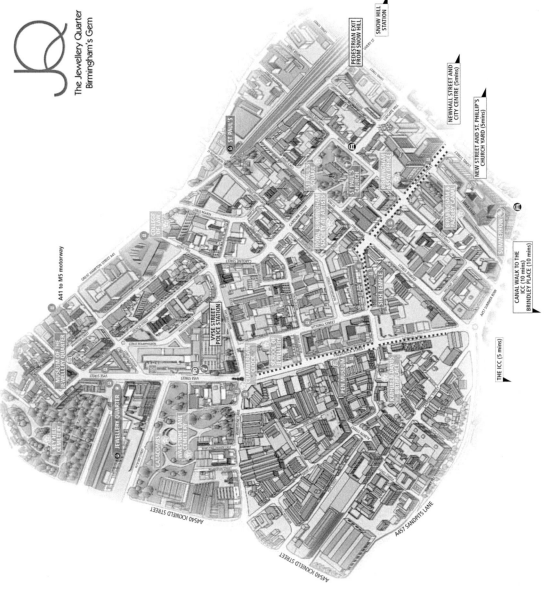

key to symbols

- Ⓜ Metro station (tram)
- ⓣ Train station
- 🚌 Bus station/stop
- ⓘ Tourism centre
- 🚕 Taxi rank
- ··· Walking trail
- 🚻 Toilet
- 🏛 Museum
- PO Post office

The Jewellery Quarter
Birmingham's Gem

SNOW HILL STATION

PEDESTRIAN EXIT FROM SNOW HILL

NEWHALL STREET AND CITY CENTRE (5mins)

NEW STREET AND ST. PHILLIP'S CHURCH YARD (5mins)

CANAL WALK TO THE ICC (10 mins)
BRINDLEY PLACE (10 mins)

THE ICC (5 mins)

ST PAUL'S
ST PAUL'S SQUARE
ST PAUL'S CHURCH
BIRMINGHAM ASSAY OFFICE
ROYAL BIRMINGHAM SOCIETY OF ARTISTS
BIRMINGHAM FAZELEY CANAL
SUMMERROW
SIKH TEMPLE
COLLEGE OF LAW
A41 to M5 motorway
GREAT HAMPTON STREET A41
MUSEUM OF THE JEWELLERY QUARTER
VYSE STREET POLICE STATION
SCHOOL OF JEWELLERY
CLOCK
PEN MUSEUM
KATHLEEN FEDDEN LIBRARY
KEY HILL CEMETERY
JEWELLERY QUARTER
CATACOMBS
WARSTONE LANE CEMETERY
A45/40 ICKNIELD STREET
A45/40 ICKNIELD STREET
A457 SANDPITS LANE
A457 SUMMER ROW
VITTORIA STREET
FREDERICK STREET
VYSE STREET

©Marketing Birmingham/Birmingham City Council, 2009

www.jewelleryquarter.net

VIII

Chapter 10

NOTE THE THOMAS IN OUR NAME

Thomas Fattorini Ltd.

One of the most interesting stories of the Jewellery Quarter, is how a successful family with a number of sons, continues generationally. With the firm of Charles Green and Sons, it led to numerous difficulties and family rivalry, most of the actual detail has been lost in time and the present

The factory as it stands today.

generation are left trying to make sense of a story that has become too vague and distant with the passing of time.

With the family of Fattorini, which has had a physical presence for ninety years in the Quarter, the divisions occurred in Yorkshire and the three branches of the family played out a bizarre co-existence from the middle of the last century, with two companies operating under the same family name in Birmingham. On occasions this led to confusions, which explains the title of this chapter, a strategy employed by this stem to distinguish itself from its familiar competitor.

The patriarch Antonio Fattorini (1796 – 1860) came from the village of Bellagio, in Lombardy. He was a refugee from the Napoleonic Wars, probably encouraged to settle in England to offset the envisaged economic downturn that was feared due to the power shifts in Europe; many were welcomed to help to drive a new wave of wealth generation through entrepreneurial enterprise. The grandfather of the present MD Mr Wilfred Fattorini wrote of Antonio coming to England:

"Napoleon was dominating Europe, causing great anxiety in Britain. To increase forces against him a Royal Mission went to Europe to recruit free forces against him. The decisive result of the battle of Waterloo came as a surprise, the statesmen of the day judged that a trade slump in England would follow the cessation of war-generated activities. They therefore changed the European Mission to civilian recruitment designed to benefit trades in Britain not fully developed. Men of good character and known skills were welcomed. These affected the energetic northern Italians, who had the added reason to wish to emigrate as their country was under Austrian domination."

Antonio was hard working and determined, and on arriving in Yorkshire became a peddler, and eventually married a local girl Maria, by 1826 he was listed as a travelling jeweller and hardware dealer in *Innocent Fattorini.*

Skipton market in Edwardian times.

Upton's Yard, Briggate, Leeds. He appears to have moved around daily to capture new markets; he is listed in 1831 as operating for two days a week in Leeds, but he was still visiting other market towns to sell his wares. A little time later, he opened his first shop in Harrogate which dealt in 'jewellery and bric-a-brac' and was quaintly named 'The Oriental Lounge'. He eventually settled his family in Bradford, and opened a second shop in Skipton.

Antonio passed his business concerns onto four of his sons during his lifetime; his eldest Innocent Fattorini (1830 – 1874) acquiring the Skipton shop, Harrogate becoming the business of Antonio Fattorini (II) (1837 – 1913) and the Bradford shop becoming the business of John Fattorini (1832 – 1909) and Edward Fattorini (1844 – 1913). Innocent died young (44 years old) and his wife ran the concern as 'I. Fattorini, watchmaker and jewellers' until their son Thomas Fattorini (1864 – 1934) assumed control and registered the company as Thomas Fattorini est'd 1827. The Harrogate concern became Antonio Fattorini est'd 1831, and the Bradford stem was registered as Fattorini & Sons est'd 1831.

Thomas Fattorini did well and used the Birmingham Assay Office to hallmark his work, from 1893 he had a punch registered there bearing his

MD Greg Fattorini in front of Her Majesty Queen Elizabeth's Bentley, with the enamelled Bentley wing made by Fattorini (by the kind courtesy of Thomas Fattorini Ltd.).

father's initials 'IF'. It became a natural progression to establish a manufacturing company in Birmingham in 1919, in order to capitalise on the growing markets for sports trophies and medals. Thomas ran this business up until his death, supported by his eldest son Frank Fattorini. Upon the death of his father, Frank Fattorini retired handing control over to his youngest brother Wilfred Fattorini (1903 – 1992); he was known to his workers a 'Mr Wilf'.

According to present Tom Fattorini (1960 –), brother of the current MD Greg Fattorini, his grandfather was a very forward thinking man. He was very sensitive to the issues of employed women during his era, especially concerned about how very often their income was not their own, either being taken from them by their parents, or husbands. He employed many women, and used to give them generous allowances for clothing damage and such like, but also he would put aside a fund for each one, for each month that they had worked; in the event that they would have to leave when children came along, he used to present them with this sum of money discreetly, in order that they could make a good start to their family lives.

Wilfred had become MD more through circumstance than design. His elder brother Tom had been tragically killed, within the last two months of the Great War (13th August, 1918), his oldest brother had suffered the effects of shell shock. Although Frank had been able to continue after the war alongside his father, he had been shattered by his wartime experiences and he felt unable to continue after his father died, and sensibly handed control to Wilfred.

Wilfred assumed a considerable amount of responsibility very quickly, and at a very young age. As well as having to keep the business solvent, he had three sisters who all needed support financially, which required a considerable amount of money to change hands. By the age of 25 he had suffered a bout of 'nervous exhaustion', which upon recovering from, gave him a whole new perspective on the importance of the welfare of those that worked for him. He was incredibly forward thinking for his time, as the anecdote of the secret welfare fund for his women workers supports. He was incredibly enlightened and realised the importance of the work and life balance; he considered that holidays were necessary for his workers, and his policy generated much goodwill amongst all of his staff, who remember him with genuine affection.

Left: Taken from the Michaelangelo marble Tondo in the Royal Academy, designed by Arnold Machin and produced by Thomas Fattorini in 1977. (By the kind courtesy of Thomas Fattorini Ltd.) Right: Staffordshire Hoard Cross – a replica in silver gilt set with garnets exactly as the real one was made approx. 1400/1500 years ago (by the kind courtesy of Thomas Fattorini Ltd.).

During the Second World War, business carried on no matter what. As with many of the companies in the Quarter, war production was paramount, and the Fattorini factory was no exception, however, they still had time to make small items to help raise money for the Spitfire fund. Small pins in the shape of the beautiful Spitfire, made not too far away in Castle Bromwich; sold to the general public to add to the fund. An interesting anecdote from the war, is how they managed to retain their factory railings that stand in Frederick Street; most metal was taken and melted down for the war effort. I know from previous research that there was much bomb damage in, and around the Quarter, Fattorini's escaped reasonably unscathed, apart from a fire caused by a direct hit of a German incendiary bomb (for which the night watchman Mr William Ramsdale received a watch from the company for his bravery that night). The evidence of shrapnel damage from the blitz, which has bent and broken the railings on the corner of Fredrick and Regent Street, is retained by the company as a memorial.

During this period Fattorini and Sons family had a presence in the Quarter undertaking more commercial work, but passing under names of concerns that they had partnered with, or acquired. By the end of the 1950's they decided to make their presence known against their family competitor, and registered as Fattorini and Sons in 1958. This set a new era of active family competition, although their markets were diverging; Thomas Fattorini specialising in more bespoke exceptional enamelling, to the commercial output from Fattorini and Sons, which tended to specialise in general items, such as, car plates; Lotus, Rolls Royce, Bentley and Aston Martin. It was at this time that Thomas Fattorini Ltd, decided to carry the following strap line on their notepaper to distinguish themselves from their competitor:

"Note the Thomas in our name, similar firms are not the same."

The damaged railings outside the factory, which stand as a monument to the bombing that the Jewellery Quarter suffered during the WWII blitz (J. Debney).

Tom's father, Thomas Fattorini (1932 – 2010) assumed control from Wilfred, and by 1964 they had opened a factory in Manchester, the original intention had been to establish another enamelling factory to make up the shortfall of all of the school badges and general insignia that they manufactured; the demand for staff in Birmingham industries in general was so great, that Fattorini were unable to employ enough personnel there. However they realised that there was a need for the production of plastic name badges, and taking a diverse course, they pioneered the new idea and developed a highly lucrative market.

More and more, their Birmingham enterprise was drawn towards their particular niche market; specialist insignia, high-quality enamelled badges, orders of merit, and chains of office. They had built up a wealth of skills and specialism, training some of the best enamellers in Birmingham. The processes remain as pure as they were fifty years ago; a metal blank is stamped in gilding metal, or precious metal, then layers of vitreous enamel are painstakingly applied. The only difference now is that the purity of the powder enamel can be guaranteed, whereas, twenty or thirty years ago, the 'old timers' would insist on taking the lump enamel, and grinding and washing it themselves to ensure the cleanliness. In the last few decades, there has been a reduction in the available range of colour, due to the intervention of Health and Safety removing chemicals such as cadmium from the recipes, it has made some colours more difficult to apply successfully.

In 1984 Thomas Fattorini Ltd were able to acquire control of Fattorini and Sons, presenting a new venture of managing two factories that carried out fundamentally different work. It was at this time that the present Tom Fattorini was persuaded by his father to move to Birmingham to manage the transition. Tom remembers the image of the Quarter that greeted him then, it was a place where business was only conducted during working hours – the UK had fallen into a deep recession. Once the doors closed at the end of the day, the whole Quarter would clear, giving the appearance of a 'ghost town' particularly at weekends. It was not a place where anyone lived, it was being very badly affected by yet another economic downturn. Tom reflects on the feelings that it evoked in him, of an old western town of the 1800's with 'tumbleweed' bowling down the deserted streets.

Thankfully times have turned now, and as with many of the companies that have survived the difficult days then, and the downturn that they now find themselves in once more, this era of famine has been managed through strategic planning and thinking. The firm has now passed to the sixth generation of the Fattorini family, with Tom's brother Greg, sitting as MD and Tom very much the face of the Birmingham concern.

He is very proud of the tradition, and heritage, that he has assumed and like many in a similar position, views his role as one of a custodian of that heritage; this inspires in him the need to protect as much of the integrity of the history, in order to conserve the overall integrity of the position of the company within the market that it occupies. He is very cautious that he gives an exact interpretation of all that has gone before, and protects for posterity the precious inheritance that his forbears have worked so hard to build. He thought that the best people to give a true account of the 'family' that his grandfather Wilfred established were two of the workers who experienced that time.

When I interviewed Grace Hill she was to turn 73 that week, and although she has retired she carries fond memories of the family that she was employed by. She began her employment for Thomas Fattorini Ltd in the early 1950's, as for most of her generation, she finished school at 15 and immediately started work. She was the third of five girls (and one of eleven children) and born at the Sorrento Hospital, she lived in Springhill until she was 29. Her father already worked in the Quarter and decided that Fattorini was the place that he wanted his girls to work at. Tom speculates that this is because of the reputation that Wilfred had built up, for being a fair and

Left: Silversmith Richard Haynes with a large mace. By the kind courtesy of Thomas Fattorini Ltd. Right: Grace enamelling a C.B.E. (by the kind courtesy of Thomas Fattorini Ltd.).

good employer particularly for women. Mr Hill considered that Fattorini would be the best place for them all to get a good start, and offer his girls the greatest stability.

Grace's father gave her a strong piece of advice before she began there, obviously conscious that first impressions mean everything, he told her:

"Don't say you know it all… ask."

A sensible piece of advice for any young person starting their first position and certainly one many could do with these days. Grace took this advice to heart and was careful to seek guidance at all times. She remembers that apart from the small pieces of instruction that she received from the foreman, that she was generally taught by the other women around her:

"We all used to muck in together."

She is one of the 'old timers' who learnt to wash and crush her own enamel, quality control was everything and started with the scrupulousness of extremely careful hand washing; any trace of grease or oil on their hands could contaminate the enamel, or the blank, and cause the enamel to fire incorrectly, wasting a considerable amount of time and costing the factory:

"You couldn't touch the top of your badges, no soap! You had to keep away from soap."

The works outing to Windsor in 1947.

She started on school badges, learning to apply one colour, then two. At every stage the most important part of the learning process was understanding the quality control. As each colour was applied, they would learn to fire off, without causing the enamel to bubble or burn – which could change the colour of the finished piece. Then they had to carefully file off the surface and polish with pumice until the finish was perfect before applying the next, or subsequent colours. Each painstaking part of the process carefully undertaken again. Only when you had mastered one colour, could you move on up to two, and only when you mastered two could you move to three, and so on. The materials were fickle, different colours require different attention; length of firing and heat control, she says that she hated the yellow because there would often be bits in it causing the whole firing to go wrong.

And sometimes things did go wrong, quite seriously. Once when working in the 'other Fattorini' factory, she stepped on some hot enamel, she had to be hospitalised and receive a skin graft, as the molten glass had burnt through the sole of her shoe in seconds.

She remembers 'Mr Wilf' with fond affection:

"Mr Wilf was a nice man, a gentleman."

Gladys, Beryl, Kay, Hazel and Grace in Matlock.

Grace retiring on October 3rd, 1997.

She remembers his grandson Thomas coming to learn to do enamelling; often this is the best way for someone who is eventually going to manage to fully understand the business that they are assuming control of.

The Jewellery Quarter of the earlier years that Grace remembers is very different to the one that exists these days. The 'muck in together' feeling that was evoked in the Fattorini factory was a common experience across the area, the feeling of belonging to a 'big family' is a familiar story to all those that I have interviewed, and the physical environments, of the honeycomb of workshops and little places, hidden from public view and interconnected by rickety stairs, are all long since gone.

'Mr Wilf' had established a good welfare policy with his staff and encouraged as much social interaction as possible between his workers, even staging works trips and outings; to the seaside in the summer, a pantomime in the winter. He encouraged in-work camaraderie as much as possible, Grace remembers fondly when there were 40 of the enamellers all working together in the workshop (whereas now there are only 8), they would often break into a sing-song which would keep all in the design room entertained.

Even when you have what appears to be the perfect position sometimes you are never satisfied, and as Grace reflects, it was a time when jobs for skilled enamellers were easy to find, and once she did leave to try working somewhere else, but she soon returned when she realised that is was at Fattorini where she felt most at home. In fact, Tom reflects with pride that the safe, happy, atmosphere generated at Fattorini led to many partnerships forming and subsequent marriages amongst the staff:

"Social glue. People do get together."

Grace herself, never married, which explains her long unbroken service; she never found anyone and preferred to live at home taking care of her parents. However, one after another, each of her sisters joined her at Fattorini; one of the younger ones, Gladys, joined a few years later; then when her sister Valarie had completed her family she came; then Cynthia joined and worked on the press; then finally, the youngest Eunice came and worked alongside Grace. So her family was very much around her, and seems to have been the policy of Fattorini to encourage this togetherness as much as possible.

(Left to right) Gladys, Valerie, Cynthia, Eunice, Grace, in the centre their mother.

Grace rose in her skills and experience, in fact Tom is very proud to say that due to the diligence of Grace over thirty years, particularly for enamelling the C.B.E., that Thomas Fattorini were able to apply for and achieve, the right to display the Royal Warrant. She worked her way up producing 'one offs' and limited range pieces, often in precious metals. She produced all of the flags, beautifully finished in detail and full colour. She once made a fully enamelled small casket. Eventually, she could apply 10 different colours with incredible skill and precision. She was the first enameller to produce the C.B.E. for Fattorini, and a framed photograph of her doing this hangs in the office where I conducted this interview.

After quite literally, devoting the whole of her life to her work at Fattorini, Grace retired at the age of 60, she says that she does miss it, but she felt that it was time to finish. Grace remembers a golden time of the Quarter's history and a very different time in the history of the country; a lot of the gentility of those moments has passed into history and leaves her with very pleasant memories.

Margaret Pritchard (nee Jauncey), can claim to be one of the oldest workers in the Jewellery Quarter, yet to look at her, with her youthful complexion and her stylish attire, you would think that she has some years to go before she considers retirement; in actual fact she is 75 years of age and has worked for sixty years, more or less, where she is now. She is not a maker, but one of the army of administration staff that have kept the larger companies ticking over for all these years. She was born in 1935, in a back-to-back in Avenue Road in Aston. Her mother had worked for HP Sauce and then Kynoch's as a munitions worker in WWI. Margaret's grandfather used to drive a horse drawn hansom cab, and would to take her mother to the stables to help him groom the horses; how different life had been in Birmingham but a short time ago. Her father had been born in King Edwards Road.

Just before the outbreak of the Second World War her parents had been advised to move from their house in Aston due to their close proximity to the Gas works; it was considered to be a very dangerous place to live with the potential of the bombing to come. Margaret may not have had such a strong recollection of this, had it not been for a rather unfortunate accident which beset her when out with her parents, getting her finger stuck in a door; she recalls being made to sit on a potty in the backroom of their house, with her finger throbbing in pain, and gazing out at the monstrously large gas cooling towers, which practically appeared to be at the end of their yard. War-torn Birmingham was a frightening place to be as a small child growing up during the heavy bombing, and she does remember the orange sky the night of the heavy Coventry blitz on the 15th November 1940.

Four Dwellings GM School Quinton in 1949. Margaret Jauncey is in the third row, fifth from the right in the white blouse.

At 15 in 1950, she left school and got her first job as an office junior at Angora Silverware in Frederick Street, she was paid £2 4/ 6d per week. It had been an import and export firm set up by Ephrim Cotton and his brothers after they had a substantial win on the Irish Sweep Stake; they then expanded into silverware. By then Margaret's family were living in Quinton, so she used to get the bus to the Hall of Memory and then walk up from there. She was determined that she was not going to remain an office junior, and took herself off to attend Queen's College on Saturdays in her own time, in order to take her secretarial qualifications in shorthand and typing. By the age of 17 she had become a secretary in Angora Silver and she began to progress steadily up from there.

This was the early 1950's, the whole Quarter was alive and changing fast, there were still works canteens in factories. Where Margaret worked she would be offered a mid-morning break when she used to like to catch a snack of cheese on toast, and real dinners at lunchtime; after the austerity caused by the war it must have been a coveted luxury for the men and women who worked around there.

Other things have changed too; the office staff never had to clock-in, being considered very professional and able to keep time well. Her hours were 9am to 5.30pm everyday except Thursday. Thursday was mail day, when all the night post that was expected to be sent both nationally and internationally, had to be made ready. Those were the days when many more office staff were needed everywhere, before the advent of computers.

In the 1960's Margaret remembers the interesting parking arrangements which came in. As many workers now aspired to their own private transport rather than depending on buses, there came an urgent need to park. There was never going to be enough parking spots to service all the workers, and by then in the 1960's, there were many more workers than now. So there was a double parking method applied all along the streets, Margaret remembers the double parking particularly in Regents Street:

"Different sides for different days of the week."

As she remembers, the whole place was an intricate network of interconnecting workshops, with rat-runs and back alleys. Some of the 'old timers' still exist now, like Roy Hancox a watchmaker in his early 80's. She recollects that down Vittoria Road were a lot of one-man enterprises; she recalls one place that she used to visit that was owned by an old Jewish gentleman, and she remembers the floorboards in particular, that glistened with particles of gold and silver, which were trapped within the grain of the wood.

Thomas Fattorini acquired Angora Silver, as like so many family businesses it had begun to fail; the whole place, plant, equipment and staff, became part of Fattorini practically overnight. She remembers how hands-on Thomas Fattorini senior had been within the factory, he used to walk round and talk to everyone. Then in the 1980's Tom and Greg were brought in and took over as their father retired. Obviously, the advent of technology has changed the profile of the business significantly, there are a lot less staff in the offices; whereas, there used to be plenty of sales staff and administration, now computers have taken the workload. But, Margaret has also viewed this as a negative in general, she feels that administratively trained staff no longer possess the command of punctuation and grammar that was drilled into her generation when they attended their commercial training. A considerable amount of the poor presentation of business letters and documents, she considers, can be blamed on the advent of texting and generally poor education at school level.

This lack of proper education, she views has not just had detrimental effects on the administration of companies, but also the engineering/artisan side. Her husband trained as an engineer when the basic engineering apprenticeships ended, and since then she has witnessed a decline in both the interest and the standard of youngsters coming through. She believes that young people are just not getting the exposure to these activities anymore, and the experiences that they are receiving are very limited, because these fail to spark their interest. In her opinion, the removal of many school workshops combined with the introduction of computers suites, means that;

"Young people just want to push buttons."

She does feel that not all the blame can be put on education, the various downturns that have happened have stopped employers encouraging young people in times of recession. Some recessions, such as the downturn in silvery cutlery, was for the most part home grown, due to a well known British cutlery manufacturer flooding the market with cheap foreign imports:

"I have a set of Angora cutlery that was presented to me as a wedding present, and it will last forever."

Margaret is one of those who worries about recent developments in the Quarter, which in her opinion have removed a great deal of the charm and character of the area; she is very sad the 'Fiddle and Bone' public house had to be closed as the 'newcomers' complained about the noise. And she feels that some nice old buildings have been demolished to make way for the development of the apartments, which in her consideration do not add anything. She hopes that the quality of the redevelopment will improve and attract families, rather than those who will not stay.

There is no doubt that Fattorini has created a feeling of safety and security for its staff, that is obvious from their longevity and affection by which they speak of working in the 'family' of workmates. Fattorini have survived many devastating recessions, family rivalry and two worlds wars; the fact that they have survived for 6 generations is due in the most part, to their forward thinking notions of the care for their staff and the fact that they have found their niche. They know what they do well, and they continue to focus on that rather, than following any course of diversification that may distract them. They are superb at what they manufacture and are sought out by many to complete bespoke commissions; as a nice gentlemen from a local authority from Yorkshire confirmed to me, as he sat in the reception with the mayoral chain of office which needed attention, waiting for the youthful Margaret to show him through.

Chapter 11

A MAN OF MEDALS

Gladman and Norman

Few newcomers have arrived with such a burning passion and fascination of the thing that they manufacture, however, Phil McDermott of Gladman and Norman has a vast knowledge and deep love for medals. Indeed, his drive towards these objects is so strong, it is hard to believe that he is not sitting behind the desk of a much-loved family firm as the third generation custodian. It may not be a company of blood ties, but that does not mean that he does not value the history of the company, in fact, he has carried out a large amount of research to contextualise the business within the Quarter. One thing that he found was that the 'remembered' history had become slightly distorted, which emphasises how within a very short time myth can develop and transform the fact, another consistent theme within this book.

Phil revealed that his research had found that the company was 100 years old as of October 2010. The original founders were Alfred Gladman and Samuel George Norman. Their firm started very close to the Great War, and of course, as was the patriotism of that time, both men considered that it was their duty to fight. Samuel Norman never made it to fight overseas for after he enlisted he contracted Tuberculosis and was discharged, he was very frail and subsequently, received a pension, dying just after the end of the war in 1919. He barely had time to launch the business with all that had gone on, he left all of his interest in the business to Alfred.

Unfortunately, Alfred had a tragic experience in the war. He was called up for the Royal Sussex Regiment and was gassed. As with many who suffered the same fate, it shortened his life expectancy considerably, and he died prematurely in 1932, at the age of 39.

Phil had purchased the business from a gentleman called Mr Clifford Hadley, who was the son of the man who had purchased it from the original owning family. Phil had been told that both Gladman and Norman had been gassed and had left the business to their respective wives, who lacking in the necessary business acumen had run the business down, hence the acquisition by Mr Hadley senior.

When he researched the various war records and civil documents, his investigations uncovered that Samuel Norman had never married, and had left his entire estate to Gladman. Alfred Gladman had married a lady called Laura, and subsequently, they had had a daughter called Grace. The two ladies that the Hadley's then purchased the business from must have been Laura and Grace, mother and daughter, rather than wives of the owners. This is a sad story but not uncommon that many of the companies in the Quarter were affected fundamentally by the devastation of the wars. Fattorini with the shell shock in the sons; the Spencer family losing all of their sons; not many of the family concerns emerged unscathed.

The business is listed in 1911 as a 'fancy badge makers' and in 1915 as a 'die sinkers' – die sinking is a very skilled trade of engraving steel to create the dies that are used in the stamping process. The dies themselves take great skill to cut by hand, being very small yet detailed, and in reverse (or the negative) of the actual finished image. Before the advent of computer aided design and manufacturing, all of the dies were cut by hand.

Left: The REME 'Sweetheart' (by the kind courtesy of Gladman and Norman Ltd.).
Right: SAS badge (by the kind courtesy of Gladman and Norman Ltd.).

The Holocaust Medal (by the kind courtesy of Gladman and Norman Ltd.).

When Mr Hadley senior acquired the firm it entered an era when it was known for its high volume of stamping, it was mainly for seaside souvenirs. Within their storeroom of dies are all of the town insignia and crests. With the advent of WWII they expanded into military cap badges, as well as, producing parts for ships and aircraft. The firm currently retains all of the tools and dies for the 300,000 cap badges per annum which the firm were producing for the War Office.

In the 1960's these cap badges had to be anodised as they were altered to be made of aluminium, added to this, demand for them was considerable, so the firm had to run 24 hour production. However, the process of anodising aluminium was then an unstable one, and produced different colour results whether it is night, or day. This caused a quality control issue which consequently caused numerous rejections, Mr Hadley decided to no longer tender for the anodised badge contract.

The business continued for some years passing from Mr Hadley senior to Mr Clifford Hadley his son. As is the case with so many families where enterprises pass to a second generation, the money that has been made previously has been lavished on the generation that assumes control, the sense of the need to drive and aspire tends not to be there; there is not the same hunger or desire to achieve. It would be Clifford that Phil would approach eventually, to persuade him to sell.

Phil's passion started early. He was born in Northfield, he calls himself a 'Ley Hill boy'. He was very much his father's son, his father had a passion for collecting coins, so Phil chose to collect medals and developed his love for all things connected with this. His business interest came about through a combination of necessity and ingenuity. It was the time of the 1980's recession, his wife was being affected by employment issues where she worked at Cadbury's. Phil felt the need to change what he was doing, so he took advantage of the Enterprise Allowance Scheme that was then operating.

He decided to set up his own business in medals, it was something he knew a considerable amount about. He understood that he had to exhibit a trading capacity to be able to qualify for the allowance, so he got a friend to have some medals mounted by him for £1 each, and thus Worcester Medals was born. In the first instance, the company dealt in medal mounting and the supply of miniature medals, and after placing an advertisement in 'Soldier' Magazine, it grew like topsy. Within six months he was registered to pay VAT.

Worcester Medals would buy the majority of their replica medals from a company called Miniature Medals, they were also big customer for Toye, Kenning & Spencer. What Phil did not know at that time, was that Miniature Medals were purchasing most of their medals from Gladman and Norman. It was only when the owner of Miniature Medals finally had enough of the business and offered to sell to Phil that he began to deal directly with Clifford Hadley at Gladman and Norman. Through these initial exchanges, and Clifford realising what a large customer Phil was for the items that Gladman and Norman were producing, eventually the two built up quite a close business relationship; putting Phil in an excellent position to make an offer to buy Clifford Hadley out. He reveals that all this occurred while Worcester Medals continued to grow, and by the time he had completed his first year at the helm, they were turning over £100,000 per annum:

"Not bad for a very small firm."

One of the first things that Phil did on taking over Gladman and Norman, was to approach the Ministry of Defence to get a licence to reproduce replica medals. They were successful in this, and became the first company to be granted a licence, and remain one of only three companies with the licence to do so. This enabled Phil to begin to establish a good working relationship with the medal office, which he now describes as 'a close affinity'.

By 2007, Worcester Medals had been awarded the contract by the Cabinet Office to produce O.B.E.'s and M.B.E.'s, all to be manufactured at Gladman and Norman, these contracts are always split between very few suppliers, in order to secure a good supply-chain and a back-up should any

The Victoria Cross was awarded to Pte Johnson Beharry for heroic action in Iraq in 2005 (by the kind courtesy of Gladman and Norman Ltd.).

one, or two, firms fail to deliver. Gladman and Norman are one of the only four firms with the contract to supply. However, this accolade and another major contribution to medal history has meant that by January 2008, they had been granted a Royal Warrant, and he was appointed as a medallist to the Queen. This has allowed Worcester Medals to display the Royal Coat of Arms in their boxes and on all of their promotional literature.

This recognition led to a further special commission from the medal office to provide the Royal Red Cross, often described as the nursing V.C.; this medal is given to nurses who distinguish themselves, or give exceptional exertions in the course their duties. The first class is a red-enamelled cross on gold, that displays the head of the reigning monarch; it is inscribed with the three words, faith, hope and charity; the ribbon is dark blue with crimson-red edge stripes. It was originally manufactured by Collingwood and it is because of the insecurity of supply that was generated by the firm's sudden closure, that the MOD has sought out a reliable firm. There are only two, or three, of these crosses presented per year, but it is a particularly cherished achievement for Phil, who considers this to be a mark of the trust and respect that he has managed to establish with the medal office.

This led to many other sub-contracts arriving on Phil's desk for the 'great and the good', and the reputation that he has formed for reliability and a high standard of quality continues to attract many new enquiries. His relationship with the medal office meant regular visits were required to deliver crosses or review performance and future requirements. On one such trip to them, they asked if Worcester Medals would assume the work for the posthumous mounting of service medals.

This role, Phil takes particularly seriously and with a considerable amount of solemnity. When a soldier dies, from any reason including active service, Worcester Medals, acquire all of that serviceman, or woman's medals, and formally mount them. They ensure that they carry out all of the collection, and then deliver the finished result to the MOD for presentation to the relatives.

Two and a half years ago, the greatest of accolades was paid to a man who is passionate about what he does. Phil was approached by the MOD to assist on a project to create what was to become, The Elizabeth Cross. For Phil, this was the highest honour that he could be recognised with, and he took considerable personal pride in the faith that had been placed in his abilities and that of Gladman and Norman's.

He had been fortunate to have gained the services of one of the most talented artist/designers in the Quarter within his full-time employment,

The first Elizabeth Cross was presented to Karen Upton in memory of her husband – Warrant Officer Sean Upton who was killed in Sangin, Afghanistan in 2009 (by the kind courtesy of Gladman and Norman Ltd.).

Dayna White. She worked feverishly for 18 months producing over 20 designs, with numerous different finishes; from these, eight were selected and manufactured into prototypes. The decision was taken on the roof of a building in Whitehall, as to which finish should be submitted to Her Majesty for her final decision of the medal. Phil had developed a special process of oxidation, to change the surface from various high metallics, through to a satin/matt black finish. The absolute jet black that they desired they have discovered since the design process ended.

The cross itself is in sterling silver, backed by a laurel wreath, and supporting the royal cypher in the centre. It is presented to the families of servicemen and women, killed on operations or as the result of a terrorist action. It is the most significant medal to have been produced since the George Cross, they have been led to believe that the Queen is very pleased with the final result.

As Phil remarks, the whole process needed a combination of exceptional design work, speed and communication, through all sorts of circumstances:

"It was a brilliant thing for Birmingham to have been awarded this contract, traditionally it has always gone to the Royal Mint."

Dayna White designer of the Elizabeth Cross (J. Debney).

The most remarkable thing for Phil was how they managed to keep the whole project under wraps:

"Unusually, in Birmingham we managed to keep the whole thing secret. It's a village and rumours abound. It is a credit to our staff that we kept this project confined to the company."

It is quite surprising that Phil did manage to maintain this veil of secrecy when you consider that he has been working closely with both Toye, Kenning & Spencer and Thomas Fattorini Ltd; as is clear from their chapters both Fiona Toye and Tom Fattorini, who both value and realise the need to work collaboratively as a universal 'Birmingham force'. However, they have their separate business concerns and it should be right that Gladman and Norman are able to celebrate their individual achievements. As a team, the three companies have achieved some successes, and as each project comes forward, the respective 'three' take their turns in leading that project to a successful conclusion. Phil believes in the importance of this collaboration, and as the relative 'newcomer' has no dogmatic traditions that tie him and the firm to a past of strict competition. He is proud that the three are bidding for the manufacture and supply of the Olympic medals and he views this sort of collaborative exercise, as one that could place Birmingham back on the map.

There is an important point to note here, that although they conduct fairly similar work in some aspects of what they do, they are fundamentally, three very different manufacturers. It can be argued that all three could restore, or supply, a chain of office for instance, but their companies skills and strengths in different areas make the choice obvious for more specialist things.

Phil is very good at creating other opportunities for the business. He was fortunate enough to get an introduction at the Jordanian Embassy in London, and gave his cards with (unbeknown to him), his personal telephone number scribbled on the back. Five weeks later, on a Sunday, he received a phone call from the King's personal envoy; they had been badly let down by a supplier of royal regalia and asked if Phil was able to help. Phil pulled out all of the stops, and managed with speed to fill the requirements, and received subsequently, requests to fill other orders of high rank within the country, one of which appears on the Jordanian banknotes.

As is often the case with these very specialist pieces, their value is limited on the open market, yet, the pieces are immensely complex and have taken considerable time to put together. This particular Jordanian award is made of multiple, hand-sawn layers, which are ornate, finishing with a piece of exceptionally sophisticated, enamelled work centrally placed.

The speed and success at which Gladman and Norman have produced such pieces have led to further introductions and contracts. Phil has a personal connection now with King George of Tonga; Gladman and Norman have produced some exceptionally fine awards for the Tongan's, which have required a considerable amount of skill, these were supplied for the coronation of King George V in 2008. This has led to Gladman and Norman being asked to supply all of the state honours and service medals.

Further to this, there have been yet more introductions, to among others, the King of Bhutan. Phil has been fortunate enough to receive an honour from both King George of Tonga and the King of Bhutan. It must be a really strange experience making your own honour for a customer, that is then subsequently, awarded back to you.

For Phil, it will always be the medals that he has come to love and prize so much, as a young lad looking through books, which will always make the hairs on the back of his neck stand up. How would he have ever known, that one day he would be making the O.B.E., or that he would be instrumental for the most significant medal since that instigated by the present Queen's late father? His eyes light up as he describes the whole experience to him is:

"Like being a kid in sweet shop."

It was because of the acclaim of the Elizabeth Cross that he was awarded the contract by Nigeria, to produce the honours to celebrate the country's fifty years of their independence.

He does think that the European market is the most difficult to break into; France tends to be a closed shop, as does Italy. The other countries have a tendency to seek their pieces within their own countries, or from the French/Italian connections, there is a perceived Anglophobe atmosphere towards British manufacturers from the Continent.

His biggest concern about the ensured future success of his business is that of Education; a theme which continues to run behind all doors in the Quarter. He has had some personal experience of the what is, and is not, on offer to young people. His daughter had initially undertaken a multi-disciplinary course in art/design, which she was not completely satisfied with. Phil suggested that she look at the School of Jewellery. When she investigated, it was suggested to her that the HND was too advanced for what she would be able to do, at that stage but they offered her an access course in engraving and enamelling initially before moving on to take the HND. Suffice to say, being the daughter of a man who owns a company that makes some of the best medals and awards in the world, and is simply nuts about medals, it could not be any surprise that she won an award for a medal, which was subsequently exhibited in Japan. But even after all of that exceptional success, she decided not to take her career in jewellery or medals any further.

Phil considers that the employers desire to bring in fresh blood, is becoming increasingly inhibited by government over-regulation, and that there is very little real consideration being made, regarding the difficulties employers face when taking on a new employee; they will have little, or no skill in the first instance, so an apprentice requires a large investment of man-hours in training and teaching (which all have an effect on production), there are no guarantees that an apprentice may stay at the end of their training.

Gladman and Norman decided it was time to look for a couple of new apprentices; at this time 25% of

'Of honour' (J. Debney).

the workforce are passed retirement age. Initially, Phil approached a few government agencies to try and find some financial support to offset the costs of an expensive process, there was none forthcoming. Then he investigated the Modern Apprenticeship route which in the first instance, had sounded quite enticing. However, on further research it was found to be in conflict with the needs of such a practical apprenticeship, which requires constant teaching and learning; Modern Apprenticeship insisted on a college-based Microsoft Office study, which is incompatible with the hands-on nature of these trades.

Finally they took the risk and advertised for 'an apprentice'. In these days of sexual and age equality, this is the legal requirement of employers, but as Phil (and many other experienced makers) have pointed out, some skills appear to be sexually divided. There is no doubt that girls of a certain age make better enamellers than men; the patience and focused work that is required seems better suited to women. Gladman and Norman received many replies to their advertisement including one from someone of 64, and as is obvious to most, to make considerable investment in someone who will have to retire is a waste of time and resources, but does lead to criticisms of ageism.

Eventually, after considerable sifting, and interviewing of the applicants they found they had two excellent candidates; a young man who they have placed in the mounting shop, and a young lady – Laura Cupples – who is beginning her training as an enameller and designer. The things that surprised Phil the most, when undertaking this whole process of seeking apprentices, was how little the applicants knew of the opportunities which lay in the Jewellery Quarter. He feels that is in part due to the lack of exposure, that young people have these days to these trades; traditionally, they were introduced to the area because their father, or mother, or other relative worked in

Craftsmen at Gladman and Norman (J. Debney).

the Quarter. Laura has now been working there for 15 months, she had attended Bournville School, where she had 'no experience' of anything remotely connected to what she is now doing, but she says enthusiastically:

"It's a nice feeling when you make something nice, very satisfactory."

Phil has been fortunate in placing the right people in his apprenticeship vacancies, he believes that on the whole luck has played a significant factor in his overall business success, particularly, when it comes to meeting the right people, at the right time. This applies to the chance, or fate, that happened when securing the services of Dayna White, the designer of the Elizabeth Cross, now the chief designer for Gladman and Norman.

Dayna has worked for 23 years in the Quarter, she has an extremely cheerful disposition and obviously loves what she does immensely. Originally, she attended Sutton Coldfield College to study a BTEC multi-disciplinary art/design course; her intention was to seek an undergraduates degree in Textiles in Cumbria. While she was in this process she decided to earn a little extra money and gain some more experience by applying to be a hand-painter at Toye, Kenning & Spencer, like many, unaware of the existence of the Quarter. She fell in love with the craft that she was doing, she describes it as an 'obsession', she believes that you have to be obsessional to undertake such work.

After her time at Toye, Kenning & Spencer, she moved on to work for Thomas Fattorini as a designer, and after several years she decided to have a go at running her own business (her work was very much in demand) but with all the output comes a considerable amount of paperwork, and very soon Dayna found herself disappearing under the mountain of bureaucracy that accompanies being self-employed. Dayna's uncomfortable position at that time, was Phil's good fortune, he had approached her to come and work for Gladman and Norman she has not looked back since.

She says, that the main part of any success story is having a good working relationship with those around you. She reflects that she had spent 15 years in various places loving what she was doing but finding herself exploited because of her passion and devotion. She did like working for herself at times, but she much prefers the safety and security of working for a company, it means that she can concentrate on what she is good at, rather than worrying about all of the extraneous issues of working for oneself.

She does shy away from recognition, this is confirmed by Phil who on more than one occasion has had to point out to others that know Dayna just how influential she has been in the field of design, however, she has not shirked her responsibilities to communicate with those that matter during the design process, such as the Generals and the Whitehall Mandarins; a situation that may put most people off but not Dayna, who is always highly professional. Dayna remains very modest, she views what she does as 'a service' to others, and not necessarily something that she should be rewarded for.

She is concerned that the Quarter has been affected by the wrong type of exposure – for the retail outlets, rather than what actually happens within the area. There needs to be greater emphasis on promoting what the Quarter actually does, and maybe less advertising altogether. She does not believe that the new breed of designer/makers who have been trained by the University are the right people to lead this promotion either, as in her opinion, they lack the fundamental business skills and experience through their own naivety.

Dayna, has given of her own time to the college as a part time lecturer, she feels that she has learnt more about enamelling by having to teach it;

Hot stamping and enamelling at Gladman and Norman (J. Debney).

because the process has to be analysed and broken down stage, by stage, a luxury a working practitioner very often does not have the time to indulge in. In her opinion, often the best lecturers at the college are those that work professionally, as they know all of the 'tricks' and ways of doing things that have been handed down for generations. She does feel that the institution does have a role to play in the promotion of the Quarter.

Phil has grown the business substantially, and that is reflected in the fact that when he acquired Gladman and Norman there were only 13 working there, now there are 23. The mounting shop used to be out-sourced, but like Toye, Kenning & Spencer, he made the investment to bring these skills in-house because they are dying off. He views, that much of the success in recent years has been due to the desire to consolidate the skills, as much as possible, under one roof. They still rely on the old tools, equipment and processes, these do not change (they were hot stamping when I was making my visit). This means that they retain much of the old plant and machinery, and the wealth of dies that they keep.

They have no dogmatic tradition, because Phil has come in rather than inherited, as such, he is far more likely to challenge the 'can't be done' attitude which means that his firm is revolutionary in adopting new ways of doing things; he is a reflection of the visionary entrepreneurs of the Quarter's past, who were always willing to develop processes. This 'man of medals', was just the person that this firm needed, the right person, at the right time. This is very much a story of personal passion, as Phil reflects with a sparkle in his eyes:

"This is not about coming to work."

Chapter 12

VOICES FROM THE WARREN

The network of the Quarter

Historically the Quarter has existed due in the most part to an effective network of skills, and small enterprise that are condensed into a relatively small area of operation. This enabled those who needed another process, such as stamping, or enamelling, or the work of a silversmith, wood turner, or case maker, to find that particular trade within a stone's throw of their own front door. Most of these businesses started because of the availability of opportunity to supply someone else and earn a living.

Traditionally, all of the industries were small enterprises once, as much of what developed there came from the advent of the small makers of the Birmingham 'toys'; snuff boxes, buckles and buttons, having workshops which were in their own homes. These developed and spread, and became interconnected with stairs and corridors. Many of these older premises bear very little resemblance to the homes that they once were.

Generation after generation, small outworkers have co-existed within the streets of Jewellery Quarter, and like a family, when one needed work they were helped by the others around them. This coalescence of sympathetic trades, based on traditional heritage continues (although vastly reduced in size) until this day. This may not be a story of a firm that has existed for six generations in the Quarter, but rather how enterprise of craft and skill has continued to survive for three hundred years.

To reflect this eclectic mix of trades and skills, this chapter collects together a number of stories from those of the complementary business sector that are either current, or as in the case of Al Trappe were once essential to the area. Some narratives are longer than others, but all are much shorter than the extensive chapters that have been compiled on the larger businesses. This too, is a reflection of the nature and the small size of these busy little places. Unlike the Managing Directors and Owners who can devote time to talking to me, these one-man, two-man, operations are pressed by time constraints, 'time is money', and they provided their tales quickly, between their work.

In this chapter, I shall introduce you to Ron Jackson, a man of considerable passion for what he does and with a tale of business success and failure; to Tony Yoemans and his workers, who found himself in the Quarter having to learn his new business in weeks rather than years; to Colin Ashford and the employees of William Downing with years of skill and experience working in an environment that hails from Victorian manufacturing; to Mary and Bill Burden, Mary being one of the most talented enamelling outworkers in the Quarter who is highly regarded by all who use her services; and to Al Trappe who worked for the original recyclers of the area a smelting firm. Each of these reflects the multifarious 'others' who operate out of sight, but keep the whole area ticking over.

Ron Jackson is featured in a previous chapter about Toye, Kenning & Spencer, but he has his main premises at the back of the old Vaughton's factory (of which it used to form part of), which he shares with Tony Yoemans. Ron is now spread across two sites because after his business partner died, he took an offer he said that he 'couldn't refuse' although in hindsight it was not the best move, and he was badly caught out in this business deal. Fortunately for him, Brian Toye valued the work that Ron and his workers did, and took over his workforce, allowing him to site them and the majority of the machines within the Toye factory.

Ron is 65, he started in the gun trade (based in the Gun Quarter) when he was 12 years of age, in those days he would walk to the Proof House with shot guns over his shoulder, he moved to the Jewellery Quarter when he was 15. He keeps a few precious machines in his main premises that he shares with Tony, where he carries out other work. He has one particularly prized machine that he has christened 'Big Bertha', it was made by John Hands in 1909. Ron says, that this machine would have been based on the ones used in the Soho Manufactory, so it is a direct link to the past of the area. His partner used to 'keep it in good nick', now that is Ron's job. It consists of a central screw and two wheels; one drives up and one drives down pulled by a belt drive; it exerts 450 tonnes of force and is a monster. Ron loves this machine is most affectionate about 'her'. He tells me that she has not been touched since the day she was built:

"Every few years, a new belt and a can of oil."

Ron knows everyone and everyone knows him, he has anecdote to tell with every other sentence that he utters, but never a bad word. He speaks of others with admiration and affection. He tells me a wonderful story about another subject of this book, Steven Green, of the Charles Green family. Steven used to be a very a generous businessman (and still is), but in those days he was a millionaire with a thriving business. When Ron and his partner started up fifty years ago, they went looking for work around the Quarter and approached Steven, who gave them £2,000 of silver to stamp, Ron stresses to me:

"He didn't know us from Adam."

Unfortunately, their big break was not as successful as they might have hoped and they ended up scrapping all of the silver, their very first job. They knew that they were in serious trouble, that Steven could quite literally finish them off, they went back and knocked on his door. Ron was shocked by Steven's generosity of spirit:

Ron Jackson hard at work.

"Tell you what lads, come back when you've got the job right."

And he took the scrapped silver from them and shut the door. To this day Ron is eternally grateful for Steven's magnanimous attitude, if it was not for that, things could have been so different.

Ron demonstrated to me the operations of 'Bertha' and some other machines that he keeps there, and he energetically operated the stampers to full effect. He tells me that in his hey day he would have had another '18 drop stampers all around the wall', all being operated:

"Now you are not even allowed to work half of them."

The reason Ron can continue without repercussions for the HSE, is simply because he is self-employed. Yet I know from my research that all of the larger enterprises depend on the drop-stamping that is done around the Quarter by men like Ron. When Ron does retire, which he is going to eventually, who will take on this role? Who will be able to take the machines over? And will the HSE allow these business interests to continue?

In the other chapter, where I discussed much with Ron, he had already expressed concerns that he believes that young people 'don't want to get their hands dirty'. He knows there is nobody showing any desire to come into the heavy metal trades of the Quarter and he is fearful for the future of what he does. Ron is a really enthusiastic man, and would more than happily like to pass his knowledge and skill on. It is these men who the Quarter must actively support to do this, before the skills that are relied on so much, die; forcing those who need stampings to buy them all from China at escalating costs, year, on year.

Tony Yoemans is a fascinating character with no tradition or connection in the Quarter, or so he thought. He had spent a year reading medicine and decided that being a doctor was not for him. One day in 1968, a friend of his came round and told him that he had bought a business in the Quarter and he wanted Tony to go in with him. Tony had no idea what he was getting into but took the chance:

"I've started writing a book about it." He tells me.

Tony's tale is one of arriving in the Quarter and finding himself launched into a dying case making business and having very little training, as the old owner was disinterested in training him, and his partner (and his sons) took very little concern to be involved. But, the descriptions of the old Quarter give an interesting insight into how things were then. The business was based in Tenby Street North, in an antiquated workshop where the only security measure was a little hatch. The parking was impossible, with everyone double and triple parked where they could, and he inherited two elderly ladies among the staff who were from a very different time, here is a brief excerpt:

"It smelt of smoke and dust however there was another smell much stronger that got up your nostrils and settled there. I did eventually become immune to it, that of animal glue which was made from skin, bones and hooves of horses and cattle."

He continues with a description of one of the old dears:

"Next to her was Bettie Underhill the same sort of age as Dolly they had worked together since they were young moving from a case maker that had closed down many years before, carrying their stools, glue pots and tools across the streets of Hockley to be re-employed by W. & W."

Dolly and Bettie were a God send, for although things were difficult, and the business did eventually fold, when they asked for a rise what they were given they were satisfied with, their salary rose from 1s 2d per hour by a few pennies more.

Tony was extremely surprised when he told his mother of his business acquisition to find that he had a very strong connection; her father had been a jewel case maker and she herself had gone to train as a jewel case liner and worked for a firm called Wheatley's; it could be said that it was in his blood. Not one to give up, and realising that although the industry was in decline, that there was a need, he kept at it. Where as at one time, there had been 30, or so, case makers – a case maker on every corner – there are only two now; Tony's business and Pickering and Mayell. Much of its demise he tells me, is due to the skills not being passed on, he made sure that he passed his skills on to those who started working for him in 1970.

It is extremely specialist work and still very much in demand, his customers tend to be the top end of the market; a flying case for the Sultan of Brunei, boxes for the King of Bahrain and the King of Bhutan. Tony is very optimistic about the future of the area, he tells me that he is busier than he has been in forty years. He does add that he thinks that may be because there are very few case makers left, but he does believe that there is a renaissance in jewellery, certainly within the Quarter.

In his opinion, the whole area has started to benefit from the 'smartening up' that has gone on in recent years. Whereas, in times gone by, the Jewellery Quarter was a 'secret'; all the high street shops were buying from other hallmarked manufacturers/retailers, yet these pieces were all made in the Quarter. He admits, that there have been some very bleak times, when many markets were lost to the Pacific rim and China, but now these opportunities are starting to return as the Chinese market diminishes, due to their own people demanding more money:

"Their delivery times are not as good as we can offer. Their economy is over-heating."

Graham Whitehouse who has worked for Tony for 20 years, gave me tour of the premises. He carries out all of the specialised wood milling; the work is extremely labour intensive and made to order, so every piece is individual even the pieces made on a limited run. Graham has to produce the carcasses to reflect the order with great accuracy. In the wood shop, the air is thick with MDF dust, which from my own experience teaching woodwork, is an incredibly difficult dust to extract, no matter what units you put in. The workshop is full of all the conceivable wood working machines; from saws and planes, drills and routers. Graham told me that they are just working on filling a return order for St John's Ambulance which always requires over one hundred a time.

I was introduced to June, whose job is to cover and fill. She comes from Shard End and left school at 15 in the early 1970's, and apart for a few years bringing up her children, she has been back for 20 years. In her opinion box making is a dying art, she works feverishly to fold the fabric and glue pieces in position even while she chats. She told me, that they have to respond to orders quickly, and sometimes there is more work than they think they can handle, but they manage. She loves her job, even though most times she never sees what she has made ever again.

Tony feels that the Quarter is a very strict community and for two years he was not accepted because he was an outsider, but once he was, life changed and it became a fun place to work. He certainly would not change what he does now:

"It is like handicrafts, and getting paid!'

The firm of William Downing, is in Spencer Street, Neil Grant of Crescent Silver (who are discussed in the final chapter) now owns the building but the work continues, in exactly the same way that it has for over a hundred years, or more. They supply stampings (pressings) to all of the other companies that require them; medallions, medals, regalia, blanks for enamelling. They have a very old premises, which has a galley feel, being long rather than wide. Part way in the galley is a deep set pit, to allow the huge drop-stamping machines to stand floor-to-ceiling, attached to an axle which provides the power; a long rope is pulled to release the full force of the press on its tremendous drop to the work, which it impacts with an incredible bang.

Colin Ashford is the owner of W. M. Downing. He is a very quiet man, which is hard to imagine with the amount of noise that is generated by all of the machines there, perhaps it is because of that and the concentration needed, he has very little opportunity to have long conversations. He has worked in the Quarter for 54 years. William Downing started the firm in 1905, I would judge from the age of some of the machines and the premises, that there must have been a pre-existing firm that William Downing probably acquired. Colin's father started working for Downing then, eventually running the business before taking it over completely. Colin started as a die-sinker in 1956, and he wished he had acquired the hand die-sinking skills that his father possessed. He currently employs four, I was able to meet two, Robert Douglas who has worked there for 40 years and Lewis Ashford (Colin's brother).

They produce a vast quantity of pieces, hundreds, and hundreds a day, as Colin informs me it used to be thousands when they employed more, and when the demand was higher. They have rack after rack of dies, dating back years and years, which cover every extent of available wall surface. Some of these dies are for commercial items, many for Masonic items. Often customers

Drop-stamping at W. M. Downing (J. Debney).

buy their dies and leave them there, they have many specifically for cufflinks which have to be produced. They used to provide stampings for Lucas, the 'L' badge at 10,000 per week, but they could not control the quality of the outworkers at that time who were enamelling. At the present time, one of their main orders is to produce the Scottish Premier League medals.

When Colin first began things were very different, for a start the rent was only £500 per year, now he pays £8,000. There were many characters around then, such as the 'one armed car cleaner', also security was not a problem. The Assay Office used to come round with a wicker collecting basket, which they would leave downstairs, and the work would still be there. He does not feel that the changes to the Quarter have been a good thing, in his opinion, the whole character of the Jewellery Quarter has all but disappeared, he believes the apartments are commanding ridiculous prices.

They have been lucky with the HSE and their drop stamps, because they are pre-existing, the HSE have allowed them to keep them and operate them, Robert laughs when he says:

"We are a dying breed. We're dinosaurs!"

The whole environment is so old and friendly, it gives an air of permanence, as if it has always been, and always will be. The walls are obscured by the hundreds of dies, which wait for use, maybe. I enquired how they knew where everything was, because it seemed some of these may not have been used for years. Robert cheerfully chipped back:

"How do you know where everything is in your kitchen?"

Mary Burden is an extremely talented and very hard working woman. She is well respected in the area for her fine enamelling work on precious metal, which is delicate and colourful. She fills the shoes of many a fine enameller who through outworking, maintained all of the larger companies; they use Mary for all of their over-spill work and she produces her own pieces. She has been in her current premises for 23 years, which she took over from another enameller of quality, Eileen Green. Previously, Mary was situated in another place nearby, but as Eileen had to leave because of her husband's ill health, she offered her premises to Mary.

Mary has been working as an enameller since she was 16, she is 64 years of age now. Her mother had been the cook at Marples and Beasley's and had heard of a job going, she told her daughter:

"It would suit you to sit around painting badges all day."

Mary was trained there in the same way, as Brenda and Grace were trained at their first employer's; on silver, first one colour, then two and so on. She was 16 when she started her training, and then she left at 21. She came back for a while when she was 28 and left again to have her son and daughter. As she had a young family and it would be difficult to keep the hours that a full-time job demanded, she decided to go freelance. To get the work she took metal enamelling, for number plates and general badges, but there was always a problem with the metal quality and it would lead to pieces having to be re-done. To make the money through general enamelling she would have to work much harder, and longer hours, so she made up her mind just to do precious metal where the rewards were much greater. She has not looked back since.

All the overflow work from factories such as Fattorini's comes to them. Their main product are cufflinks, which have to be handled

Mary Burden with Donna (J. Debney).

very carefully especially when they are being linished (which is polishing on a continuous wet belt of carborundum paper) as this process can change the colour. They have recently completed five of the medals for the papal visit, which were mounted on the cross and chalice. She calls her husband Bill, 'the filer', he is her man-Friday. When they used to work on general enamelling most items could be polished by the machine, but the delicacy of the items that they do now demands a more 'hands on' approach and Bill is content to file each piece to a high level of finish. While I was there he was cheerfully grinding enamel with a pestle and mortar.

Mary relies on having other pairs of hands to work with her, which is always difficult to find, but particularly now with the new regulations on advertising. She cannot advertise for a 'girl' as that would be breaking guidelines on sexism, however, as many others have stressed girls tend to make the best enamellers. She has Donna working alongside her, who is now 27 and has worked with Mary for 10 years, normally there is another enameller. Unfortunately, at the moment Mary is facing a particular problem, as the young lady that has been with her for 9 years is on maternity leave; by law Mary has to hold her job open.

As a consequence, the two of them and Bill, are working flat-out, including weekends, to fill their orders. Mary's daughter and son have popped in from time to time, to help out but they are finding it quite demanding, so she has to find another girl to train up.

She says that she prefers to get school leavers, who have no experience and know nothing, then she can train them from scratch, with no bad habits. She has tried taking more experienced help on before, who have generally been trained in metal enamelling and think that it is the same. They tend to be too heavy-handed; piling the enamel on; overfilling and filing to save time, and very often, they try to melt the enamel with a blow torch, which will just burn the enamel.

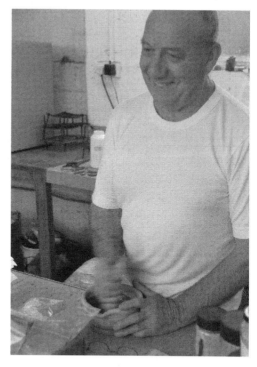

Bill Burden (J. Debney).

My visit was brief as 'time is money' to all the workers such as Mary, and I sensed the urgency of the situation that they are facing presently, with mounting orders, and one member of staff missing. However, I was able to watch for a while, as Donna deftly applied the enamel, and a kiln was heating another batch, while one cooled; Bill with a smile, continued to pound the enamel; and all with the radio playing in the background.

The last of my collection of voices is that of Al Trappe's he is retired now, and although he was not a craftsman, as such, he worked for a firm which provided a very valuable service to the area, and clearly defined the term 'recycling', long before it became fashionable to do so. Alan was born in Ladywood, his father worked for Henry Wiggins and his mother worked for a leather company off Ladypool Road. Later they moved to Kings Heath, where Al attended Wheelers Lane School. When he left there he started in a factory making machined parts for cars, then he was in the forces for his National Service. A chance meeting with a pal in a snooker hall, gave him a job re-laying a driveway for a man who worked at John Betts the smelters.

This man was the foreman at that time, Jimmy Scott, he suggested to Al that 'he could have a job for life' if he went to work there; at that time John Betts (which was a fifth generation firm) was employing 30 people in the refinery. John Betts came to see Al personally and liked him, offering him a job, Al remained with the company for 54 years. He started as a general yard hand, but they taught him to drive and he became one of the collectors.

He would travel all over the country collecting precious metal scrap, such as; gold frames from the Bristol Art Gallery and photographic film from all of the studios, anything that contained precious metal. He often visited the hospitals and collected all the scrap X-ray film, and boxes and boxes of household objects; knives, forks, spoons from all over the country. Eventually, he would spend three or four days a week on the big artic lorry, wheeling 10 to 15 tonnes loads from the Hatton Garden depot for Kodak in London.

After a while, he settled just living and working in Birmingham in the Jewellery Quarter, he describes it as 'one big family'. No one really knew his name was Alan, and most assumed that he was called Albert, but he never minded, although he says that it used to drive his wife mad.

They often had some very unusual collections to make, such as concrete floors, with the silver veins running through them; if it was incinerated to ash then the precious metal could be refined. Of course, they would make regular collections from all of the workshops and factories for the lemel (the off-cuts of gold and swarf) from the benches. The remains would be emptied and melted into a bar and the firms would be paid by weight. Sometimes they would have to collect whole floors, he says that:

> "You could see the wooden floors shining, then you would take the floorboards and burn them. One company who concentrated on diamond cutting had carpets on the floor (Johnson Mathey now Cookson) and they were paid £35,000 some years ago for their carpets."

He remembers the decline starting in the 1970's, he says that many left then because of the escalating rents and prices, and all of the hidden costs of parking, and started working at home. In 1972 he was the victim of a robbery while he was at his home. It was during the time of the power cuts and he often took the keys with him from the works, on this particular occasion he had not. The criminals waited in the communal garage area behind his house, and as he pulled his car in they jumped him, coshed him and tied him up. They were determined to get the keys and drove him around, luckily for Al he was able to kick the door open and run to a strangers house to alert the police.

Towards the end of 1970's, John Betts did suffer a massive robbery, or at least a systematic one from the inside. Where their premises were in

Charlotte Street had a back wall, and £1,000,000 in gold bars went over the wall, in dribs and drabs, but unfortunately, by the time the crime was detected it was too late for the firm to absorb the loss. They moved their place to another quite nearby, but because they had to leave their windows open there were too many complaints about the fumes and the smell, the company ended up relocating again, this time to Oldbury.

In the 1980's he remembers how empty the Quarter became, especially on Sundays. He would still go into his routine of making collections from them all; Charles Green, Deakin and Francis, Len J Millington. Like all of the trades in the area he was never paid very much, which is why like so many, he had to work seven days a week.

Al remembers a lot people that he used to know with affection, he had a particular friendship with Alan Davies (the husband of Brenda from KJD Jewellers) they were best pals; he tells me sadly, that Alan died of cancer at an early age. He remembers his first place in Vyse Street, where the business started at the top and they moved down two, or three places.

In 1983 Al found himself caught in a bit of a bind. Betts was sold to Canning's, and Al was instantly offered a job by the new boss Mr Probert. Steven Betts had already approached Al offering him a directorship in another company. Al found it difficult to choose, but his wife was in failing health, and he knew he needed the money and the security, he chose to stay with Betts, always feeling like he had failed the old owner, but as he says:

"But you have got to live."

This chapter gives a flavour for the diversity of trades and experience that cover the whole of the area, some things continue, but are dying off, such as, stamping and casket making, some things have gone like the heavy refining, and others continue as they are needed like enamelling. There are many other trades that exist now, or have existed previously, that have helped to shape the Quarter and make it the place it is today. There is no doubt that this entwined hidden network is essential for the overall survival of what currently exists, and it would be a shame if it were allowed to dwindle to nothing, much of what makes the character would die with it.

Chapter 13

CHASING A STORY
– GIL BROADWAY

W. H. Darby Ltd.

This is not so much a history of one particular company, in this case W. H. Darby, it is the tale of how one fine craftsman now finds himself working there. One theme that has been drawn out during this study of the Jewellery Quarter is how so many different companies have become tangled, through closure, merger and acquisition. Gil Broadway who is the main subject of this chapter, is one such individual, who has moved jobs on occasions and then fallen into another position as the original company that he worked for Vaughton's was bought up by Darby's. I have met many around the Quarter, who work under the roofs of other companies that have acquired their own small business or their parent company, that they have been working for; they have continued doing what they have always done, and simply been moved to a new place. It seems to be an accepted state of affairs for most, as it appears to have been something that it has always happened, throughout the history of the Quarter.

Steve Hobbis the managing director of W. H. Darby informs me that he acquired the firm from David Hepinstall who was married to the last Darby, Sally. Steve runs Darby's as very much a family concern, with his wife, daughter and son-in-law all working in the main offices. Darby's specialise in medals and trophies and were established in 1886, their original business was die-sinking, and carving their hand-made dies which then produced the embossed images through stamping. David had acquired three other companies in the last fifteen years before Steve took over the firm. One of these being a company of a similar nature with a longer heritage, Vaughton's. Vaughton's was established in 1819, and from the census returns the Vaughton family has several branches operating in the Jewellery Quarter. One Philip Vaughton of Lozells Road, died in 1863, at approximately 61 years of age, he is recorded as a 'jeweller in gold' and left an estate just under £4,000. Edward Vaughton is listed in the 1861 census as living in Warstone Lane, he had a wife and a few small children at that time, and is recorded as a 'manufacturer of jewellery, employing 6 boys'. Another Philip Vaughton is recorded in the 1901 census as a 'medalist', he was 34 years old at that time and living with his father Thomas (74 years of age) and his wife Rosina; Thomas is described as gold jeweller. So there is no doubt that the family had very strong connections in and around the area.

A typical chain of office.

Vaughton's built their reputation on the manufacture of medals, regalia, and chains of office. They were renowned for the high quality of their workmanship and their attention to detail, to such an extent that their work was sought out. There are examples of three of their medals held in the Victoria and Albert Museum. In 1890 the original English Football League Cup was manufactured by Vaughton's and was used up until 1992. In 1908, Vaughton's made the Olympic Commemorative Medallions and in 1911 started manufacturing the Football Association medals.

Gil Broadway who is 69 years of age, came with Vaughton's, when it subsumed into Darby's. He is an engraver of some merit, and commands a considerable amount of respect within the company. He is a fine example of the workers who were trained well by others and experienced much of the change in the Quarter of the last fifty years. He has a lineage of family that have traditionally worked in this and associated fields, that goes back four generations, and he has had a very varied career.

Gil's ancestor, which was either his great-great grandfather or his great-great uncle, was a writer of letters for Birmingham Corporation for letters patent. These were the official letters issued by the local government, which were beautifully ornate, and informed the reader of decrees or laws, or granted authority, or title. Gil considers that he has inherited his talent for handwriting, and I would say his accuracy within his own field.

His grandfather, William Broadway started a firm of silverware manufacturers in Spencer Street, he eventually had all of his own sons working for him. The art of die-sinking is related to engraving, but it is a much heavier process, requiring the die-sinker to carve into a block of steel, and of course, in reverse – the negative of the positive. There were four sons; Gil (senior), Roland, Gil's father and Richmond, who all took their place in the family firm. Although, Gil's father 'felt like a change' in the 30's and went to Canada and proceeded to work his way across, before returning and working for the firm once more.

The family were doing particularly well, and managed to move from Hall Green out to leafy Marston Green. This required the boys to have

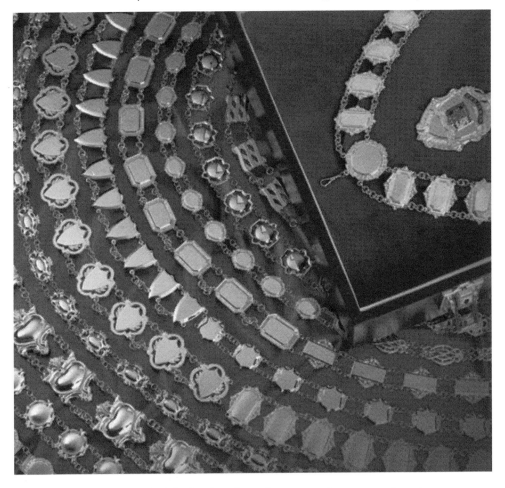

A display of miniature shields for the winner's name to be engraved each year.

motorcycles. Gil was born during the war, his father volunteered to join the Royal Engineers, but was refused because of being in the metal trades; he was in a reserved occupation. He told Gil later that he spent a great deal of time fire watching during that war, and he thought he was making parts for Sterling Bombers but no one ever actually told them. On Gil's birth certificate his father's occupation is given as 'a viewer of aircraft parts', although, he was a silversmith by trade. Gil confirms that the Quarter 'took a hell of a pounding during the war'.

As his parents lived near to Droitwich, when Gil left school his very first job was making gloves in Worcester, which had been his mother's trade. Then he joined W. B. Broadway the family firm, which at that time were producing items such as dressing table sets. He was trained

Gil Broadway at work (J. Debney).

up as an engraver, he thinks now because the family wanted him 'on call' for their engraving work, however, Gil had other plans and decided to branch out on his own. He reflects now and considers that he would have liked to have been more involved in the design side, as he had a particular interest in fine art.

It was when he started in his first position in the mid-1950's out of the family concern, that he had a chance to extend his talents. He started working for a company called James Harrison, there he trained alongside an old chap called Reuben Hathaway (a cousin from the firm Hathaway and Murreyman). While he was there he was able to attend the School of Jewellery; he enjoyed that experience to be able to be more creative, and he says that most of the prizes that he won were not for engraving but for the design work that he did. He was able to specialise considerably in heraldry which he particularly enjoyed; it honed his skills, and he benefited from the teaching of 'one of the best' lecturers there – Mr Colin Toon. He was also able to practise his engraving to a high degree, and was able to draw an

A display of Rotary regalia.

arabesque line in a particular style. Gil had a fascination for all things medieval and was always interested in church and ecclesiastic work.

After a few years there, he moved further, to a company called Turner and Simpson, they used to do a lot of work for the Crown Agents; the Crown agency serviced the whole of the British Empire, they were the body that would procure all of the goods and services; in this case, it was producing the dies and other items for embossed papers and enamelled regalia. He worked alongside Ian Campbell the famous Scottish folk singer, who had come from the printing industry where he had engraved blocks for printing; Ian had two famous Birmingham sons, Robin and Ali from the pop group UB40.

Turner and Simpson had many women employed in 'making up' and they had an enamelling shop next door, which was staffed by women. The supervisor was a woman called Miss Pearse, she turned out to be the cousin of the Irish patriot Patrick Pearse who was executed following the Irish uprising of 1916. Most of the places of work for Turner and Simpson were in and around St Paul's Square.

Gil then moved on briefly to Thomas Fattorini, where he worked mainly in a design capacity. He remembers 'Mr Tom and his vintage car'. He revealed to me that it was the only job that he was ever sacked from, 'through no fault of my own, may I add'. From there he went to work at Deakin and Francis for a number of weeks. Where to Gil's surprise, he found his great Uncle Tom (his grandmother's brother) was working there as a jeweller and silversmith, though their paths never crossed.

At that point Gil tried what many of his contemporaries of the time ventured into, taking a 'bench for while' of his own as an outworker. He said that he enjoyed the freedom but 'he could not be bothered with the paperwork'. By now it was the late 1960's and Gil sought refuge back in employment for another firm, this time it was A J Harris, there he stayed for a few years where he did 'some lovely small cast charms'. While he was at A J Harris, he used to help out an old gentleman (Mr Lee) who worked for Vaughton's with his engraving work; he was able to do lettering and heraldic work and enhance the design work that they wanted. At the beginning of the 1970's, he joined Vaughton's – due to the merger of A J Harris after Mr Lee passed away. Gil had made himself indispensable to the company because of the vast range of skills that he could offer, in his words:

> "In this trade it pays to be adaptable. I cannot set stones, at least not very well. The one thing that I cannot do, that I really wish that I could is chasing."

He worked happily for Vaughton's for twenty-seven years, it was obviously his most stable and content period, he has been moved again twelve years ago, when Darby's acquired Vaughton's, but fundamentally his job has not changed. He tells me that he was 16, when he came into the trade, he has now been working for fifty years. More than anything else, Gil has to carry on working for financial reasons. He does enjoy his job greatly,

A flagon with decorative chasing.

but believes that there should be a chance to enjoy some sort of retirement in the long run, he hopes to achieve that by working part-time eventually.

Gil possesses a wealth and diverseness of skills yet has never been approached by local schools to come in and work alongside young people. One of the aspects of this book which I am very close to professionally, is the encouragement of young people towards working in the trades which are dying through the lack of interest now shown by youngsters towards them. There are many like Gil, Ron, Bill and David, who are incredibly talented and devoted to what they do, there appears to be a loss of opportunity here which the various business concerns could capitalise from by exploiting the

Finished municipal regalia.

service and enthusiasm of these craftsmen towards forging links with education at Secondary School level.

His trade as an engraver, has very few dangers. He does have visitors coming in to see him work from time, to time, he always gets asked the same question, has he ever cut himself? He replies that it does not happen very much now, years of experience have taught him not to; it tends to be the index finger of his left hand that takes the punishment. Gil is not comfortable using a power engraver, he was trained in the old ways. He prefers the control and originality that hand engraving ensures; to him, all the designs that tend to originate through computer methods have 'lost their style'.

The size and complexity of each piece of work determines the time that it takes to engrave, and consequently, his rate of output; he has just finished a piece of work which was a replacement jewel and chain for the Kingston-Upon-Hull Council. The original, he describes as 'a beautiful piece of work dating from 1857, with some elaborate chasing'. The council had decided that it was time to retire the original to a bank vault, and commissioned Darby's to produce a replica. Gil has produced the finished engraving to look as much like the original as possible, despite that there are very different techniques involved, this took four weeks to complete. His next task that he has been given is to work on a chain of office from Belfast, which requires all the many shamrocks that are engraved on it, to be deepened to take enamel; Gil estimated that this might take him a day or two to

Left: Ornate polished spoons. Right: A medal for Rotary International.

complete. Some of the Masonic jewels which he has to work on can take only a few hours, which would mean that he could produce several finished pieces in one day. He finds that some days pass quickly and some not:

"When the job goes well the time goes well."

Gil is full of many interesting and witty tales from his working life, these reflect his time of life and the different times of the Quarter. When he started in the Quarter he was not termed as an apprentice but as his trainee, and he told me that the 'boss' at that time who was an old chap who had served in the First World War used to tell him that on his indenture (the boss) it read, that he was not allowed to carry ale for his master.

Gil's hours then were from 8 o'clock in the morning until 6 o'clock in the evening, and with the overtime that he would do, he did not usually finish until 8 o'clock at night. When he was young high jinks were the order of the day, he once got himself into some trouble with his tom-foolery. He used to use 'buffsticks' a small polishing implement that was employed to polish burrs. He remembers, that he and his young colleagues used to take great delight, when they were bored firing them across the workshop, until one day Gil got it wrong and it landed in a pan of diamonds which scattered across the floor. He says:

"Holy hell broke out then! I was very lucky that the setter didn't go to the boss!"

These boisterous activities were sometime very dangerous as Gil revealed to me. When he had his time at James Harrison, he worked with a lad who had just come out of the army, and had brought some souvenirs back with him, including a small amount of some sort of explosive. One of the less savoury practices of the men who worked in the Quarter (as most did not smoke) was a communal snuff tin, which would be passed about. Often the call went round from some old chap or other:

"Reuben! Send the kid down with the box."

One day, the ex army lad decided to play a trick on one of the men. The toilets were across a yard, with doors that did not reach the ground. Sometimes a humorous notice would be pinned on the bottom of the door 'beware of limbo dancers'. This particular chap, used to have a habit of vanishing off to the toilet for long periods of time, and very often would fall asleep in there. On one of these visits, the lads noticed that the old man had not returned, and a shout went up:

"The old so-and-so's asleep on the khazi! Quick, get the grenade."

The grenade was made out of one of the old snuff tins, with explosive secured in, and a short fuse from a model Jetex (jet motor) kit attached. Quite an effective, if a little deadly bomb. Gil says that someone lit it and threw it, unfortunately not judging the angle as accurately as they should, and probably without the intention to do what happened next. It bounced off one of the walls in the courtyard and went under the door and then there was a loud bang. The perpetrators disappeared promptly and resumed their seats in the workshop, the visions of complete innocence. Minutes later, a somewhat dishevelled and disturbed old gentleman appeared and let fly:

"Percy them bloomin' kids are throwin' fireworks!"

The error of their ways was pointed out to them, but it was not the last explosion to be heard in that workshop, there was also the time of the exploding, home-made ginger beer!

Gil, like others, misses the old Quarter when the character was still there, when high-jinks could happen because the health and safety culture had not taken over. He remembers fondly the old back-to-backs in Pope Street and 'Bullpits' (where they made Swan Kettles) as he used to walk to Turner and Simpson, 'Just like Kathleen Dayus says'. He misses his old work pals, and he has tried over the years to keep in touch with 'many an old comrade' who has left.

He would like to have aspired to the same occupation as that of his ancestor and been a maker of letters patent. His love for history is a real passion and he particularly likes to visit old churches, a hobby he intends to indulge in once he does finally retire:

"It would be nice to retire. The boss said 'you wouldn't like to sit around all day and make model aeroplanes?' – yes, I would...well not all the time."

Retirement is something he looks forward to greatly. He has friends who share his love of churches. He likes to go and look at the craftsmanship and try and work out, how the tombs were carved, and how the brass plates were engraved. As he pointed out to me, the tools and the processes have remained the same essentially:

> "They were probably using the tools that I use in the 15th century and the 14th century and the middle ages... Albrecht Durer used the same tools that I use every day, square and diamond section, cut to a facet for fine lines, flat if you want to chisel the background out."

He still has another passion which he enjoys greatly, that of building working model planes that fly.

The saddest tale that Gil relayed to me was about how little someone of his skill and craftsmanship could hope to command as a salary for the long years that he worked in the Quarter. When he started he was on £2.50 per week, even when he was at Vaughton's all those years later he was still only earning £80 per week. Gil lived with his parents all of his life until they died, as he says it was not because he did not have a chance to venture into married life, it was always the money that prohibited him:

> "It was the reason that I could not marry because I couldn't afford to. It broke my engagement, I don't blame her, I mean I couldn't give her the life that I would have wanted to."

Despite this sad event, which has ultimately shaped the course of Gil's life, he remains a remarkably cheerful person, with plenty to say, and a passion for all things historical. When he does retire, which will no doubt be in the next few years, he will be a sad loss to his trade and a great loss to the Quarter, as another of the characters will leave.

Chapter 14

THE SPIN OF SILVERWARE

L. J. Millington

Few silverware companies from the last forty years have survived the various up and downs of the economy over that period, never mind the Bunker Hunt scam, which practically wiped out the market for silver goods during that time. Those that did, had to take serious actions in order to continue to exist, as many chose to get out while they still could. For L. J. Millington their good fortune was being a young company in the first instance, with a son eager to prove his worth and keep the family business surviving, this required breaks with traditions; whether, that be the way by which silverware companies such as theirs had traditionally done their business, combined with a risky move from the confined safety of the Quarter itself. This is the story of one firm's survival through all the adversity, by adopting new strategies and diversifying into new methods of using the internet to create enterprising markets for their point of sale.

Leonard John Millington is by trade a metal spinner, and very good at what he does. By the late 1950's he had specialised in silver; this foresighted action coincided with the birth of the industry in silverware spinning, so he was able to capitalise on his skill and his place in the market. In the early 1960's he was employed by a firm called Sanders and McKenzie, where he honed his skills in silver, and gained as many contacts as he could. He was a very enterprising man, for despite having a very young family – his son Steve had been born in 1962 and was followed two years later by his younger brother – he made the leap to set up his own business at the end of that decade. It was quite a revolutionary thing for someone to do, because although he set up business in a workshop 6 feet square in Hockley Street, he had bigger ambitions and was already visualising a much larger business concern.

From a very young age, Steve's memories are fixed on the Quarter. He can vividly remember his brother and him being picked up from school by his mother; he recollects getting the bus to the Jewellery Quarter and:

Left: A paper weight. Right: A baby's rattle (images by the kind courtesy of L. J. Millington Ltd.).

"climbing the rickety old stairs."

The most evocative memories to him are the same as many, including myself, they are those of smells. Often the smell of something that was most enjoyable, or that you have achieved the greatest satisfaction in, are those that evoke the most enormous feelings of well-being within us. There is no doubt that workshops hold a distinctive smell; whether that be the combination of engine oils and grease, or the heat of metal which is having some process applied to it, or just the well-aged floor, ingrained with its dirt from times gone by. There is something that makes me feel at 'home' so I empathise with Steve when he remarks that to him it was probably the verdigris of spinning:

"and you think oh yeah…and it takes you back."

By the early 1970's, Leonard had moved to Pitsford Street, a road that runs adjacent to the cemetery. He remained a 'one-man band' at that point preferring to rely on the army of 'outworkers' around the area, to complete the various items that, by then he was making to order, as it was known at that time a form of 'cluster networking':

"You can't do everything; you use engravers, chasers, polishers and engine turners for different things."

At 15, Steve did not consider himself to be academically clever, but he was naturally gifted with his hands; he would have had plenty of practical experience over the years when visiting his father's workshop. He was considered to possess good commonsense and an ability to communicate extremely effectively. He had an ambition to be (of all things) a lumberjack; not that there is much call for that activity in the West Midlands area. He remembers actually visiting his schools career office and discussing his future plans, and rather than deriding him as many might have, he was told he would have to go to Scotland, and he 'didn't fancy that', it was at that point that it dawned on him that 'there were not enough trees in Sutton Park'.

A candelabra (by the kind courtesy by of L. J. Millington Ltd.).

His father made him the offer to train him as a metal spinner, in their shed at home; with Leonard needing all the hours he had to earn his living in the Quarter (and Steve still at school) it would have been impossible for him to have been trained there. As this 'home' training started a while before he finished school, he was able to supplement his pocket money in the late 70's by doing some metal spinning jobs for his father. As soon as he finished school in 1978, Leonard put Steve to work alongside Kevin the polisher (who still works for the company now). Leonard encouraged both the lads to attend the School of Jewellery, the idea was that they were to attend one day a week, but unfortunately at that time the School, was offering a very limited range of courses; such as, gem setting and horology, which were inappropriate to the business that they were now working in. Steve settled into learning the trade alongside his father, and the outworkers that were being called on, and spent six years building his own contacts.

By 1984, Leonard became convinced that the company was being limited by the small number of people that were employed; they could never take on larger orders, or multiple orders, as they were restricted by the number of pairs of hands available to carry out all of the necessary tasks. It was at that point, that Steve was able to persuade his father to let him come off the bench and move into management, so that he could look to developing the company and helping it grow, by exploring ways of raising the turnover. Leonard was somewhat sceptical, but allowed Steve to:

"realise the opportunities that were available."

Steve was somewhat limited in his business experience at that time, but fortunately for him, the British Jewellery Association had started to run a suite of courses which were just right for that purpose. He took a particular interest in marketing, and along with a friend who was from a sales background, Steve was able to apply what he had been learning to begin to build the business up. It required Steve to spend a considerable amount of

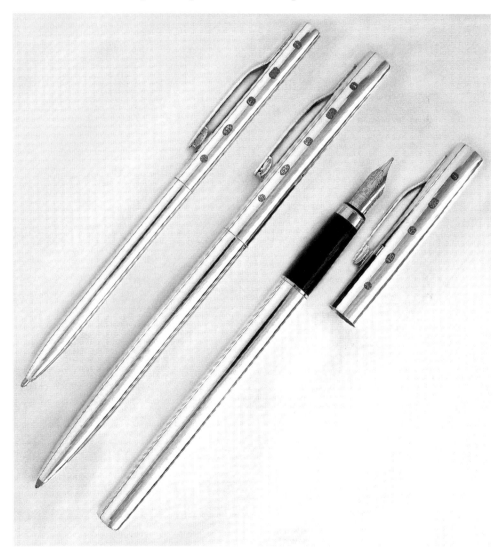

A set of pens by Jo Mason (by the kind courtesy by of L. J. Millington Ltd.).

time on the phone, to begin to network effectively and open the doors to opportunities previously unexplored. This created considerable friction between himself and Leonard during this six month period regarding the raised phone bill, but the constant bombardment of the wholesalers and other marketing opportunities began to bear fruit.

They discovered their first major shortcoming was that of their rather antiquated premises of the late Victorian/Edwardian age. The original workshops of the Quarter had been private houses that had been converted over a period of a hundred years, or so, into a warren of workshops; these premises usually grew as the individual business concerns grew, but never to any great extent, always being limited by the physical capacity of each of these places. These 'rabbit warrens' expanded, as newer enterprise occupied the premises left by departing businesses, consequently, ending up with a 'hotch potch' of rooms, with ramshackle interconnecting corridors and too many stairs.

By the early 1990's, L. J. Millington were occupying the whole of one such building and were employing nine workers. Father and son, decided it would be necessary to make some major refurbishments to the premises to make them more fit for purpose, and they made an approach to the landlord to buy the property outright. Unfortunately, their landlord was intransigent and would not sell. Not to be deterred by this, the company decided that they had to find some suitable premises that they could buy.

The Quarter was under the threat of developers during this period, it was a property frenzy due to the financial and business sector moving outwards from Newhall Street engulfing St Paul's, and any premises which were available were being snapped up at ridiculous prices; others who were considering retiring were finding men in suits turning up with suitcases of money in order to gain a lucrative purchase. There was simply nothing available within the confines of what was then designated as the Quarter.

As has so often been the case in this area, the misfortune of one firm often becomes the good fortune of another. S. J. Rose a well established silversmiths and goldsmiths, went into liquidation, their property was slightly out of the area, bordering on Lozells, in Nursery Road. However, it was the ideal opportunity to secure a purpose-built building, for their own silversmithing business. They then had to play the waiting game for the property to go on the market, as soon as it did, they immediately made an offer and bought it.

Their timing of the purchase was a little flawed being October 1993, and the impending Christmas market bearing down on them, this meant that it

Silver and crystal match striker and a christening cup (images by the kind courtesy of L. J. Millington Ltd.).

would be impossible for them to move during that period, but they were able to focus their attentions on streamlining the production process, to make the most effective use of their new space, when they eventually did move in. They also had to work harder and longer during that time, to build up enough stock and fill enough orders to cope with the six-week planned down-time to facilitate and complete the move.

What faced them on 3rd January 1994, was floor-to-ceiling boxes, nothing in any sort of sense or order; it was a mammoth task to unpack and organise, but within six months they had got back into full production and the future looked very bright indeed. Steve looks back on that time with great nostalgia, it was a dream and they had secured it, it truly was a golden period for the firm, from the mid 90's until 2002/03. During those years they were employing 15 people and nothing looked as if it could possibly go wrong.

Indeed, they had reached new heights, the company had achieved an annual turnover of three quarters of a million, but they knew that they had over-extended themselves. Once a company that has been manageable reaches a certain size it becomes unmanageable and the stress that is then generated, causes the whole thing to implode if action is not taken before it gets out of control. Steve and Leonard took the much-needed decision to downsize. The pressure on all aspects of their lives was just becoming too great. As they had made a conscious decision to do so rather than a

Paul spinning metal (J. Debney).

reactionary one, they knew they could manage the contraction through natural wastage, it was the only way to ensure the sustainability of the company. It is true to say that the events of that decade really have precipitated the present economic downturn. This in turn has set many more challenges at their door, each they are meeting head-on and trying wherever possible to plan strategically. They are the first to admit that the last few years have been a 'real struggle', they are not alone in this assessment, there are many in the Quarter who could retell the same tale of the pain of recession and they have survived by wit or luck, more often, than shrewd business judgment.

L. J. Millington now directly employs six personnel. Leonard is 82 and still works, and his wife Mary does the books. Steve's cousin Paul joined the company two years after he did and is employed as a spinner, now with 30 years experience. Kevin the polisher who Steve worked alongside in the early years, is still employed by the firm. David is the youngest and has been with the firm for approximately 10 years, he mainly carries out soldering work. They also sublet workshop premises to a designer/silversmith, Adam. The company is now a manageable size and easier to oversee. Their primary process is spinning and through this they produce a range of items, from coasters to mustard pots, candle sticks, photograph frames, even silver lids for Marmite pots.

They have continued to cut their cloth to fit, but this has not stopped some timely expansion into other markets and a certain amount of diversification within the area of sales. They have expanded their products through an acquisition of William Manton Ltd, manufacturers of silver pens. The two companies had tended to work on parallel tracks. When William Manton fell into difficulties, and subsequently became available for purchase Steve kept a watchful eye, and eventually acquired the firm and their business interests. It was a worthwhile exercise, once the firm shut three years ago, it took one lorry to move the products from Caroline Street, with that came Paul, the sole Manton employee, who continues to make the Manton pens.

Millington's are very conscious of all of the good firms that they have known that have not survived and gone to the wall. They take comfort in the fact that they have always managed to diversify to seek new avenues to develop, and this they believe is what has kept them in business. Rather than falling into the trap that so many have, of sticking rigidly to a dogmatic tradition of having always done things in a certain way in business. Their philosophy has always been to enhance their core business whenever that has been possible; they have even acquired an engraving business in recent times.

As long as fifteen years ago they had aspirations towards the retail sector and could see real potential of finding a route into some sort of direct selling, this was when the internet was still in its infancy, and ecommerce had not been developed. They realised with this avenue for sales they could reduce their own overheads very significantly. Millington's were one of the first companies in the Quarter to develop an ecommerce arm to their business, launching in 2001, Silverpuresilver.com; this investment has resulted in another strong income source and they have since created further impressive margins by personalising items. They knew that the major investment would be the improvement of their packaging, something that a direct customer would expect as part of the service. Steve views the advent of ecommerce as a quality filter, for those who were not able to adapt and adopt new methods, as inevitably, these short-sighted companies have been unable to compete against those that do.

Originally, they operated as all firms had in the Jewellery Quarter, through the wholesale buying network which was controlled by middlemen, however, this did remove any need to consider marketing or public perception. A middleman would arrive at their door, make an order for so many of each particular product, pay a cheque direct to the firm and then leave. All of their orders were operated in this way, and then the trusted middlemen that they had worked with for years began to leave and were replaced by others who did not have the same appeal to the big retail outlets. To the extent that one rather large point of sale, contacted Millington's directly and asked to deal with them directly; however, the expectations would be that packaging must be to a high standard and the overall presentation was now the concern of the manufacturer. Steve reflects that despite the further erosion of margins, that they are still in business, he knew that it was necessary to follow the strategy of 'adapt or die'.

They have developed the markets of 'drop shipping', where other internet companies now trade on their products. Their own contract is to supply the product which has been ordered online through this third-party supplier, and then ship directly to the customer's door. The third party supplier, never has any contact with the product, or the shipping of that product from the supplier to the customer. This process of internet sales has become a very lucrative market.

Carrying stock is a notion from history for most manufacturing firms. Those that did, have now moved over to the policy of 'just in time'; no longer are materials housed in big warehouses which cost overheads, of atmospheric and environmental controls, heating and lighting, manpower to staff. Now things are ordered in, to arrive on production lines just as needed, and at the end of the process wherever possible shipped directly out to the customer. Historically, precious metal bullion cannot be held because of the weekly fluctuations in the bullion market, what could be £400 a kilo one week could be £350 the next, and during the time of Bunker Hunt, items made, became too valuable to sell (not that anyone could have afforded to buy them).

Steve has witnessed the demise of my own industry, glass, firsthand. An industry which was plagued by old-fashioned practice and dogma, those that worked in it were waiting for a mass-extinction like tired dinosaurs. It was a practical trade, the 'gaffers' were old timers, most would not have not known how to turn on a computer, never mind use one. When large outlets started to request orders by BACS transfer; boxes to be bar coded and correctly labelled; the small glass industry of glasshouses in Stourbridge simply caved in under the bureaucracy; it finished all of those that were still hanging on and that were at that time only just surviving. Much the same did happen to many of the old firms in the Quarter, those that have survived have had to change and apply new methods.

Steve does have a problem with the education and training available. He is concerned that the silversmithing establishments in the UK place too much emphasis on the craft aspects of the trade, leaving graduates with fantastic skills upon graduation but very little or no knowledge of how to survive in, what is a very difficult industry to make a living from. He prefers 'in-house' training schemes (all Steve's employees over the years have been trained in-house), but these schemes have not been available for many years, the last being the 'YTS' the Youth Training Scheme of the 1980's. It does now appear however, that there are new 'in-house' training initiatives in place, funded and managed through local government –

Dave silver soldering (J. Debney).

although well received by industry in general – Steve fears it might be too little too late to have a long term effect on the industry in Birmingham.

His thoughts as to the future are not those of further expansion, or even passing the mantle to the next generation. He considers that too many of the once closely held British Markets have now gone to the Far East where overheads and margins are particularly low. In his opinion, the average UK manufacturer can simply no longer compete on price alone. Volume producers in the UK and particularly in the Jewellery Quarter are in serious decline. The only companies that are attempting to challenge this position are those that have a niche market, but as fast as those markets are enabled and become profitable the designs are cloned and produced overseas.

Steve is also aggrieved by the disadvantages heaped upon British Jewellers and Silversmiths by changes to the Hallmarking Act during the last decade. Prior to the change, items of jewellery and silver imported into the UK were hallmarked with an 'import' mark, distinguishing the item from British made products. He feels that European legislation swept away the requirement for a 'level playing field'. This allowed manufacturers from all over the world to send items into the UK for sale complete with a British hallmark as though it were 'made in Britain'. His words reflect his obvious concerns:

"The Assay Office must have been quietly delighted by this move, the resultant increase in the number of items being hallmarked through the Assay Office must have been great business for them and it does now seem rather bizarre to me that although the Assay Offices were introduced hundreds of years ago to protect the consumer, their role nowadays seems very different, as the consumer has more idea where his block of cheese from the supermarket has come from, than the £1000 wedding ring that his wife wears on her finger."

Despite all of this, Steve remains optimistic that there is still work to be had, and where it is they will find it and make it work for them. He is a realist who has seen the best and worst of times in the Quarter's recent history. He will not artificially speed up the end of L. J. Millington's, rather manage the business as the markets dictate. A very sensible strategy, given the volatile nature of the current economic climate. As Steve wryly notes in the meantime:

"You have got to cut your cloth to fit... and then use ecommerce!"

Chapter 15

BOOM AND BUST
– ONE MAN'S STORY

Steven Green

There are many around the Quarter that could testify to the precariousness of the trade that they work in, especially, in the times that they have witnessed over the last thirty years. Thirty years ago the markets crashed due to monopoly and manipulation, this was followed by a relative boom time, and once again, a global crisis has caused the jewellery trade to descend into a recessionary abyss. During the 1980's, many watched as the area became a ghost town, when not a soul was to be seen outside working hours. Company after company, suffered near total collapse as the Bunker Hunt brothers tried to corner the silver markets globally, and quite a few did lose everything. Those that could diversify, or had an niche market to exploit, did so, those that only had a silver trade on a small scale watched helplessly, as their whole livelihoods were wiped out over night. One man who ran a very successful business then, still remains in the Quarter, and works as an outworker now, mainly self-taught, he has seen the wealth and the poverty that his business can generate. He comes from a family that is at least six generations of success in the Quarter, and his cousin still runs the successful parent company.

Steven Green is an enigma in every sense of the word. He could be described as eccentric, especially, when he greets you in his workshop, which is an eclectic jumble of all sorts of tools and materials that he has squirreled away, in a room he rents from Deakin and Francis. He concentrates on the restoration of silver dressing table sets now, and when he has time, has a line of his own, which has a contemporary rustic quality, very reminiscent of Scandinavian silver. He is very well educated and deeply knowledgeable, he loves to travel, particularly in China. He is a Guardian of the Birmingham Assay Office, with a strong opinion as to the place of that institution within the context of the modern Quarter.

I had shared much of the family history with his cousin Tom Green, when I visited the company Charles Green. Steven has a slightly different slant on everything as might be expected, but there is no family rivalry as such, in fact, the cousins are very good friends. They have discovered a mutual love for trying to uncover as much of their common family history between them.

Steven informs me that he is of the opinion that there was a Charles Green working in the Quarter in the early 1800's, as the indenture of George Coley in 1824, the apprentice to Charles Green (which Tom holds) confirms this. He believes that it was similar to other family stories from that date, a migration post the Napoleonic Wars to seek productive trade. Steven is also particularly keen to investigate the Captain Cook connection further, the Charles Green who repaired the sextant, following the incident in Tahiti, must have had astronomy/horology knowledge to be able to make an accurate restoration. All Tom knows to date is that he died in Jakarta.

Steven and Tom, share a common great-grandfather, it was he who had a large family of four sons, it is safe to say, that although the business was successful, that in itself could not hope to support all of them. Despite their great-grandfather being responsible for many a pro-active development of the Quarter when it was in a time of deep recession, it is said that he was not the best of businessmen. However, he was one of the main figures of influence in the launch of the Birmingham Jewellers' and Silversmiths' Association, followed by the foundation of the School of Jewellery; subsequently, he sat on the Chairman of the Guardians for the Birmingham Assay Office, as well as being involved with the City Council. Tom's other grandfather Tom Millward Banks, assumed the role of Chairman of the Birmingham Jewellers' and Silversmiths' Association later.

Steven now sits as one of the Guardian's, a role he treasures, however, because of his previous concerns within the trade he used to have to follow very strict rules when attending meetings there. A Guardian with vested interests is not allowed to see what their rivals are doing, and he had to be led through the office with a velvet blindfold on. Steven has heard it said, that his great-grandfather was such a bad businessman, that he could have been led without a blindfold and it would have made very little difference.

Charles Green and Son had their premises in Augusta Street, he expected 'the boys' (his son's and workers in their 30's and 40's) at the factory at 8.15am, however, he would never arrive on time and he would have the keys. Additionally, he would allow no one else to deal with the post, which would be waiting for his arrival:

"Whoever controls the post control the day."

He would allow them to take small amounts of work home in their 'skins', but it was never enough to keep them actively employed until he turned up, the majority of all the work was retained in the safe, this would lead to 'mumbles and grumbles'. Obviously, his tardiness would cause many problems, having not turned up until at least two hours later and not allowing his sons to deal with the business at hand, not only created problems for the business itself, but created family tensions which would eventually lead to rifts.

The story passed down, is that Steven's grandfather decided to break from the family in 1903, the exact reason is not clear, but he made an agreement with his father, not to go into direct competition with the parent company. His father paid him the sum of one hundred pounds, and Steven's grandfather set himself up as Charles S. Green and Co. Ltd, dealing in silver rather than gold. There was also a rumour circulating that the family had to pay off a large gambling debt that amounted to £5,000 the equivalent of between one and two million today, and although his grandfather did have a history of gambling it is unlikely he could have amassed debts of that nature. It is an accusation that is strongly denied by Steven.

Whatever the truth, there is no doubt that his grandfather was determined to prove himself a businessman and although now extremely poor, he went after his dream in earnest. He had an added advantage to be ably assisted by his wife, who was Winifred Carr, whose photograph frames are widely sought after these days. She had won the gold medal at the School of Art in 1896; the last year in the life of William Morris.

Steven's grandparents rented a very small place (one up and one down) in Pemberton Street. Charles subsidised their impoverished state, by selling off his furniture, including his dining chairs to the man who would later become his brother-in-law. Charles then assembled a range of ladies toilet-ware which were all factored. He would eventually set his telegraphic address as 'tolietbirmingham', whereas, the parent company was 'signetbirmingham'.

It appears that Charles junior was able to capitalise on the goodwill of many in the Quarter, who had sympathy because of his perceived isolation from his family, and others who just revelled in family rifts and trouble. Within two years he had gone from absolutely nothing, and close to dire poverty, to clearing £5,000. It was enough to build a very successful life, even if he only actually made money in two further years. His business grew tremendously and they were able to move to St Paul's Square and rent a factory. By the time the Great War came he was able to turn a profit in 1911 and again in 1914; the demand for photographic frames throughout those years was extremely high.

Much later the family were hit by tragedy while they were still living in Pemberton Street. Steven's father was the second son, being named Michael Pemberton Green, in honour of the money that had been made while the family had lived there. Unfortunately, the eldest son Steven, contracted 'cancer of the bone' and died at the age of 20. Unfortunately, Steven's grandmother never got over the agony of losing her eldest boy and 'took to the bottle', and his grandfather 'took a mistress'. Charles had also developed a taste for the high life, racing in particular, and used to be regularly seen at race meetings accompanied by his other woman, Mrs Brown. As Steven jokes:

"Mr Green took Mrs Brown to the races."

At this point, he was able to own a couple of race horses and a Rolls Royce, his racing colours were sea green, a very apt play on his company name and his.

That is not to say that there were not difficult times, the Great Depression of the 1920's were tragic for most, but Charles had so much personal wealth it made very little difference to his lavish lifestyle. Steven told me that his grandfather's answer to particular downswing in 1929, was not to go hunting once a week, as had been the case, but to go three times a week, as 'there was no point going into the factory'. He was not the only family member to adopt this somewhat laissez-faire attitude, another uncle bought some salmon fishing to fill his empty hours, as Steven remarks, 'this is something that one would definitely keep quiet about these days'.

By the time of World War Two broke out, Steven's father was at loggerheads with his own father, probably regarding his 'carrying on' and after a monumental fallout, left to fight. Tom's father was also an active serviceman and badly injured, and subsequently captured at Dunkirk by the Germans. Steven's grandfather, had his racehorses shot, and married his housekeeper (the mistress was retired). Tom's father was eventually repatriated, and because of the extent of his injuries was granted a 'desk job' for the duration of the war.

Steven's grandfather had made his money during a time when taxation and the general cost of living had been extremely low, as a consequence of this, he was able to live very well for the duration of his life; in comparison to many other businesses in the Quarter at that time, which were not as successful, or at least, not as successful as they first appeared to be.

The workshop of Steven Green (J. Debney).

As with all of the other firms in the area, the war had a devastating effect on trade. The Total War Economy that had been proposed by Bevin in order to keep pace with the need for arms and armaments, meant that every manufacturing place, or industry, had to turn all of their personnel available and their premises over to war production. Most of the smaller companies had the added problem of losing all of their men of serving age to fight on the frontlines. As most of the businesses in the Quarter were what we would term today SME's (small to medium enterprises), traditionally staffed mainly by men, it is not hard to see how the area soon became bereft of manpower. Some of the skilled men were in reserved occupations, as Gil Broadway's father had been, but many were called up.

For Steven's grandfather this was no different, he was stripped of workers and left with skeletal workforce; his answer was to go and 'wine and dine' a few men from the labour office, this won him some war work, which began to shape the business post-war. The contract that he gained from the Government was that for polishing rota blades. This arm of the business then developed into producing specialised car components. Eventually, this led to contracts with British Leyland to produce carburettor filters and a fuel filling pipe for the Honda Acclaim, and later a considerable amount of work for the new Rover which was selling particularly well in the USA.

In Steven's opinion, there are always misconceptions about the boom and bust times that the Quarter has experienced. Due to the cycles of recession and upswing, most depressions are felt generationally, and some merely cause a drop in profits rather than the devastation now experienced, as with the depression of the 1920's. However, there have always been these cycles and particularly post war, this was as true after the Napoleonic Wars, the Boer War, the Great War, and WW2. When many returned from the last war, they expected business to resume 'as it always had been' but that was to a devastated war-torn Birmingham, where reconstruction became a necessity. Most people were not in a position to consider the luxuries of life, and jewellery and silverware certainly were luxury goods. This made the business case to Charles S. Green and Co. not to place all of their eggs in one basket, but to expand the engineering skills which had been sought.

The business continued until the 1980's with two sides to the offering, they still managed a reasonable trade in silverware, and at the same time they looked to profit on the lucrative car contracts that they had established. Steven was active in the business by this stage, and by the reference of others that I have spoken to, well respected by this time. Ron Jackson's tale of knocking on his door and asking for work, and then not making a very successful job of it, but finding Steven very gracious in his attitude to Ron and his partner's disaster. For a while the business boomed, and there were some extremely big clients purchasing their products, the Sultan of Brunei among them.

The problems for the company were experienced in the 1980's, as with most business a certain amount of success has to attributed to luck; being in the right place at the right time, or offering the right product to the market at the right time. The reverse is also true, if bad luck and bad timing hits, unless there is another strength to the business to offer, very little can be done.

The case of Bunker Hunt has been mentioned on several occasions in this book, as others suffered the consequences of the scam to hold the market to ransom over the price of silver. Millington's rode the storm, Deakin and Francis melted all of their stock and paid off their army of outworkers; effectively putting the pain onto their suppliers.

In the case of the Charles S. Green and Co. Ltd it became no longer viable to operate, and the business in silverware was sold. Steven is very reflective about this, but has no regrets, it was the necessary thing to do at that time and he has numbered many who have gone in the same way. He moved all of the production of the company over to the engineering side, confident that it could survive as the demand for car components was high at that point. This caused some internal disputes within the company, and the engineering workers went on strike demanding increases in their wages. Then Black Monday happened on 19th October 1987, the whole of the car manufacturing interests were hit dramatically. The USA stopped buying the Rover, the Rover Group itself never fully recovered from the devastating blow that the stock market crash precipitated, the whole supply chain network, Steven's firm included, were effectively killed off.

Steven was left with nothing, except the 'family', he had a number of relatives still working in the Quarter and the many friends and business colleagues who rallied around him. David Deakin was a major supporter during this time of crisis. Steven's father had always warned him not to get involved with repairing brushware, but he met a friend of his in London who suggested that they might work together on supplying some new brushware for Tiffany's. Additionally, when he had made the sale of his silverware business a condition that was stipulated, was that he would accept liability for any returned goods; he was confident of the quality and repair and knew that he could make a charge for it. David Deakin offered him a room upstairs to the rear of the Regents Place, where he has been ever since.

He has a chaotic workshop, which fills the eye with the busy atmosphere of eclecticism, the place is simply full of every tool, or small machine, that a silversmith could desire. He has carved himself, a small place, in between the multitude of things, in which to work. There he busily, disassembles bristle brushes, and restores them back to their original condition. He is self-taught, and has learnt much through trial and error. He also produces a personal range of work such as, spoons, and combs, they have a rustic charm and appeal, and are particularly evocative of much of the silver which hails from Norway. He has found his buyers, and attends a farmers market, every second Sunday of the month, at a place called Knightwick (between Bromyard and Worcester). Steven told me, that he finds being a maker 'particularly satisfying'. He obviously feels an affinity with the material that has been so much part of his life.

He believes that one of the most difficult things for a maker is having to turn 'work' away, because of the under valuation of the 'renovation' by the buyer. I think this story is true of many an independent outworker in the Quarter, the only difference between Steven and many of his contemporaries is that he has been on the other side of the fence, and knows what the true values are. Whereas, in general, the outworkers have traditionally under-sold themselves very often living, what only can be described as, a-hand-to-mouth existences. As Steven holds a niche market, with perhaps only one competitor, he does not have to fight to keep his margins down, which puts him in an enviable position as compared to most others.

Perhaps because he has been on each side of the employer, employee divide, combined with his family heritage and the positions of responsibility held by himself and others within his siblings, he possesses very strong opinions about the Jewellery Quarter. Many of his opinions run counter to those expressed by the majority of outworkers in this book, and are more in tune with those in the larger enterprises.

In his role as a Guardian to the Assay Office, he puts the case for the new face of the Assay Office. He feels that people have misjudged what the office is about and how it is run. In the modern day and age, it has to operate as a business concern. They do not pay a dividend, as they have no shareholders, and they have to be funded, which means that in the bad years this must come from the reserves. This has consequences that the Office must charge for the work that it carries out, and speculate for work from other sources; they do carry out work for other countries, for a fee. He believes that rather than getting 'hot under the collar', about proposals for hallmarking deregulation, that others should be supporting the Office in their fight against the competitive offices in foreign parts that cannot be policed. In his opinion, the Birmingham Assay Office is in a much stronger position than the majority of Assay Offices in England and Scotland and should be recognised as such by the dissenters in the Quarter:

"It protects the Quarter and provides security."

He also has incisive criticism for those who complain about the property speculation and the contraction of the area. He believes absolutely, that if the business interests were strong and dynamic enough, that they would be buying stretches of land that become available to expand, rather than complaining about the developers who do:

"Property development is a fact of life, and not necessarily due to any fault on behalf of the City. It is more to do with the contraction of the Jewellery Quarter itself."

He gave an example of W. H. Collins moving their personnel, plant and equipment out to Worcester and training up new workers within their new locality. In his opinion, it is inevitable that businesses will move to where they can reach the best potential to maximise their growth.

For him the Quarter still holds its value as a tight knit group of workers, all able to exchange their skills, all within close proximity of one another, and ultimately the City centre itself. This notion of 'cluster networking' does enable a considerable degree of collaborative enterprise, which would be lost if the businesses became scattered across the city, as would their business advantage, not being able to turn to a neighbour for the next process, having to source help further afield at inflated costs. This inevitably would push all of the prices up, causing the final product outcome, to be too costly and not viable.

Steven's answer to the issue of parking is to live in the Quarter itself, as he does, that removes the need to travel anywhere by car, and as he points out, rent and Council Tax relief is given to those who choose to. For him, the workers are being placed at greatest disadvantage from increasing over-regulation by the Health and Safety authorities. The escalating costs of insurance and employer liability are the charges that are doing most damage to otherwise viable business concerns.

Steven does share the feelings of most, that the Jewellery School is allowing the students it teaches to leave with unrealistic expectations of what they can actually achieve. In his opinion, they have inadequate knowledge of production techniques and costs; very often, they leave with 'fanciful notions of setting up in their own studio, which they wont survive in for five minutes'. However, there is a need to generate a discourse for the highly technical nature of the work that is done, rather than the dismissal through the label of 'craft'. In much the same way as the discourse of engineering has to generate a professional recognition, as it does in Germany, so the work of the Quarter which could be defined as 'artisanal engineering' and thus elevate the status through language and discourse.

Steven has a very optimistic vision for the Quarter, he does not see that it will fade and vanish, but rather exist in a new form. Many of the troubles that are currently faced there have been generated through mass manufacture, he believes that the over-accessibility of products have given the general public unrealistic expectations and false perceptions, of what price an object should command for retail. The problem has been generated through the demand to get more, to want more. In his opinion, 'society is no longer content with acquiring objects of beauty', but have changed to more physical pastimes, such as foreign holidays. He considers that the money is still there, it is just being spent on more esoteric activities.

This lack of interest in physical objects has caused a contraction of the volume manufacturers due to the continual undercutting, by competitor against competitor until the business is no longer viable. In Steven's opinion, the volume manufacture will not return, rather, the situation has left two avenues for the area; the niche markets served by Fattorini's and Toye, Kenning & Spencer and the like, and the bespoke products of Crescent Silver; he visualises these, existing amongst the bijou apartments, coalescing happily, a working Covent Garden art market perhaps?

There are drawbacks to the contraction, the biggest of which has been the loss of skill and the loss of industry. Without the industry there is no demand for the skill, and without the skill the industries cannot be reactivated. There is a general realisation amongst many, that this situation needs to be turned before it is too late, which means that there needs to be some sort of industry remaining, in order to keep the skills 'of some sorts' alive.

Chapter 16

THE ARTIST AND CRAFTSMAN – A PORTRAIT OF A MAN ALONE

Bill Haynes

Bill is a very quiet and unassuming individual, which when you consider the work that he has done and has been responsible for is quite surprising, but in another way it is not. Most individuals may self-promote their skill by showing and revealing what they have achieved, but he is a modest and humble character, who is very glad of the gift that he has, but hides his achievements.

He originally came from Wednesbury but moved to West Bromwich. His father was a skilled engineer and was paid low wages of about £4 per week, so to supplement his income he used to make cigarette lighters in his home workshop. Bill took a fascination in this little workshop when he was about 7 or 8 years, and his father decided to encourage that fascination by purchasing some little aluminium moulds to cast lead soldiers in. As Bill stresses, this was quite a dangerous activity to do because you had to melt the lead to quite a high temperature, it was normally carried out under the strict supervision of his father. However, once Bill decided to have a go himself, he burnt his fingers quiet badly, but as he says, sometimes you have to do this:

"You learn don't you?"

He obviously had a talent for the materials and the three dimensional form. Very often, people can be good at two dimensional realisation through drawing and painting, but struggle with the appreciation of three dimensional form, Bill was a natural in these aspects of visualisation.

Bill went to a Secondary Modern School and found his niche in Metalwork where he excelled, and despite the fact that his Form Master had had a reason to 'tick him off' earlier in his school career, Bill did very well in the last two or three years. He found that he had a natural gift with materials, 'it all came so easy'. At that time, schoolboys had to undertake standard projects that they had to carry out in those days, such as, a garden trowel and hand fork etc, but he never found any difficulty and really enjoyed the work.

"If I didn't get it right first time, I usually got it right the second time. It is either something that you have got or you haven't."

Each year the 'lads' would have to display their work in large display cabinets in the main part of the school, then came the year that eighty percent of all of the work in those cabinets was Bill's. He says, that he does not believe that he had come to the Headmaster's attention until then. One day he was in a Geography lesson and his Form Master appeared instructing Bill to report to the Headmaster in the staff room; Bill was extremely worried as he made his way there, trying to remember what misdemeanour he may have committed, it had turned out that the school inspectors (who were making their regular inspection) had praised the high level of work that he had produced.

As he was 15 and due to leave school it was very fortuitous timing for Bill, as he had been working with the local Careers Office to find him a job; they had neither been particularly concerned, or had cared to offer him an appropriate placement. He knew that generally the only work on offer in the locality was foundry work, and all the Careers Office presented him with, were a job in a wood yard, a job in a steel drawers, and a few other dead-end

Bill Haynes chasing sterling silver monstrance face plate c.1962.

vacancies. However, his Form Master had noticed Bill's hard work and dedication and sought out a better position for him; he arranged an apprenticeship for him at Barker Brothers in Snow Hill. There he would start as a junior undertaking all of the menial tasks and then work his way up to the level of a chaser, it was 1956 and his starting salary was £2.50 for a forty-four hour week. His first problem was the long journey to get there on the buses from West Bromwich to Snow Hill:

"It used to take a hell of a long time."

Most of the work carried out at Barker Brothers was destined for the Middle East, particularly Arabia. They worked mainly in Electro Plated Nickel Silver (EPNS) and Bill remembers the piles of work which used to cover the floor there. His first job as a new employee entailed him to make the place ready for work; this involved making sure that the big cauldron of pitch was put on the heat, first thing, so that it was melted and ready for the pouring into the lined-up hollowware ready to start work. He had other sweeping duties and general running around keeping the floor clear. From his vantage point, he could observe the whole process of the various aspects of applying decorative techniques to EPNS.

The system depended on always 'working a day in advance'. All of the hollowware had to be marked out and then filled with pitch the day before it was worked on, to allow it harden over night, ready for the next day. When the pitch was solid it would mean that the chasers could work (with considerable force in some cases) without deforming the shape of the vessel that they were working on.

On particular vessels before they could be filled, the 'snarling up' would take place. This process enabled the designed pattern to be applied to the surface and then the outline raised. Specific hollowware items such as; teapots, and sugar bowls, would have a special piece of steel bar with turned up ends inside it, and then the bar was held firmly in the bench vice. A perforated piece of tracing paper pattern was then applied to the surface, that a thin layer of oil had been painted on, and the pattern was dusted through the perforated holes with Plaster of Paris. The pattern was then removed and the chalk dots used to act as guide for the image to be drawn using a metal scribe. The 'snarling up' happened with the constant whack, whack, of the hammer against the snarling iron to raise the pattern. As Bill reflects, most of the men smoked:

"But once you had been snarling up all day, you couldn't hold a cigarette."

The next stage was to fill the vessel with the pitch ready to decorate, various different size rings were used to help restrain the object from moving. The following day, the work was handed on to the decorator who would use an amazingly simple contraption to hold the work called a 'leg rope'. The rope was a continuous loop that passed through two holes in the bench and enabled the worker to firmly hold the work down on the bench, by holding the rope down with the force and weight of their foot; leaving both hands free to decorate the work. It also fitted the work perfectly, whereas a bench vice could misshapen or mark a delicate object; a rope would follow the contours to hold the work more sympathetically:

"You could work away as quick as lightening, each piece being priced."

Obviously, these techniques had been developed in generations gone by, and as I have emphasised throughout this book, despite what people may think, the processes and tools have barely changed, because they have no need to change. They serve the purpose and complete the task well; a thing, tool or object, is only designed when it is needed and all these ways have been developed to be the best and most efficient way of doing things and Bill agrees:

"these things go back hundreds of years."

Bill was at Barkers for six years, but during that time he did progress; firstly, his travelling became considerably easier. He had become quite seriously involved in cycling and had a very stripped down racing cycle, which had a fixed wheel, and no brakes, and could only be stopped, or slowed, by back-peddling. He got his journey time down to a fine art, whereas, previously it had taken an hour by bus; now he was managing to get to Snow Hill in a record seventeen minutes. He achieved this by utilising the slip-stream of the buses to ride behind, on one occasion, he did get it slightly wrong when not paying his full attention, and rode straight into the back of the bus which had stopped in front of him.

Barkers allowed him two half days a week to attend the School of Jewellery and Silversmithing in Vittoria Street, Bill loved this he immediately joined the chasing class; obviously with the ambition to try and move himself on in his employment quickly, however he still had some time to finish his work as a trainee on general tasks despite his ambitions to do otherwise. He also took advantage of the many classes available in his own time in the evenings, he did three nights:

"because I absolutely loved it!"

Within his very first year, he had achieved a 2nd in chasing, and in his first annual exhibition he had done extremely well. He may have had an inkling that he would lean more towards the design and art side; at secondary school he had been encouraged to attend the Royal and Memorial School for Art for one afternoon a week, where among other things he had learnt photography which would prove useful at a later date.

Left: H M Silver gilt replica of Elizabeth I Lambard cup and cover c.1578 London. Right: H M Sterling silver model of lighthouse at La Corbiere Jersey (images by the kind courtesy of Mr William Haynes).

Most of the teachers who taught during the evening sessions at the School of Jewellery and Silversmithing were practising trade crafstmen and in some ways he found them better because they taught with the needs of production in mind, and knew all of the tricks of the trade. During the day classes he studied silversmithing and design, which was very important to him to have this opportunity to appreciate the aesthetics of making. Eventually, he moved on from chasing and concentrated much of his efforts towards silversmithing, this would be where he really came into his own.

Much of his inspiration came from one particular teacher in the evening called Joe Hazeldeane, he was a chaser and modelmaker. Joe had actually been trained by William Bloye, famed across the city for the statue of the three most influential citizens – Boulton, Watt and Murdoch – that stands outside the old Register Office in Broad Street. Joe was an old chap even then, having been a Great War veteran, but an extremely talented chaser and sculptor and model maker. Bill had discovered that he had a particular love of these areas and had won prizes for his model making when he attended evening classes in sculpture at the Birmingham College of Arts and Crafts. Bill was fascinated by Joe's work and skills and they formed quite a friendship, Bill used to visit Joe's workshop and do some work for him from time, to time.

Bill had made it clear to Joe that he did not feel settled in Barkers and he wanted to do more, after all, he had gathered many more skills and he wanted to use them; he could not visualise himself staying where he was only required for chasing. Joe listened and did some quiet investigating and found Bill a contact at H. Samuel's; they had a large warehouse and manufacturing departments on Hockley Brook. Joe told Bill to have a word with Mr Neville – who was another evening lecturer who had a special trophy department within Samuel's.

Unfortunately, in Bill's youthful enthusiasm he revealed his secret to another apprentice at Barkers, who told the bosses. Then a bit of a 'to do' erupted between Bill's firm and the College, Barkers were not happy that one of their workers had been effectively poached due to the actions of one of their staff members. Bill has always felt terrible about his momentary lack of discretion, for poor old Joe Hazeldeane was subsequently carpeted by the college principal – Mr Backsindale.

He did make the move to Samuel's, but it was one of a number of short-lived jobs. He was to do the model making, which he really enjoyed and Frank Neville would do the design work, however, Bill would find that Mr Neville 'would clear off' at the drop of a hat leaving him to do everything, Bill decided to move on again and just after the departments within the manufacturing section closed.

He eventually ended up at A Edward-Jones where he remained for 10 years. He was interviewed by Major Crisp Jones, who having left the forces, had taken up the reins of the family firm and decided to run it as a military operation; Bill found him calling on his other talent as a photographer for their in-house marketing. Bill loved the work that this firm handled because it was mainly ecclesiastical silverware; alms dishes and chalices etc. Bill found himself with many different hats in that firm; he was the resident designer, a chaser, a silversmith and a photographer, 'it was hard work' and the major was a 'stickler'.

The upside was it was where he met his wife forty-six years ago, she was working in accounts; little did they know what a perfect team they would make later on. They became a 'celebrity' couple within the firm, being the first couple to get engaged and subsequently, the first to tie the knot and get married. But for many newly weds this is when the drive to do better really begins to take hold. Before long Bill had his first son and as he says 'the money had never been that good'. When it came to his departure and the reasons that he finally decided to leave, he reflects that it was 'twenty-five percent the money and seventy-five percent the foreman'. Finally, Major Crisp and his constant policy of keeping everyone in their place, and letting them know their place.

Bill remembers the blackboard that used to hang on the wall inside the drawing office, on which the Major had drawn an organisational hierarchy of his company, with himself at the top. He used to bring groups of visitors around and take them into Bill's area, and in front of him drive home the place of each in the firm; this finally chipped away at Bill a little too much it was time to move on. Bill found new employment with M. Gordon (MFC Silversmiths), a middle-aged man who had rented premises in Warstone Lane, and was effectively running his business down because he had been doing it since he was 14 years of age. Mr Gordon ran a small concern in manufacturing and silversmithing and restoration work and in the first instance Bill worked for him. Mr Gordon was impressed by Bill's level of skill and the love that Bill had for his work, and they soon became great friends. On his retirement, Bill bought the business from Mr Gordon as a going concern, and continued the good trade; he specialised in highly skilled, commissioned work, and antique restoration for regular customers who required a high standard of workmanship; his wife ably assisting him by managing the books.

Occasionally, Bill had the company of an older worker part-time who was just out to make a bit of extra money to supplement their incomes. He worked 6 days a week for 20 years, it must have been a very solitary, but focused existence, and for some it is this final tranquillity of being 'solo' that gives them the peace and the satisfaction that they have been seeking and a chance to use their mastered skills to their full potential. He would do his design work at home on a Sunday. For instance, if he had to make special items (a silver rose was an example that he gave me) the design drawing would be completed at home in order for him to work at his bench the next week.

It was while he was at these premises he encountered two, or three, funny moments, due to the underground crime that filled the Quarter at that time. On one occasion, the police used his office room to put the premises opposite under surveillance for a number of weeks, in order to secure evidence on the five men who were receiving stolen goods and melting them down; it was quite a racket!

Bill experienced the difficulty of parking that others have referred to in this book, and had been through the double parking era, that was followed by officious parking wardens marking tyres; he ended up paying a fortune in fines over the years, Another time he parked his car near the Chamberlain Clock and not only received a fine for doing so, but high winds blew the tiles off the roofs and they damaged his car very badly – that was an expensive day for Bill.

By this time, he was occupying the whole of the top floor of a multi-occupied building, which sat on the grounds of where James Watt's garden had used to be opposite the 'Big Peg'. As he was located fairly close by, he did try to park in the multi-story a few times, this led to the theft of his car on several occasions, and once the theft of his boot.

These humorous histories are part and parcel of the Jewellery Quarter and are some of the tales he tells me predate Bill. The original premises that he had occupied with Mr Gordon – which he subsequently had to move a few doors down from when the rent escalated because the engineering firm to the rear of the property sold out – had an interesting incumbent during the Second World War, his name was Mr Morris, another silversmith.

Mr Morris senior had been in the Great War and had both of his legs shot off, naturally this had caused his son great angst, and with the advent of World War Two he became a conscientious objector, uttering that 'there was no way the bloody government is going to get me'. So he had made an agreement with Mr Gordon's father and he went into hiding in the top floor, the room is marked by a circular porthole. He remained there for the duration of the war, never being found, or suspected, only sneaking out at night on rare occasions.

Bill is well known in the Quarter, although he has now retired. The nature of the business meant that so many others were inter-dependent on one another, it was a mutual exchange of skills, time and knowledge, which kept all of the businesses surviving. This closeness has often been described throughout this book as the feeling of 'family'; all being there for one another and knowing each others lives; joys and sadness. Bill knew of Neil Grant's (Crescent Silver) father and told me that he had been a prisoner of war in Changi a fact that had not been relayed to me; he was aware of the problems that had been experienced by Steven Green, another tale of the Quarter. These shared stories are a tribute to the network of 'friends' that has always existed.

Bill's work is remarkable, and he is very modest about what he does and what he has achieved. Following the dreadful fire in Windsor Castle, which destroyed St George's Hall, Bill was approached by recommendation in 2002 to help in the restoration work there. He had to reproduce the beautiful, if large, knobs, handles and back plates which were a feature of the chamber, which included an intricate design of St George slaying the dragon. Bill took all of this in his stride, and faithfully reproduced exact copies of the commission which had been laid before him.

He has had a career of undertaking a large amount of commissions for other companies and individuals that have gone unrecognised, such as a very wide range of architectural work and military models of intricate workmanship, many of his clients were extremely concerned

One of Bill Hayne's commissioned classical pieces in H M Sterling Silver.

when he announced his impending retirement. He has also been responsible for the modelling and production of prosthetic implants for medical purposes; something which does require a considerable amount of care, accuracy and attention to detail.

He has also made some local works of considerable interest, using his skills as a sculptor. The biggest piece he undertook was entitled the 'Tipton Slasher' and was commissioned in 1992, it was a life size model statue of the bare-knuckle boxing champion of England (1850-1857). The sculpture was unveiled in Tipton on May 3rd 1993, Bill reflects with much pride:

"I was King for the day!"

Bill was also responsible for the manufacture of the British Quality Foundation Awards and National Television Awards annually. A process which was very labour intensive and he took great pains to get right. The original design for the award which was outsourced from Thomas Fattorini Ltd, consisted of a brightly polished stem, which was then planished and chased, in order to add texture and added enhancement to the ball-shaped top. This process would always culminate around the same time every year, mid-summer, and there were 20 pieces to finish. The heat was always too much that time of year, and Bill would have to work with the window open. Unfortunately, this led to complaints from a neighbouring firm of solicitors about the noise.

This has become a common issue across the Quarter, those who try to work receiving complaint after complaint about the noise, or the smells they generate; or the irregular hours that they keep infringing on the lives of the recent 'newcomers'; whether that be non-associated business interests, or the new inhabitants. It is a question that has been raised again and again, is this a 'Working Quarter' or is it not? If the interests of Birmingham Council are to promote, and by that fact, support the business that is carried out in the Quarter, then they must put those workers first and make allowances for their noise and nuisance. The Quarter must be promoted as a place with individuality and a peculiarity; as such any irritations that are perceived now should be viewed as the essential qualities and idiosyncrasies of the place and celebrated as such.

When Bill finally retired in 2005, the area lost one of the best artisan/ craftsmen that they had ever had working there. He did not want to retire, as is often the case it is very much 'in the blood' and part of the reason to live in many. The six days a week, with Sundays to complete design work, had been so much part of his life, for so long, he finds himself at a bit of a loose end and missing his many friends. He still puts in the odd day for Lunt's in order to keep his hand in, and retains a little workshop where he lives in the Black Country. He has kept all of his work from school all those years ago, and is very proud of his lifetime's devotion to his work.

Bill is not the last, but he will be one of the last. He is a dying breed of craftsman, who will not be in evidence again, the product of a very different time in education and society. He misses the place where he worked for so many years, but he misses the old days more than what the Quarter has become. Most importantly he misses 'the family', all of the characters who made the Quarter, after all it is the people who make a place, not the fabric and the buildings.

Chapter 17

THE MEN WHO MADE
THE WRITING REVOLUTION

History from the Pen Room

This is not a tale of a company that has survived for generations in the same family, as some are in this book, or even a firm that has reinvented itself and passed into the hands of others. This is a story about an industry which Birmingham was famed for the world over that only really existed in glory for about eighty years, the mass manufacture of steel 'pens'. The men who made this industry what it was, quite literally revolutionised writing, and made it more accessible to everyone. The major manufacturers sited themselves in, or, near the Quarter, so this story is very much a part of the area, but now it is a history, of the past and not connected with the present. That is to say directly, for there has been a desire to re-tell this history and keep the story ever-present.

The Pen Room is a museum which has been sited in part of what was an old purpose-built pen factory of William Wiley. It is now the Argent Centre – a business development centre. Within that museum, much of what is left of the memorabilia and artefacts have been carefully displayed, and the written history has been archived and catalogued. Mr Larry Hanks is the curator and is ably assisted by guides such as Mr Nicholas Tulloch. On the day that I visited, Nicholas explained the contents of the museum and various anecdotes associated with it, he also showed me how to make a pen, with the few hand-presses which they have managed to save. A pen in these terms is not the fully functional object that we describe as such now, it was then the nib, the machined part that functioned to write once dipped in an ink pot, it was the successor to the sharpened point of a quill pen, usually a goose feather.

Machined pens in other forms have a history as far back as the Roman times, and various methods, such as the shaping of precious and semiprecious stones have been used as a way to achieve the desired point with which to write. However, these pens were very specialist and required a considerable amount of time to fabricate, the results were not always as accurate, or as dependable, as the good old quill. The high cost of producing such a manufactured pen precluded their usage to only those that could afford to commission them. The quill remained the only device that was accessible to most, that too, restricted many of those who may have learnt to write and in turn this kept overall levels of competent literacy low.

It was due to a combination of astute entrepreneurial drive accentuated by the hunger to achieve, and the technological developments in machining (which find their roots in Birmingham), that the pen industry was born. It is hard to imagine now the hotbed of enthusiasm and invention that the particular time, and the particular place, gave rise to, but it was the generation of mass-production, and the city led the way in pioneering new and exciting methods to make things better and in vast quantities. Much of this rapid evolution owes its provenance to Matthew Boulton's visionary enterprises in the Soho Manufactory and the Mint; his need to produce in

The Pen Room – The Argent Centre (J. Debney).

volume to the highest quality drove a considerable amount of engineering inventiveness. This gave Birmingham the place that it had in the history of the times of the pen manufacturers, the kudos of being the only city with the creative capacity to make these things a possibility.

Nicholas tells his stories with great love and enthusiasm, introducing me with great rapidity to the pen making process, filling my head, with facts and dates, names and places, of all the great milestones in pen development in the city. There are a number of family names that come to the fore as those who have made the most significant contribution within the context of Birmingham, they are Josiah Mason, John and William Mitchell, Joseph Gillott, James Perry and William Wiley, but there were others not so influential, who added to the vast volume of output that was generated in this field.

The first of these, Josiah Mason, is famed as great benefactor of the city, putting his name to Mason Science College, which would later become Birmingham University. It was at a speech that he gave there, that he talked of the first man that he knew that had made a specialised machined pen, his name was Mr Harrison, and Josiah referred to him as 'a good friend'. According to The Birmingham Mail of the 24th January, 1905:

"The pen made by Mr Harrison was for Dr Priestley, and it was destroyed during the Priestley riots, when the doctor's house was sacked."

It was to be expected that the 'Lunar Men' of whom Priestley and Boulton were founding members, should be those who the aspiring, inventive engineers should approach with their ground-breaking ideas. This pen had been given to Priestley in about 1780, and was referred to by Mason, as the first pen to be made out of cheap metal. According to the Mail, these pens were only turned out in small quantities until 1820, it was at this time, or a few years before, that three enterprising individuals headed towards Birmingham and changed the course of pen manufacture, though which of those three is to be ultimately credited with the industry's transformation is a matter for some debate.

Certainly, the most information that remains is associated with Joseph Gillott, as Nicholas informed me:

"He walked from Sheffield with a penny in his pocket, which he spent, he was illiterate, yet became a multimillionaire. The massive irony, he made thousands of pens, and employed hundreds of women, yet the thing that made him rich he could not use. The same for the women, as far as they were concerned they were making bits of metal."

From the information available during his life time and subsequently to his death, he was a very interesting individual. It is fair to say that he saw an opportunity, and worked very hard to make that a reality and assumed as much credit for it as he could; that is not to say that he was not a fine employer, who did more for his workforce than any of his contemporaries. Most of the evidence describes him posthumously, as a very quiet individual, and not one to self-promote, though it is apparent that these rules did not apply to his business interest which were marketed vigorously.

He was by trade (according to the Birmingham Sketch August 1962):
"about 16 years old and already a skilled operative grinder with several years of working life behind him."

He set out for Birmingham from his hometown of Sheffield, which had been badly affected by the economic downturn caused by the Napoleonic Wars. There was at that time some infant trade in pens in Sheffield and it is likely that someone of the skills that Joseph possessed is liable to have had some experience in the manufacture and maintenance of such items.

As did another Sheffield refugee, Mr John Mitchell. He was born about the same time as Gillott in 1798, and according to his son Henry Mitchell in 1872, is to be credited with not just the invention of the steel pens, but also with the invention and development of the associated machinery for the manufacture of them. He started his working career as a pen knife manufacturer in the back streets of Sheffield; a complementary trade to this is grinding, to sharpen the blades.

It would be rather fanciful to surmise without actual evidence that these two arrivals at the same time in Birmingham, who were approximately the same age, who both hailed from the same place, and were both associated with the same transformations of an industry, may just have been friends; who not only worked together in Sheffield, but set out on that long walk, accompanied by John's younger brother William (who became part of the Mitchell firm). On arrival in their new city, they probably shared a common goal to develop the methods and experiment with new ideas and techniques. What can be proved is that Joseph Gillott married their sister Maria Mitchell in about 1823.

The dates at which these men became established in business would come some years after their arrival in Birmingham, but we know from the dates that are available that they started their pen making concerns in close proximity of time and location. On their initial arrival they would have worked in other areas probably, as there is evidence that Joseph Gillott, set about making the steel 'toys' that Birmingham was famed for; the buckles and trinket boxes and such like.

John Mitchell became established in his business in 1822, and some dates conflict as to whether it was 1820 or 1823 when Joseph Gillott

Displays from the Pen Room (J. Debney).

established his concern. The Mitchell's are recorded as selling their first pens, at 30s per dozen, Gillott sold his at half that price a year later. The families obviously had some connection eventually, through marriage, and the rivalry of future years would have stopped any such marriage from occurring, so it is fair to argue that their connections were very close at one time, and this may have led to some hot debates as to who exactly should be credited with the evolution in the pen industry. However, John Mitchell did establish his business in 1822 in Newhall Street manufacturing limited quantities of pens in the first instance. Whereas Joseph established himself in Bread Street (now Cornwall Street). That same year he married Maria, and as hard working as he was, so was she, for the morning of their wedding they set about 'making a gross of pens, which after the ceremony they sold to their guests for one shilling each, bringing a useful £7 4 s in for their first week's housekeeping' (Birmingham Sketch – August 1962).

With the speed at which 144 pens were made that morning, and knowing how long and laborious the process had been prior to this, it is safe to argue that he had already found some successful methods for machining the nibs. His brothers-in-law had been making them by hand on their arrival, and Joseph Gillott is noted as commenting that he had witnessed this, and it had inspired him to seek other means. Whatever, the story of who developed what, the collective brothers-in-law had been exposed to various buckle and button making presses now available in Birmingham, which had been innovated by the previous generation of entrepreneurs. It was not difficult to someone of 'like engineering-mind' as these men were, to see the potential and begin to adapt these machines to their material advantage.

By 1831, Joseph Gillott had registered a patent for a process for placing elongated points on the nibs of pens, this is one of many of the future improvements that he made and registered. Whether, the Mitchell's had been before him, they had failed to register their achievements. This maybe is where the bone of contention of future years lie, however, the industry was a relatively short-lived one with both the fountain pen and the ball point pen being patented in the 1880's. During that fifty year period there was an explosion of pen production to feed the world's desire to write, nearly all of these pens coming from Birmingham.

The process that these men pioneered, involved using machine presses for the various actions, combined with the foresight to sub-divide the manufacturing tasks into grouped areas for ease of production; there is no doubt that in the earlier years, Gillott was better at this than his in-laws. He also recognised that the best form of labour (the reason given was their dexterity and nimbleness of fingers) were women. It can also be argued that he chose women because they could not be unionised, and as such did not command as high a wage as a male operative (Morgan 2001).

Gillott moved twice before he established his principle factory, firstly to Little Charles Street, then to Newhall Street, before the building of a magnificent factory in Graham Street in the Jewellery Quarter, known as the Victoria Works in 1839. At its peak he was employing between, 600 to 700 people (mainly women) and producing tens of thousands of pens per day. The adoption of the revolutionary mass-manufacturing techniques had brought the price of a pen down substantially; what once had cost 1s each were now costing 1½d per gross.

The first stage of the process involved rolling the sheet metal then heating and 'pickling' it, in order to make it soft and malleable for working. In any process of metal production, as the metal is worked it becomes brittle (work hardening). The more it is worked the more fragile it them becomes, until it fractures and breaks. Sometimes certain items require softening a number of times before the object is finished, this process of further softening is called annealing. The next stage was 'blanking' or the cutting out of the blanks, it required the least skill, so paid the lowest wage. Girls usually started at 14, and were lucky to earn 7s per week for cutting out 130 gross or 18,720 nib blanks per day. There were generally about 50 girls set to this task.

Then the blanks were passed to the 'marking' stage, where the blanks had incised letters and images, such as, the Queen's head embossed on them, sometimes with many different hand punches. The machine that applied this decoration generally was a small kick-stamping press, where the operator had her foot in a stirrup which operated a pulley wheel. This operation required a considerable amount of manual dexterity and attention, for one momentary slip of concentration could lead to the poor girl having her fingers trapped in the machine, not released again until the counterweight was depressed. In the small pamphlet by Robert Stanyard entitled 'Tales from the Pen Room', he relays an account given by one such young lady:

"We had a piano at home it was inherited from my late uncle he was a pianist, in the inns, and the concert halls, sometimes, I learnt a little of how to play. I liked to play. Unfortunately my fingers had been crushed so many times in the stamping press I doubt if I could play the piano anymore."

From his own publication entitled 'Messers Joseph Gillott and Sons' Steel Pen Manufactory Birmingham' produced in 1880. The author makes light of the process in these words:

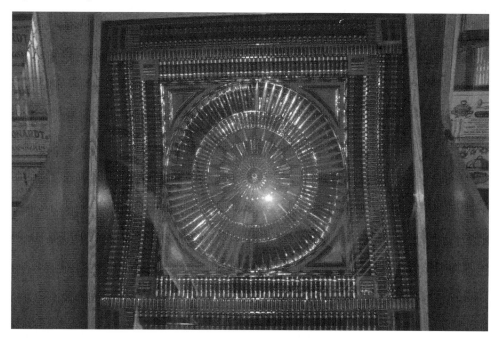

Displays from the Pen Room (J. Debney).

223

"The nimble fingers play in and out under the heavy stamp hammer with airy indifference to danger, which quite reassures the spectator, though it is evident that the slightest miscalculation of time or distance would make a case for the nearest hospital."

From the marking, to the piercing of the hole, a one-handed operation, enabling the worker to pass the work to the piercing press with one hand, while operating the press with the other. It meant that the output remained high and kept pace with the amount of work arriving at the piercing operation, but according to Robert Stanyard's research it was considered to be the most boring and repetitive of tasks.

Then the pens were hardened and tempered. Hardening to return the metal to the original state, this was achieved, as described in Joseph Gillott's own pamphlet:

"When heated to a sufficient degree of redness (not one scintilla more, or it will be burnt), and then cooled as suddenly as possible, it will attain its maximum degree of hardness."

This cooling was achieved by plunging the work into a bath of oil. The tempering was to restore a degree of flexibility for the specific purpose that the pen would be required for, usually reheated to a dark blue, enabling the greatest degree of elasticity and then cooled slowly to keep that temper.

Then the pens were pickled in a bath of sulphuric acid to remove the oxide and scoured in a barrel that turned continuously with an abrasive medium in it, this removed any of the extraneous burrs that had been acquired through all of the actions of cutting and piercing. The pens were then ground, by girls operating steam driven grinding wheels which had

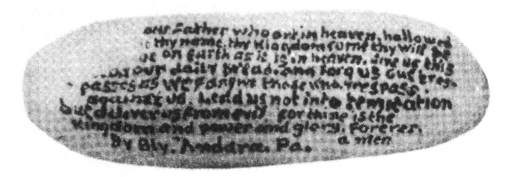

Reproduction of the Lord's Prayer written on a grain of rice with a Gillott's 2000 superfine pointed pen.

emery cloth attached, this achieved a high level of polish and cleaned the metal. It was essential that all of the operatives were scrupulously clean, as grease, or moisture could have contaminated the metal, and any girl who failed at this was summarily dismissed. As Robert Stanyard reveals:

"Jane was only seventeen. She had been a grinder for three years and worked hard exceeding the others 'lots' by several thousand! She needed the money. She had lost her mother and father and had two younger brothers and a younger sister to look after. Jane, was unwell, not one to complain she continued with her work. That afternoon something happened the owner of the factory came to the Grinding Room he stopped each of the girls in turn and asked to look at their hands, Jane was perplexed by this odd behaviour. Finally Jane's employer came to her bench. She stopped grinding. 'Show me your palms!' he demanded. Jane turned and showed him her sweaty palms, he looked at them and touched them. 'You're dismissed.' He growled. 'But, why?' questioned Jane. He produced from his pocket a ground rusty nib."

The next process, that would require possibly the greatest attention to detail, was to cut the slit. This was done with a bench shear, and had to be accurately made to the correct length. The cutting of the slit determined the flow of the ink, and the writing of the pen; ultimately, even its performance for the task it was intended to do. Some pens would require multiple cuts which would take the greatest degrees of accuracy of the cutter, from Joseph Gillott's pamphlet:

"As proof of what may be done by skilful hands in this way, we may mention that we have seen a number of pens which had six distinct slits within the width of an ordinary point, each being perfectly clean and sound, and, as shown under a microscope, at uniform distance from each other."

Then the pens were subjected to a final treatment in the 'barrel' to polish them to bright steel finish, before being colourised if necessary and then having a layer of varnish applied to them. After this, a quality control viewing process was used to check for the accuracy of the manufacture and finish, those that were not up to standard were rejected. Then the pens were carefully packed in boxes, but most of the pens were sewn on cards by armies of 'outworkers' in their homes; very often these were women with families who could not work and every penny counted; so all of their children to the smallest that could hold a needle, were used to fill the cards; it was piecework, paid by the finished cards produced for packing.

Despite the revolution that these processes brought to manufacturing, it is not difficult to see how exploitative mass-manufacturing was, and some manufacturers had better reputations for fairness than others. Working conditions varied enormously, some surveys done on factory work at that time paint a very different picture of working conditions from one to the other. For instance, the Pen Room have a description of the John Mitchell premises at 48 Newhall Street in 1864, which describes a very unpleasant working environment:

> "These premises are of the kind so common in Birmingham – old street buildings with small yards and shops at the back adapted to manufactory. But unusually gloomy. Two places in which two boys work are more vaults or cellars unfit for human occupation. This whole atmosphere is pervaded by the smell of vitriol (sulphuric acid) used to cleanse the steel and the rancid smell of oil. The acid is so strong that it tends to destroy the clothing of the boys involved."

From the same year, a report of the Gillott Manufactory by the 'Birmingham District on the Manufacture of Steel Pens', the author Mr J. E. White describes a very different environment, he informs the reader that:

> "246. These are very large works, conveniently arranged, and the work rooms clean, fresh, and cheerful.
>
> 248. In one press, worked by steam, I noticed a simple contrivance for protecting the fingers, by means of a guard.
>
> 249. *Mr. Gillott, jun.* – We have a rule not to employ any children under 13, and have very few under. There are many girls under 18, but they are a small proportion of the whole number of persons employed, which is toward 500. The majority are young women of from 18 to 25 or 30. The day's work is 12 hours with two hours for meals, except in winter, when it is from 8 till 7… Washing places are provided for the workpeople."

There exists other evidence of the Gillott Manufactory being a fairer place to work than most, there were works outings for the employees. One such outing consisted of 50 cars 'laden with about three hundred smartly dressed females, and the workmen', originally setting out for Kenilworth, but making a detour to a previously preferred place for their outings – Lickey Hills in Bromsgrove. They were accompanied by two of Joseph Gillott's sons, and an 'instrumental band', later, Joseph Gillott and his three daughters joined them to great welcome. They took refreshments on the hills, and danced, afterwards they descended to a local inn, where:

> "the good things of life were spread out on three extended ranges of tables, the master himself presiding at one, while his sons were indefatigable in their exertions to promote comfort of all."

At the height of the glory for the pen manufacturing trade, there were 700,000,000 pens being manufactured in Birmingham per year, and it supplied the whole world; out of that figure, Joseph Gillott was manufacturing 150,000,000 pens per year. Mitchell's and Gillott were the first, but there were at least a dozen more. Notably, Josiah Mason who manufactured Perry's Pens (Perry and Co Ltd. Manchester and London) at his Lancaster Street Factory. Then on opening the college in his name, he was able to recount the story of Mr Harrison's pen for Dr Priestly. Perry and Co. took over three other companies in 1876 and by 1880 and were producing 360,000,000 pens a year. In 1914 they employed 1,200 women (Pen Room).

In 1852 two manufacturers established a partnership of Hinks Wells, and by 1864 had a large factory in Buckingham Street. They were famous for their 'J' pen, and at their peak were manufacturing 1,820,000 gross per year. They were the first firm to adopt the nine hour working day, and John Hinks paid for his entire workforce to visit places of interest in London. By 1920, they had amalgamated with William Mitchell and Co to form British Pens (Pen Room).

Another contemporary in age to the Mitchell's and Gillott was a man called John Sheldon. He was born somewhere between 1800 and 1802 and died in 1863, and was typical of many of the small 'toy' manufacturers of the city, who set up in business making; boxes and buckles before seizing the opportunity to branch out into pen making. He moved premises from Lancaster Street to Great Hampton Street in 1846, where he was listed as manufacturing a number of items from; pens, pencil cases, cutlery, snuff, cigar and card boxes. He was quite a diverse manufacturer which probably accounts for his lack of status as pen maker per sae, however, he was very careful to patent all of his many associated products including a patent in 1843 Pocket Escritor; which was a miniature writing desk comprising of; almanac, inkstand, blotting card and memorandum pad, pens, wax tapers, and a promethean light.

William Wiley had been a gold pen manufacturer at 34 Great Hampton Street, so his was a specialist pen, but never a real competitor to the steel pen industry; the gold pen was the luxury end of the pen market. Wiley built a factory opposite Joseph Gillott to manufacture his pens on Frederick Street, he called his the 'Albert Works' as opposed to the 'Victoria Works'. It is a vast and impressive structure which is almost a palace to pen making, having towers, and impressive windows. It cost him £5,000 to build and was such a notable structure there was an article written on it in a copy of 'The Building News' of 1863. Wiley wanted to add further to the feeling of luxury, and maybe was a farsighted individual wishing to recycle the heat that his premises would generate, he sited a lavish Turkish Baths on the top floor. He established himself as a manufacturer, and became the largest manufacturer of gold pens which retailed at 5 s each in the first instance. It was too special a pen to compete against the volume of steel pens, and with the advent of the new technologies in pen manufacture (such as the patent of the fountain pen) subsequently, had a very short time in existence. By 1876 Wiley had become the largest shareholder in Perry and Co, probably already deciding to wind his business down. In 1880 the Albert Works were empty and the manufacture of pens was never to return; it is now the site of The Pen Room Museum and the various business units within the renamed Argent Centre.

Most pen manufacturers had seen their best years by the 1920's but continued to operate for a few more years, most joined into larger ventures such as British Pens. Gillott's passed to the fourth generation, the great-grandson of Joseph Gillott – Nicholas Gillott was in control from the middle of 1950's to the end of the 1960's. He did his best to promote the company

An unusual treatment of an oriental scene. A very effective treatment of flowing grace in black and white, giving the effect of stained glass.

"THE LAST RUN OF THE SEASON" (after E. Landseer).

SPECIMENS OF BLACK & WHITE DRAWINGS EXECUTED WITH JOSEPH GILLOTTS SUPERFINE PENS.

Examples of work by Gillott's Pens (J. Debney).

strongly, which he relocated to new premises in Dudley. He marketed the prestige of his pens well, the connections to Walt Disney (the Burbank Studio only buying Gillott pens for all of their animation work), the Lords Prayer having been written on a grain of rice with a Gillott No. 2000 superfine, but by 1969 he too had succumbed to the amalgamation with British Pens.

There is no doubt that the original men of this relatively, short-lived industry, had spectacular vision, drive, and determination, as to whether they were and remained illiterate for all of their lives, I would assume some semi-literacy in the beginning to be able to understand engineering drawings, and sales ledgers; then as most being self-made men they would have progressed no doubt. My Scottish great-grandfather was taught to read and write by his wife when he was in his early twenties; he became a most able businessman. In one of the obituaries written after the death of Joseph Gillott who died in 1872, it was acknowledged that he truly had risen higher than any, for as the author pointed out James Watt had been a trained engineer, Gillott was not:

"Mr Gillott was a self-made man, but no man of merely mediocre talent could have made himself in the same way."

There are those in the Quarter now, that may argue that it is a working area and should be promoted as such, and not act to conserve, thus giving the impression of decline from a glorious past. To some extent this argument is a fair one, and indeed if the Quarter is to regenerate it should be seen as a dynamic place of forward-thinking enterprise based on hundreds of years of strong business within precious metal trades. I would argue that we should not forget the significance that this industry has had on Birmingham, coming directly from the heritage of the Birmingham 'toys', and generating a sizeable amount of wealth for the city as a whole. This industry enabled thousands of women to be employed on relatively good wages (for women at that time) when very few were employed in anything other than sweated trades. It created personal prosperity which through philanthropy of those men, benefited Birmingham greatly, and geographically it can be argued that the home of this industry was in and around the Jewellery Quarter. If this museum had not been developed in the location that it has, then a trade which the city owes much to, would be consigned to history and inevitably forgotten.

The Pen Room is developing constantly, collating new information, saving as many artefacts as are made available. They view themselves as an educational resource open to all, and in particular, the many school parties which go there. People now visit the Quarter far more than they have in the past thirty years. This museum provides an 'open door' to encourage people to visit, and then they see the other on-going, dynamic aspects of that area, and most important of all, young people are coming and some will have the light of realisation of the opportunities that the Jewellery Quarter may offer them, and come back. When many who have contributed to this book have been discouraged by the lack of interest that youngsters have towards their trades these days, it is perhaps important to consider the need for, and the use of, such places like the Pen Room in attracting that enthusiasm back.

Chapter 18

THE CRESCENT OF ALCHEMY

Crescent Silver

The diversity and difference of the Quarter never ceases to amaze me and it is a tribute to the place and the people, and the immense talent of those people, that so many diverse business enterprises can co-exist in such a relatively small area. Crescent Silver is not a company that spans numerous generations, neither can they boast a particular niche in a market, it is more a coalition of the old and the new. Neil Grant the owner, has brought together under one roof, a collection of new designer/maker blood, alongside the complementary old traditional industry and skill. It is a happy partnership that works very well and epitomises all that the Jewellery Quarter once boasted in the perfect setting.

The buildings in Spencer Street are from an age of Georgian grandeur, a small shop leads off the street into a warren of rooms and workshops, interconnected by rickety stairs and corridors. Some of the rooms in the house are converted into offices-come-design rooms, where Neil and others exist in a haphazard environment with an eclectic feel. Then further, leading into the neighbouring property, there is a gem of a find to anyone researching the area. A collection of workshops under the auspices of William Downing, where stamping machines of a great age, are sunk into a pit, and operate to produce the countless stampings and pressings still needed by many. The walls are filled with rack, after rack, of dies which date back hundreds of years.

Neil feels that he has a duty to keep all as it is. That it is a true reflection of everything that the Quarter is about and one of the last truly authentic working environments. Neil owns four of these interconnecting buildings and rents rooms and areas to designer/makers and craftsmen/women, for a peppercorn sum, for it is his desire to encourage the wealth of skill to continue in the area and not be put out by the escalating high costs. He does not have an actual training in the skills that he now uses aplenty, but rather he has absorbed and acquired techniques as he has gone along. It has not been a hindrance for him not having a formal training in the first instance, because this makes him more flexible in how he might solve a design problem, and more adventurous and able to experiment.

His father used to be the Works Director at Cavalier Tableware, a 100 yards from where he now sits. He never dreamed that one day he would be doing what he is doing in these buildings. It is safe to say that Neil had other intentions and was pulled back to the place through a mixture of circumstance and opportunity. Neil had studied a HND and was planning to set up a business restoring Morris Minors, but found that there was too much competition, it was then that his father approached him and suggested that Cavalier were seeking an engraver; they had a large order to fill for 2000 trays for the Avon Cosmetics – Circle of Excellence Award.

Mount Gay sailing award.

At that time Cavalier were a large company employing 400 people, they manufactured a diverse range of silverware of which his father was a Director, most of the items that they produced were principally for export. The products at that time ranged from tea sets and trays, which were highly popular then. Like many companies at that time, they eventually lost their markets due to cheap foreign competition, particularly from the Far East.

Neil decided to try his hand at engraving, bought a machine and moved out to Evesham, where he completed the orders and went into business specialising in trophies and awards in 1976. With the demise of Cavalier Tableware, Neil moved to the Quarter and decided to set up Crescent Silver. He did not know at the time, but the name that he chose had a significance in the trade in which he has now established himself; the crescent was the old alchemist symbol for silver.

From the outset, Neil decided that he had no intention of being caught in the rent trap and that property equity would ultimately grant security. He bought first one then another building, eventually totalling four. He applied himself to renovating the premises with the intention of renting them out to others, principally; jewellers, students, lecturers. He retained number 85 for manufacturing, to enable his own commercial enterprise.

Crescent Silver produces bespoke items for their customers. He has a number of exclusive clients and has produced work for Highgrove. He has recently completed a large order for the Emma Bridgewater Pottery in Stoke on Trent, to complement one of their mug designs – a miniature mug in silver that is to retail at £350. The court of the King of Bahrain has placed an order for three awards for their upcoming air show; when the orders mount up or require considerable attention that is when Neil needs all of those he works with to be involved.

He employs a handful of people, and he has an in-house spinner and a polisher. He out-sources his stamping work to Downing's who are one of the firms that Neil is landlord to, he also outsources his casting work. He has a good working relationship with a plating business which is based in Sutton Coldfield. Depending on the type of commission that comes, Neil tries to ensure that any tasks that they cannot complete in-house are kept within the area; because of the individuality of the orders that they fulfil they have a need for a full range of production techniques in various materials.

Neil feels that they are in a dying industry, but because of the adaptability of Crescent Silver they will always find work. They produce very individual and sometimes very eccentric items dependent on the customer who has placed the order. An Award for the Ghurkha's required a very thoughtful approach to the production, especially as they had to produce 200 in 2 weeks. They utilised CAD/CAM scanning the original model and reducing it in size. Then they modelled the figurine in resin, before producing rubber moulds for casting in pewter.

They have endeavoured to maintain a balance between the different orders

An award produced for well known stock car driver Colin Higman.

that they accept, to keep an equilibrium between the general items and the high quality articles. They often carry out renovation work on old pieces, which require the use of a multiple of skill sets and alternatives. Sometimes clients have an unrealistic perception of the cost of a particular commission and when Neil has availed them with his guide to the knowledge needed, and time involved, the reality of the situation makes the order impractical to the customer.

Neil considers that there is a lack of young blood willing to come into the industry and train as apprentices, this emphasises the change of the times, as his father used to run a highly successful apprenticeship scheme, for which he received The Freedom of the Worshipful Company of Goldsmiths (City of London). Now Neil often finds himself doing the little jobs because of the dearth of apprentices to undertake such tasks, and many of these original small occupations only existed due to the availability of low-

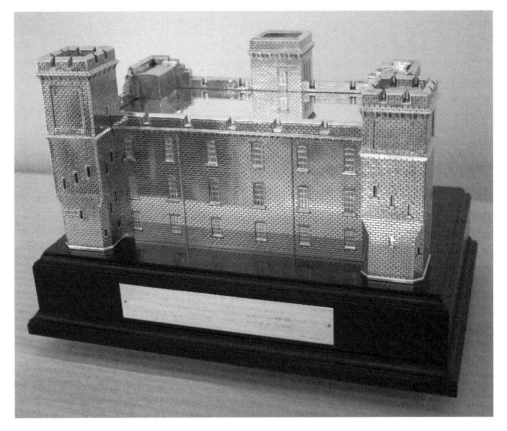

A model of The Keep at Whittington Barracks, Whittington, Staffordshire.

skilled labour. As a consequence, many of the methods of fabrication have changed and been adapted from other methods which has caused a loss of simplicity; he is always thinking of alternative practices to solve problems, which of course lead to offshoot jobs to accommodate the excess produced.

Neil fears for the future of the Quarter due to the dying off of the trades. It used to be that the main trades in the area were in silversmithing and jewellery, now it is mainly jewellery with some designer silversmithing; there are very few manufacturing companies left. He has concerns regarding the transformation of places from working businesses, to museums and apartments; the Quarter must be promoted as a working environment and

Severn Trent 'Water Aid' Cycle Challenge Award.

not as a tourist destination. He is concerned that the loss of the throughput of youngsters learning the trades will have dire consequences in the future. Ultimately, the businesses have only continued due to those that train, keeping the availability of skills at a consistent level, there will be no one left to take on the firms that remain as people move on or die.

He too, shares the concerns of many in the Quarter that the 'School' trains individuals at a level that is impractical for actual commercial business. The emphasis on design rather than product viability, leads to items which are made in inappropriate materials, with no intrinsic value; such as, copper, which once the product is finished cannot command the price for the piece demanded by the time and labour involved. There are some of the designer/makers that he can see succeeding, but many will struggle to find a place in the industry, because they have no real idea how business operates.

Neil wishes to encourage as much of this talent to stay, which for the most part is transient because they have no sense of belonging to, or ownership of, the place. They are generally students from out of the city, who have not got the appreciation of the Quarter's need for the students to remain. After all, the original intention of the School was to generate the much-needed throughput of skills to keep the business concerns in operation. This is why Neil has kept his rents low, to try and attract as many as possible to remain, and to encourage some businesses that have relocated elsewhere in the city back to where they are most needed. One of the most important aspects of the Jewellery Quarter's success and its future survival, depends on a tight network of skill-sets all within one area, that are accessible and available.

The Mick Saxby Memorial Trophy.

The buildings are a magnificent situation for any designer/maker who does find the idea of staying appealing. It is an environment full of character, being old and eclectic, rather than a sterile suite of office-like studios; this is a most inspirational setting. Neil is endeavouring to retain as much of this character as possible, even down to the wonderful Adam-style fireplace made in Coalbrookdale, with a Minton tiled surround, which is the main feature of his office. Also, the wonderful workshops next door which house the firm of William Downing the stampers.

He does tend to find that this drive to maintain the 'old' is often against all of the odds. In these days of the health and safety culture, he is finding constant blocks being placed in his path, even when he aims to keep practices that have always been in place. He was recently challenged by fire officers, as to fitness for purpose of the buildings and the siting of inflammable gas tanks appropriately. This does tend to create a whole load of new challenges, which cost time and money to rectify and comply with, however, it cannot be avoided and once it is done it is another hurdle achieved.

William Downing, who currently have four individuals working in their atmospheric workshops that date back hundreds of years, would not be allowed to be built in this current day and age. The stamping machines would be prohibited from installation. Fortunately, because they are pre-

An intricate wax carving created by Bethan Williams (reproduced by the kind courtesy of Silver Birch).

installed and no other new workers are employed they comply to laws of Health and Safety. The fact that the business has existed through several owners as a stampers, with no serious accidents, is living proof that some might consider that these over-officious regulations may now have gone too far, and infringe on businesses operating and surviving, rather than encouraging them.

On my visit, I was able to talk to Colin Ashford the current owner of Downing's and some of the people that currently work for, and, in partnership with, Crescent Silver. As I have dedicated a chapter 'Voices from the Warren' to an eclectic mix of stories, to reflect the entwined nature of interdependent small business that benefit the survival of the Quarter, I have included a fuller interview with the employees of Downing's there. Mike is part of Crescent Silver, though the relaxed approach that Neil has towards his employees, he prefers to appreciate his employees as multi-talented people that he works with.

Mike Ball who is 45, originally trained as a jeweller and is now working as a silversmith. When he was a lad he used to do a lot of swimming, and he was always finding jewellery at the bottom the pools which stimulated his desire to learn to be a jeweller. This was combined with an enjoyment of studying metalwork at school, and particularly the encouragement that he received from his teacher, who was more of a silversmith than a jeweller. Mike decided to study at the School of Jewellery, he enrolled on a City and Guilds course. In the first year he experienced the three main trades; silversmithing, jewellery and engraving. He decided at the end of his first year to concentrate on jewellery.

Although, he learnt many skills in his three years that he spent there, he felt that he knew very little by the time he had completed his course. His main criticism of the training that he undertook is although he may have had a good grounding of skills, his experience of actual production techniques was very limited. In his opinion, a student would be unable to make the transition successfully

Original sketch for a Gurkha award.

between education and work without additional experience. He found his own limitations to be quite acute when he left, but he was fortunate to secure a position in Bath; he lacked the speed that is so necessary when you are working in the commercial sector. He was lucky enough to be working alongside a girl who had acquired that speed through technique, and he was able to learn much more from her that made him feel more confident in his own skill-set.

He returned to Birmingham after a while, and started work for the firm of Bushnell's and then for a small Indian firm for a further twelve months. By 1989 he decided that he would like to try going self-employed with his brother; they had a contract with one specific customer which provided their initial income and they set to work trying to establish themselves as a

Left: Wax model for the Gurkha award. Right: The finished artifact.

business interest, and build up their own customer base. They would concentrate on making master patterns, which they cast into rubber moulds, and then using investment tubes, they would apply a centrifuge-casting method. He enjoyed those initial years and the freedom of being his own boss, but it was an uphill struggle for eight years.

In their last year of trading, he only managed to turn over £17,000, he was deeply disheartened. After all those years working and trying, combined with all the skills and knowledge that he had, he just could not make it pay, or earn his true value as a craftsman. As he says, he had to walk away because 'the money was crap' and he was 'fed up', all of his time was taken 'continuously chasing payments, it is notoriously bad for paying'.

Another more elaborate Gurkha award.

He decided to take whatever he could and ended up shop fitting, which although was not his chosen path, paid considerably more than he had been earning; he managed to earn £27,000 in one year. Unfortunately, this did not last as long as he might of hoped, and he found himself being laid off in 2009. He returned once more to the Jewellery Quarter, were he initially started working for another company for a few days until he found out how little he was being paid, and promptly left. It was at that point that Neil offered him a position as his silversmith and

A detailed wax carving of a butterfly.

although it is not his first skill, he has found that he has remembered more than he has forgotten. He has ably turned his hand back to this form of work, and because he is not tied to technical training, he can often use very different techniques for solving a problem; particularly, when it is on a work of restoration.

He defines the biggest problem for those who try to go into business on their own as that of retail. The small firms that tend to do well have premises that have a shop, which allow them to attract passing trade, which makes a considerable difference to their income. It is something that has changed the Quarter quite significantly, Neil has a small shop at the entrance to his 'warren' of premises, yet he remembers the days when manufacturers would not sell direct to the public. The company his father worked for, would not entertain the idea; they kept their supply strictly to retail, thus protecting their costs by ensuring the intrinsic value of the item.

Mike considers that people on the outside of the trade have a very unrealistic perception of what happens. He often meets others who assume that because he works in the jewellery trade that he must be doing well. They have no idea that the money that can be earned in the industry is so poor, that it can barely support the craftspeople who work in it:

"The first thing to go in a recession is jewellery because it is a luxury item."

He knows that many youngsters have no interest in coming into the business at this time, and he would be the last person to encourage them having experienced all that he has experienced. However, he was shocked to find out that his own school has lost all of the metal work facilities and the teachers, it does add to the problem of young people coming forward as they lack exposure to the skills. Unfortunately, the students coming out of the School of Jewellery have too little appreciation of the needs of the trade, although they can make their own pieces. He believes that although they are competent in some ways they are not going to be the solution to filling the skills gap.

In a neighbouring room, which I can described as a very self-contained studio, I met Bethan Williams, she is a fine example of a designer/maker who has adapted admirably to life and work in the Quarter; she is self-employed and is one of those individuals that Neil encourages to remain in the Quarter by renting space to work in Crescent Silver. She is a very quietly spoken individual who possesses a cheerful disposition, she is not one to 'sing her own praises', but Neil has already explained to me how enormously talented she is. Her 'cubby hole' of a studio, evokes a feeling of self-containment, solitude and sanctuary, which is obviously Beth's preferred place to be.

Beth hails from Anglesey, she arrived in Birmingham in 1983 to study a course in Silversmithing and Jewellery. She had a desire to work in metal and while studying at Birmingham, she was able to explore where her talents truly lay, and although she enjoyed the jewellery side of things, she found her preference was for design and silversmithing. She took part in various competitions in the three years of her study and particularly enjoyed one where she had to design medals. She did not know at that point that she had a forte for carving, because she had not been taught how to, however, during her design course she was given her first block of wax to work with, and that is when she found her natural talent. She was able to visualise in three dimensions and translate her ideas very adeptly through carving a form in the round. The material being wax and being easy to carve, meant that she was able to quickly realise her ideas.

She saw herself, first and foremost as a jeweller and although she did not enjoy all aspects, such as stone setting, she loved many other processes in her course. Upon completion of her degree she applied to the Royal College of Art to study a post graduate course, unfortunately, demand for places at the RCA are extremely high and Beth was unlucky, so she attended a die-cutting course at Birmingham part-time.

In 1987, she decided to start her own business; she was able to rent a space with a bench at the top of the building from Neil's father. There she set to work producing her own range of jewellery which were flat pieces in a Celtic style. Neil's father offered her some wax patterns to dress up, that is

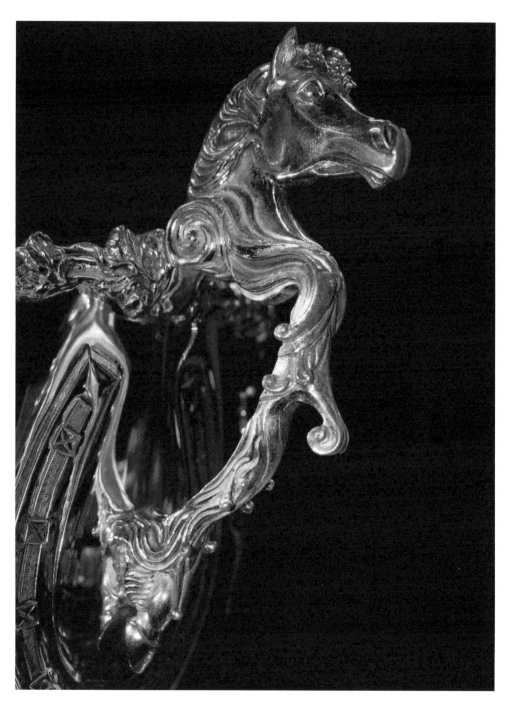

A silver horse's head produced by Crescent Silver.

when everyone discovered that Beth was particularly good at it, and consequently, the word soon got round, and she found others coming to her with waxes to refine.

At this point she was able to establish her company 'Silver Birch' formally. She tells me that she owes a great deal to Neil and his father, who both offered a considerable amount of support in this endeavour. They were able to network with many others in the Quarter, which put Beth's name and reputation with the right people at the right time. As she says, the whole area operates extensively on 'the word of mouth in the community'.

Now she produces individual commissions as well as her own interests, and work for Crescent Silver. She believes that for her it is a 'continual learning process'. She is a

The Queen's Medal for Music, obverse and reverse view, and the original wax carving, all created and produced by Bethan Williams of Silver Birch (the images are reproduced here by the kind courtesy and permission of Buckingham Palace and Highgrove).

kinaesthetic learner, who gains most by experience of the actual medium, in other words, she learns, as she does. She says, that she is challenged by both dyslexia and perfectionism, which can make her a very hard task master on herself, and highly self-critical of all that she does. She loves working with her medium of preference, wax. She is a highly-responsive maker who will attempt different ways to solve a problem, as she stresses:

"There is no right or wrong way of doing things."

I believe that this flexibility of the designer/maker who comes from the School of Jewellery is often overlooked by the critiques of the training there. There is no doubt that Beth and others like her, bring a quality that is often missing in those that have been more rigidly, technically trained. These craftspeople have a greater creativity, and because they have learnt through the creative process, they are not constrained by the dogma of 'this is how we do this, and this is how it has always been done'. The designer/maker is more able to experiment, try new things, adapt methods, and applications used in other contexts to the particular job in hand.

As Beth points out, every new job presents a whole new set of challenges, and initially that generates within her a wealth of enthusiasm. Then she encounters the hurdles, the problems to be solved, and she has to achieve a solution, her internal drive for perfectionism will not let her do anything else. All this can lead to a state of both physical and mental exhaustion once the job is completed. But unlike a student who can sit and recharge, for her there is no respite, once one task is finished she must move on to the next.

She has become part of the Quarter, it is under her skin, she has been consumed within the tangled web of talent and skill that coalesces together; operating almost like a hive of bees, one handing the work to another for another process. That has always been the way the area has survived, the multitudinous amounts of outworkers, who have the skills that are not always available in the bigger concerns, or can offset peak demand, by taking the work overspill. It teaches the designer/maker, the ex-student, to work in cooperation rather than isolation. The economy of the trade is demanding all to be 'less precious about their areas and more open to ideas'.

She fears for the continued existence of the Quarter, not necessarily through the death of the trade, or the loss of skill, she believes that the location of place is the curse that it carries. It is prime land adjacent to the heart of the city and constantly under the threat of encroachment of unscrupulous developers. That is why all must work to protect the Quarter for the 'Jewel' that it is, whether that be the various conservation and trade groups, or the City Council and local people. All that care for the history of an area – that is still very much a beating, working heart – must make a stand to protect and promote its importance daily.

Crescent Silver is founded on the heritage which made the trade and the location famous. Neil is a very principled individual who wants his vision of protecting the working traditions to continue, but he is also a pragmatist, he will do what he can do, for as long as he is physically able, and like all of those who have had these small concerns that they have held for one or two generations, he would hope that there will be a safe pair of hands to take over and continue the process after him.

Conclusion

THE WAY AHEAD

In this book, I have tried to encapsulate what I understand to be the quintessential Jewellery Quarter of Birmingham, I have explored the past that evolved the trade and discovered that many of those previous cycles of economic upswing and downturn have been played out in the Quarter throughout its history. Creating times of great prosperity, interspersed with general hardships in an industry that depends on wealth of people for its own survival. I have tried to frame the diversity of skills and processes that make it such an exceptional area of manufacture; condensed into a relatively small geographical location.

The most significant contributions given in the previous chapters, are those provided by the companies and individual people, who so kindly gave of their time and their stories. They have provided us with a 'snapshot' of what the Quarter is today, and through their reminiscences, what it has been in the last half century. It is just a point in time, and like all views, subject to change from another viewer (reader). Many reflect on a 'golden age' remembered, maybe in the 1960's or again in the 1990's, and some yearn for a return and fear that will not happen. The one thought I carry with me after my brief exploration of the history prior to 1950, is that it always changes and transforms; often it is an adaptive change to fashion and circumstances, sometimes it is a forced change brought about by recession and war. Nothing stays the same, nor should it. These concluding notes are not written to suggest that it should remain as it is, but it should stay, and should be granted the status and recognition that it deserves. The questions primarily driven through this text, are in what form should this complex and diverse place address the future? Is it a museum or conservation piece? Will it be promoted strongly as an area for tourist attraction by the Council? Is the area a working Quarter, dedicated to the production of items of intrinsic value? Does education form a part of the regeneration for the place? And, can the Quarter offer a model for 'whole-city' economic regeneration?

There are many forces both inside and outside the Quarter that operate to shape and challenge its existence. In this conclusion I will attempt to highlight those issues that are to be applauded and the resistors to the overall success, that in my opinion, need to be managed for the benefit of all. It is important to view all of what is following holistically, it is not the individual companies, or the workers, or the various support groups that can make a significant difference at this stage, it is a much wider concern, that ultimately affects the prosperity of the City as a whole, and should be viewed in such a way.

One of the greatest challenges facing the Quarter at the moment is one of identity, between what it is fundamentally, and what it is evolving into. As Marie Haddleton discussed in her chapter, prior to the whole conservation area being designated, it had corridors which were open to exploitation and property speculation. That has caused an influx of inhabitants. Some in this book are very doubtful about the idea of having residents there, but there is little anyone can do because it is as it is now. Some see the arrival of residents as a good thing, that will encourage an elevation in the overall profile of the area, giving the place a smarter image. There are voices that fear, that the size and quality of what has been developed will only encourage transient (passing through) individuals, and not the families and the community that needs to be established. There are tensions that underlie all of this, in a Quarter that needs to work in manufacturing enterprise; make loud noise and odd smells, sometimes at anti-social times. There needs to be compromise from the 'incomers', they have chosen to live in an eccentric part of the City, that possesses oddity and charm; in the same way that some choose to live near a football stadium, or a railway, there has to be an acceptance, that business has to be conducted, without it, there is no Quarter.

In the same way, there needs to be an acceptance by the businesses that they operate in a highly historic part of the City. It has attractions, some of which are still to be developed. The conservation groups in operation are conducting sterling work in their efforts to conserve all that remains, and the fruits of their labours are evidential through the support shown by English Heritage. I am not arguing that the Quarter should be preserved in aspic, there has to some give and take, to allow the businesses to expand and develop within reason.

The industry has existed on small operation and small-medium enterprise, there was only large scale employment in a very short period of history. The industry cannot function as a large scale employer. However, companies need to be able to expand if necessary, whether that be providing parking for their employees which is by far the biggest nightmare for most.

Equally, there must be a respect for the work of conservationists, the two museums do attract visitors and offer educational opportunity. The Pen Museum, preserves the memory of a most significant industry in Birmingham's history, that without the museum would be all but forgotten.

The biggest drawback for the Quarter is the prime location of the site, it will always be under threat from some speculation or other. It exists in an uneasy truce, of conservation areas, protected only because individuals and groups fight to save it. There is only so much that these groups can do, and so much they can afford to do, or ask for in sponsorship. There is a great deal that could be done by the City to improve the general accessibility to the Quarter. Again, parking, it is designed only for those who are there briefly. Most parking meters demand constant feeding on a four-hourly basis; if you are a worker, that means having to leave to top-up the meter at least once a day. There are still many workers in the Quarter and visiting clients, which makes it extremely difficult for all other visitors (particularly tourists) to find anywhere to park, and the multi-story has a reputation that can deter.

The companies are doing a great deal to make their premises more accessible. They are opening doors, to what has been traditionally a closed-shop, to try to attract direct custom and interest. In so doing, they are working hard to improve the frontages and present a modern image, while retaining character and obeying any grade listings. It would be a nice touch, if the local authority would consider general environmental improvements. With the conservation of Warstone and Keyhill Cemeteries high on the agenda – because of their many famous incumbents – this presents an ideal opportunity, for gardens and benches, and tranquil places to sit and soak up the ambiance and history of the area.

The workers and companies that operate face two challenges at this present time, which if unchecked, will change the 'working nature' of the Quarter fundamentally and in some cases, finish businesses entirely. The first is Health and Safety, a necessary body in an age of litigation, but many of the premises which are the very essence of what makes the Quarter so special, where acquired during a time when it was not an issue. I write acquired, because they are generally the old residential properties which were converted. There are very few left, what has not been bulldozed by the developers, or remodelled by the Luftwaffe during WW2. It would be a shame, if the only way these exciting little workshops could be retained is as museum pieces. As I have argued in the book, these places have operated for one hundred and fifty years, with no accidents in living memory, the words restraint and compromise need to be considered, when these properties are viewed by officialdom.

The most pressing issue is the shortage of skills, and this needs to be addressed pro-actively. From my own personal experience having taught metalwork for fifteen years, these opportunities in the school curriculum are dying rapidly. As qualified, skilled staff like myself leave, they can no longer be replaced. When school workshops lie idle, and a governing body needs to develop classroom space, the workshop becomes decommissioned (at a very small reclamation value). If there is a desire in the future to replace what was, the costs of substantial investment become prohibitive to any head teacher.

Many of the characters in this book, had some formal training at school before being apprenticed, and attending the School of Jewellery to improve their skills. The experience and exposure at school now is minimal, the opportunities for apprenticeship within the trade are difficult in recessionary times; training is always the first thing to be cut in an economic dip (Debney, 2007). The Modern Apprenticeship Scheme, is not 'user-friendly' for working businesses in the Quarter. Added to this, The School of Jewellery has an excellent reputation at degree level, but these students do not tend to stay, and have no emotional attachment to the area. Many business individuals, regard the students as possessing unrealistic expectations of what they can do and what they can achieve, post-degree level. I must support this view, as I undertook a similar education in Glass, and I had limited knowledge of production costs or processes.

The School of Jewellery was opened to provided technical education to the army of workers that the Quarter needed to train in order to survive. Many of the courses are still available, but there is not enough money generated at this particular time, or school leavers coming through to join apprenticeships, that stimulate further growth. Effectively, the technical training at craft level in the jewellery trade is in a period of stagnation and needs some inward investment to stimulate movement in the right direction.

The vision shared by Toye, Kenning & Spencer and others, for a more pro-active response needs further investigation. There are some who consider that investment towards specialist education could promote skills not just for the Quarter but for the whole of Greater Birmingham. This may be the right time to embolden that vision; a centrally located, school of excellence with a practical, vocational, theme, that dedicates the mission statement towards the promotion of manufacturing and understanding manufacturing processes, which in turn could help regenerate many sectors of the City.

The history that I have analysed of Birmingham, clearly points to the greatest economic successes being produced through small-medium enterprise. There are many these days who mark the passing of big industry in the City as a deathblow, when we should look to history and see that the City was built on small-scale, high-quality manufacturing, in that way, the Quarter itself is an excellent model for re-generation. The whole concept of complementary manufacturing processes, sitting cheek by jowl and working collaboratively, is one that should be mirrored as much as possible. We were fundamentally 'the manufacturing city' in the manufacturing economy. Many would say that manufacturing is dead. I would argue that without manufacturing, wealth and prosperity will dwindle to nothing, and that we have to do everything that we can to revive what there is before it is too late: we cannot survive as a nation of service industry and tourism; and service industry needs a manufacturing base to service.

The Jewellery Quarter is an important part of the history of Birmingham, it forms a most significant part of the present, but it also teaches lessons that once learned, could help to move local industry forward to a highly rewarding future. The diversity, hard work and determination, that shaped the Quarter persists today. Those that continue need to be supported in every way in their endeavours, as they are facing many challenges. How can the importance of the Jewellery Quarter to the City and its necessary survival be assessed? The intrinsic value of anything cannot be measured in a simple economic equation, it is a question of philosophy and ethics. In the same way as it is impossible to equate the intrinsic value of a precious piece of jewellery created in the Quarter. On the other hand, the instrumental value to the City of Birmingham has been obvious throughout history and continues to this day. The Jewellery Quarter is in every way a "jewel" of our City; it is the crown that adorns the king and it must be preserved, celebrated and promoted at every opportunity for the effective future of Birmingham.

BIBLIOGRAPHY

Books

Allen, G. C. (1929) *The industrial development of Birmingham and the Black Country* 1st ed. London: Cross and Co.

Andrew, J. (2009) Was Matthew Boulton a steam engineer? In Dick, M. (2009) *Matthew Boulton – a revolutionary player* 1st ed. Warwickshire: Brewin Books

Andrew, J. (2009) The Soho steam-engine business In Mason, S. (2009) *Matthew Boulton – selling what all the world desires* 1st ed. Birmingham: Birmingham City Council

Black, C. (1907) *Sweated Industry and the minimum wage* 1st ed. London: Duckworth and Co.

Baggott, S. (2009) 'Real knowledge and occult misteries': Matthew Boulton and the Birmingham Assay Office In Dick, M. (2009) *Matthew Boulton – a revolutionary player* 1st ed. Warwickshire: Brewin Books

Ballard, P. Loggie, V. & Mason, S. (2009) *A lost landscape – Matthew Boulton's Gardens at Soho* 1st ed. Sussex: Phillimore

Cadbury, E. & Shann, G. (1907) *Sweating* 1st ed. London: Headley Brothers

Cadbury, E. & Matheson, C. M. (1907) *Women's work and wages – a phase of life in an industrial city* 1st ed. Chicago: Chicago Press

Cattell, J. & Hawkins, B. (2000) *The Birmingham Jewellery Quarter – an introduction and guide* 1st ed. English Heritage

Cattell, J. Ely, S. & Jones, B. (2002) *The Birmingham Jewellery Quarter – an architectural survey of the manufactories* 1st ed. English Heritage

Chinn, C. (1999) *One thousand years of Brum.* 1st ed. Birmingham: Birmingham Evening Mail

Dayus, K. (2006) *The Girl from Hockley* 1st ed. London: Virago

Debney, J. (2006) *Engineered Careers? A study of women engineers in the offshore oil and gas industry.* Ed.D Thesis. British Library. (unpublished)

Debney, J. (2010) *Breaking the Chains* 1st ed. Warwickshire: Brewin Books

Debney, J. (2011) *The Dangerfields* 1st ed. Warwickshire: Brewin Books

Demidowicz. G. (2009) Power at the Soho Manufactory and Mint In Dick, M. (2009) *Matthew Boulton – a revolutionary player* 1st ed. Warwickshire: Brewin Books

Dick, M. (2009) *Matthew Boulton – a revolutionary player* 1st ed. Warwickshire: Brewin Books

Drake, B. (1917) *Women in the engineering trades* 1st ed. London: Fabian

Gledhill, A. (1988) *Birmingham's Jewellery Quarter* 1st ed. Warwickshire: Brewin Books

Haddleton, M. (1987) *The Jewellery Quarter* 1st ed. Birmingham: YBA Publications

Hodder, M. (2004) *Birmingham The Hidden History* 1st ed. Gloucestershire: Tempus

Hopkins E. (1998) *The rise of a manufacturing town – Birmingham and the industrial revolution* 1st ed. Gloucestershire: Stroud

Hutton, W. (1783) *An history of Birmingham* 2nd ed. Wakefield (reprinted 2008)

Hutchins, B. L. (1907) *Home work and sweating – the causes and remedies* 1st ed. London: Fabian

Hutchins, B. L. (1915) *Women in modern industry* 1st ed. London: Bell

Jones, P. (2009) 'I had l(or)ds and ladys to wait on yesterday...' visitors to the Soho Manufactory In Mason, S. (2009) *Matthew Boulton – selling what all the world desires* 1st ed. Birmingham: Birmingham City Council

Jones, P. (2009) Trading a liberté: the commercial token and medal coinage of Monneron Frères In Clay, R. & Tungate, S. (2009) *Matthew Boulton and the art of making money* 1st ed. Warwickshire: Brewin Books

Mason, S. (2002) *Guide to Soho House* 1st ed. Birmingham: Birmingham Museum and Art Gallery

Mason, S. (1998) *Jewellery Making in Birmingham* 1st ed. London: Phillimore

Mason, S. (2009) 'A new species of gentleman' In Dick, M. (2009) *Matthew Boulton – a revolutionary player* 1st ed. Warwickshire: Brewin Books

Morgan, C. E. (2001) *Women workers and gender identities, 1835-1913* 1st ed. London: Routledge

Nott, S. N. (1987) *The Birmingham Jewellers' Association – 100 years of service* 1st ed. London: Prangnell-Rapkin

Ryland, A. (1866) The Birmingham assay Office In Timmins, S. (1866) *The resources, products, and industrial history of Birmingham and the Midland hardware district: a series of reports* 1st ed. London: Hardwicke

Skipp, V. (1987) *A history of greater Birmingham* 2nd ed. Warwickshire: Brewin Books

Symons, D. (2009) Matthew Boulton and the forgers In Clay, R. & Tungate, S. (2009) *Matthew Boulton and the art of making money* 1st ed. Warwickshire: Brewin Books

Timmins, S. (1866) The Birmingham steel pen trade In Timmins, S. (1866) *The resources, products, and industrial history of Birmingham and the Midland hardware district: a series of reports* 1st ed. London: Hardwicke

Tungate, S. (2009) Technology, art and design in the work of Matthew Boulton: coins, medals and tokens produced at the Soho Mint In Dick, M. (2009) *Matthew Boulton – a revolutionary player* 1st ed. Warwickshire: Brewin Books

Uglow, J. (2002) *The Lunar Men – Five friends whose curiosity changed the world* 1st ed. London: Faber and Faber

Upton, C. (1993) *A History of Birmingham* 1st ed. Sussex: Phillimore

Ward, R. (2005) *City-state and nation – Birmingham's political history* 1st ed. Chichester: Phillimore

Williams, D. (2004) *The Birmingham Gun Trade* 1st ed. Gloucestershire: Tempus

Wright, J. S. (1866) The jewellery and gilt toy trade In Timmins, S. (1866) *The resources, products, and industrial history of Birmingham and the Midland hardware district: a series of reports* 1st ed. London: Hardwicke

Internet resources
www.visionofbritain.org
http://bobmiles.bulldoghome.com – Explore the Birmingham Jewellery Quarter.

Pamphlets and Journals
The Assay Office Birmingham – Independence, Integrity, Innovation.
British Jeweller – September 1935
British Jeweller – October 1935
British Jeweller – April 1937
British Jeweller – October 1937
British Jeweller – October 1940
British Jeweller – February 1941

BY THE SAME AUTHOR

If Only, ISBN 978-1-85858-460-7, £6.95
The Dangerfields, ISBN 978-1-85858-464-5, £14.95
Breaking the Chains, ISBN 978-1-85858-470-6, £14.95